THE BOOK

of a

THOUSAND
PRAYERS

Other Books by Angela Ashwin

THE BOOK

∽ *of a* ∽

THOUSAND
PRAYERS

Compiled by

ANGELA ASHWIN

ZONDERVAN™

GRAND RAPIDS, MICHIGAN 49530 USA

ZONDERVAN™

The Book of a Thousand Prayers
Copyright © 1996, 2002 by Angela Ashwin

Requests for information should be addressed to:
Zondervan, *Grand Rapids, Michigan 49530*

Library of Congress Cataloging-in-Publication Data

The book of a thousand prayers / compiled by Angela Ashwin.
     p. cm.
    Includes indexes.
    ISBN 0-310-24872-8
    1. Prayers.   I. Ashwin, Angela.
BV245.B584 2002
242'.8—dc21

2002012744

First published in Great Britain in 1996 by Marshall Pickering.

Angela Ashwin asserts the moral right to be identified as the compiler of this work.

Interior design by Todd Sprague

Printed in the United States of America

---

02 03 04 05 06 07 08 /❖ DC/ 10 9 8 7 6 5 4 3 2 1

For Wendy

CONTENTS

INTRODUCTION

In the hope of making this anthology more than just a collection of old favourites, I have cast my net widely, finding prayers which are poetic, prophetic or even passionate, as well as adding a number of my own. As a result, the prayers vary considerably in topic, style, source and age, and I hope that readers will find it an interesting and stimulating mixture.

We do not always need another person's words when we pray. But there can be times when a prayer by someone else expresses our concerns and desires better than we could do ourselves and becomes a source of inspiration and strength. Or we may 'grow into' a prayer which has tremendously high ideals, such as the one by John Wesley: 'Lord God, I am no longer my own but yours.' Even though we have not ourselves arrived at such dizzy heights of self-giving, the very act of using a prayer like this helps us to come closer to its aspirations.

There can also be a sense of freedom in using a set prayer, because the words are given, and we simply let go into their flow and meaning. This is especially helpful in times of stress or doubt. The familiar words of a well-known prayer, or the challenges of a modern one, bring us back to our roots in God and remind us that we belong to the great body of Christ's people. A written prayer links us not only with its author but also with all the other people who have used it, so that, in a sense, we are never alone when we pray.

We usually think of prayer as an offering that we make to God– and so it is. But it is much more. Prayer is God's gift to us, a banquet of good things to feed our inner life as we respond to the invitation to his feast of peace, forgiveness, challenge and love.

 презентация

I have arranged the prayers so that those at the beginning of a section tend to be personal in tone and content, while later ones are more suitable for group or public use (using 'we' instead of 'I'). But there is no hard and fast line between the two, and most prayers are interchange-able, with a bit of flexibility and imagination.

Occasionally I have kept the old form of English (with 'thee' and 'thou') because it seemed an essential part of the prayer's poetry. Over the question of whether to use masculine or feminine pronouns when referring to individuals, I have kept to the original form (usually 'he') in copyright material, but have used 'she' in other prayers.

Here are some ways in which this anthology could be used:

PRAYING ALONE

One or two prayers from different sections could be used as part of a regular pattern of personal prayer. Some people light a candle or play music as part of the slowing-down process. When deciding which prayers to use, you might find it helpful to work through certain parts, such as the thanksgivings, or prayers of self-dedication to God, taking one from each section every time you have a chance to be quiet with God. Obviously, if any specific concerns are on your mind, the contents and index point to prayers on a wide range of topics.

While you are using a prayer, an individual sentence or phrase may strike you. If this happens, it is worth staying with it and letting those words lead you into quietness.

PRAYING WITH ANOTHER PERSON

When two people pray together, they generally find their own words. But it is worth experimenting with set prayers too. For example, after a time of extempore prayer, you could have a period of quietness intro-duced by a prayer from Part 9, and end with a blessing (Part 13). Using prayers out of a book like this has the advantage of freeing you from having to think of suitable words yourself.

PRAYING IN A GROUP

Many prayer groups are so informal that prayers from an anthology would only hamper the flow of spontaneity. But some prayer-meetings can benefit from a specific introduction, with one or more written prayers offered slowly and thoughtfully. Some groups start with extem-pore prayers, followed by a short reading and a set prayer leading into a period of corporate silence. One person keeps an eye on the clock and closes with a blessing or an act of self-dedication.

If you are responsible for a house group, certain practical measures may help:

- arrange chairs carefully, if possible leaving an empty seat near the door for any late-comer
- have gentle lighting, with lamps rather than a central light
- some groups like a central focus to look at, such as flowers, a candle, an icon or a cross
- put the answering machine on if you have one
- ask people to turn watch alarms off
- arrange for one person to answer the front door
- serve coffee at the end; sometimes people value the opportunity to share anything that was important to them during the meditation or shared silence (though no one should be forced to talk about this if they don't want to)

OPENING AND CLOSING A MEETING WITH PRAYER

This prospect fills some people with panic! A few tips can help:

- have the prayers for beginning and ending the meeting written out beforehand (either your own or from a book)
- make sure that you will be heard; don't bury your chin in your notes but speak in a way that will be clearly heard by those at the back of the room; if you are using a microphone, practise with it beforehand if possible
- if a particular issue comes up during the meeting and you are going to lead a closing prayer, try using the index of this book to find appropriate material (e.g., bereavement, community conflict, anxiety about the church's witness, worries of parents, concerns about war and violence, etc.)

PRAYERS IN CHURCH

There are prayers suitable for public worship in most sections of this book. Many have responses in bold type, which work best if printed out on an order of service. Part Six contains longer orders of intercession for use in church services as well as individual prayers of intercession for various needs. Further thoughts about leading intercessory prayer are given at the beginning of Part Six.

CONCLUSION

Nothing is outside the care and concern of God. He is totally involved in his world and is waiting for us to offer ourselves as channels of his love and to be transformed into the person he created us to be. So come now, taste and eat!

> *On this mountain the Lord of Hosts will prepare*
> *a banquet of rich fare for all the nations.*
> *Then the Lord God will wipe away the tears from every face,*
> *and remove the reproach of his people.*
> ISAIAH 25:6, 8

Our Father in heaven,
hallowed be your name;
your kingdom come;
your will be done
on earth as it is in heaven.
Give us today our daily bread;
and forgive us our sins
as we forgive
those who sin against us;
lead us not into temptation,
but deliver us from evil.
For the kingdom, the power
and the glory are yours,
now and for ever,
Amen.

part one

OUR RELATIONSHIP WITH GOD

SEEKING GOD

You will seek the Lord your God, and you will find him, if you
search after him with all your heart and with all your soul.

DEUTERONOMY 4:29

1   O God, you are my God,
                   early will I seek you.
               My flesh longs for you,
               my soul thirsts for you,
     in a barren and dry land where there is no water.

Psalm 63:1

2   Late have I loved you,
O Beauty so ancient and so new.
You called, and broke through my defences,
and now I long for you.
You breathed your fragrance on me,
and I drew in my breath
and now I pant for you.
I tasted you, and now I hunger and thirst for you.
You touched me,
and I burn for your peace.

St Augustine of Hippo (354–430)

3   Lord Jesus, I am not an eagle. All I have are the eyes and the
heart of one. In spite of my littleness, I dare to gaze at the sun
of love, and I long to fly towards it.

St Thérèse of Lisieux (1873–1897)

4   Holy Spirit
dwell in me,
that I may become prayer.
Whether I sleep or wake,

eat or drink,
labour or rest,
may the fragrance of prayer
rise, without effort, in my heart.
Purify my soul and never leave me,
so that the movements of my heart and mind
may, with voices full of sweetness,
sing in secret to God.

after St Isaac the Syrian (seventh century)

5   O sweetest love of God, too little known,
        whoever has found you will be at rest.
     Let everything change, O my God,
        that I may rest in you.
     How sweet to me is your presence,
        you who are the sovereign good!
     I will draw near to you in silence,
        and will uncover your feet,
        that it may please you to unite me with yourself,
        making my soul your bride.
     I will rejoice in nothing until I am in your arms;
     O Lord, I beseech you, leave me not for a moment.

St John of the Cross (1542–1591)

6   Lord,
     this moment is yours;
     mine for you,
     and yours for me.
     I need you,
     I cannot survive without you;
     and yet I go on rushing through life
     as if I could do everything in my own strength.
     Forgive me.
     I know
     that you care for me at all times,
     and that I am always in your hands;
     but I still need to pause

and let my heart and spirit
be loved by you
into loving you again.

A.A.

7   As a deer longs for flowing streams,
               so longs my soul for you, O Lord.
                        Psalm 42:1

8   Lord, teach me to seek you,
           and reveal yourself to me as I look for you.
       For I cannot seek you unless first you teach me,
           nor find you unless first you reveal yourself to me.
                   St Ambrose (340–397)

9   Eternal Trinity, you are a deep sea,
       into which the more I enter the more I find,
       and the more I find the more I seek.
       The soul ever hungers in your abyss, Eternal Trinity,
       longing to see you with the light of your light,
       and as the deer yearns for the springs of water,
       so my soul yearns to see you in truth.
               St Catherine of Siena (1347–1380)

10   I put aside my weighty cares and leave my wearisome toils for
       a while. I abandon myself to you, O God, and rest for a little
       in you.
           I enter the inner chamber of my soul, and seek only God and
       the things that can help me in my quest for you.
           Come then, Lord my God, teach my heart where and how to
       look for you, where and how to find you.
                   after St Anselm (1033–1109)

11   O Father, give my spirit power to climb
       To the fountain of all light, and be purified.
       Break through the mists of earth, the weight of clay,
       Shine forth in splendour, you who are calm weather,

And quiet resting-place for faithful souls.
  You carry us, and you go before;
  You are the journey, and the journey's end.
Boethius (c.480–524)

12   Be thou my vision, O Lord of my heart;
Naught be all else to me, save that thou art;
Thou my best thought, by day or by night,
Waking or sleeping, thy presence my light.
Eighth century Irish hymn, trans. by
Mary Byrne (1880–1931) and Eleanor Hull (1860–1935)

13   O Christ,
tirelessly you seek out those who are looking for you
and who think that you are far away;
teach us, at every moment,
to place our spirits in your hands.
While we are still looking for you,
already you have found us.
However poor our prayer,
you hear us far more than we can imagine or believe.
Brother Roger of Taizé

14   O God,
whose beauty is beyond our imagining,
and whose power we cannot comprehend:
show us your glory
as far as we can grasp it,
and shield us
from knowing more than we can bear
until we may look upon you without fear,
through Jesus Christ.
Janet Morley
Exodus 33: Moses in the cleft of the rock.

15   O Lord,
         Open our eyes to your Presence
         Open our minds to your grace
         Open our lips to your praises
         Open our hearts to your love
         Open our lives to your healing
         And be found among us.
                        David Adam

16   O Lord our God, grant us grace to desire you with our whole
     heart,
         so that desiring you, we may seek and find you;
         and so finding you, may love you;
         and so loving you, may hate those sins
         which separate us from you,
         for the sake of Jesus Christ our Lord.
                  after St Anselm (1033–1109)

17   O gracious and holy Father,
         give us wisdom to perceive you,
         intelligence to understand you,
         diligence to seek you,
         patience to wait for you,
         eyes to behold you,
         a heart to meditate upon you,
         and a life to proclaim you,
         through the power of the Spirit
         of our Lord Jesus Christ.
                  St Benedict (c.480–c.547)

S E L F - D E D I C A T I O N

Here am I; send me.

ISAIAH 6:8

⌒⊙ ⊙⌒

18   Lord God, I am no longer my own, but yours.
Put me to what you will,
rank me with whom you will.
Put me to doing, put me to enduring;
let me be employed for you,
or laid aside for you,
exalted for you
or brought low for you;
let me be full, let me be empty;
let me have all things,
let me have nothing.
I freely and wholeheartedly yield all things
to your pleasure and disposal.
And now, glorious and blessed God,
Father, Son and Holy Spirit,
you are mine and I am yours.
So be it.

John Wesley (1703–1791)

19   Lord,
let my life be a space
in which you can work in the world.
Clear away my inner rubbish,
and fill me with your Spirit
of healing, delight and peace,
so that everything I do
may be the fruit of your life in me.

A.A.

20   Ask what you will, and give what you ask.
                St Augustine of Hippo (354–430)

21   O gracious God,
      accept my offering, though it is incomplete.
      Accept my time, though it is often broken,
      my energy, though it is often frail.
      Lead me, guide me, hold me
      in your straight and simple way,
      and let me shine in the remembrance of your love,
      one holy whole,
      knowing peace in the still flame of my soul.
                        Julie M. Hulme

22   Lord of my life,
      I give you my time,
      my reputation,
      my worries
      and my desires.
      Thank you
      that you receive whatever I offer
      and transform it,
      so that this gift of my life
      is taken up
      into your great energy of love.
                              A.A.

23   My Father,
      I abandon myself into your hands.
      Do with me as you will.
      Whatever you may do with me,
      I thank you.
      I am prepared for anything,
      I accept everything,
      provided your will is fulfilled in me
      and in all creatures.
      I ask for nothing more,
      my God.
      I place my soul in your hands,

I give it to you, my God,
with all the love of my heart,
because I love you.
And for me it is a necessity of love,
this gift of myself,
this placing of myself in your hands,
in boundless confidence,
because you are
my Father.

Charles de Foucauld (1858–1916)

24 O Christ my Beloved,
each day you embrace me,
each hour you honour me,
each moment you cherish me.
I do not deserve it,
but through your grace,
I accept that I am,
in your eyes,
lovely and beloved:
so fill me with your Holy Spirit,
that I may take
each present moment, hour, and day
to embrace, honour
and cherish others.

Julie M. Hulme

25 How shall I not give you
all that I have,
when you, in your great goodness,
give me all that you are?
Source unknown

26 O God
be all my love,
all my hope,
all my striving;

> let my thoughts and words flow from you,
> my daily life be in you,
> and every breath I take be for you.
> *after St John Cassian (360–435)*

27   Lord, take as your right, and receive as my gift,
all my freedom, my memory,
my understanding and my will.
Whatever I am and whatever I possess,
you have given to me;
I restore it all to you again,
to be at your disposal,
according to your will.
Give me only a love for you,
and the gift of your grace;
then I am rich enough,
and ask for nothing more.
St Ignatius Loyola (1491–1556)

28   Lord, in union with your love, unite my work with your great
work, and perfect it. As a drop of water, poured into a river, is
taken up into the activity of the river, so may my labour become
part of your work. Thus may those among whom I live and work
be drawn into your love.
St Gertrude the Great (1256–c.1302)

29   It is a comfort, Lord, to know that you did not entrust the fulfilment of your will to one so pitiable as me. I would have to be
very good if the accomplishment of your will were in my hands.
Although my will is still self-centred, I give it, Lord, freely to you.
St Teresa of Avila (1515–1582)

30   O Lord my God, take away from me all that blocks my way to
you; give me all that speeds me towards you; rescue me from
myself, and give me as your own to yourself.
Nicholas von Flue (1417–87)

31   Have thine own way, Lord,
       Have thine own way;
       Thou art the Potter,
       I am the clay.
       Mould me and make me,
       After thy will,
       While I am waiting
       Yielded and still.
                         A.A. Pollard (1862–1934)

32   Dear Jesus,
       help me to spread your fragrance everywhere I go.
       Flood my soul with your spirit and life.
       Penetrate and possess my whole being so utterly
       that my life may only be a radiance of yours.
       Stay with me, and then I shall begin to shine as you shine,
       so to shine as to be a light to others;
       the light, O Jesus, will be all from you,
       none of it will be mine:
       it will be you, shining on others through me.
       Let me thus praise you in the way you love best,
       by shining on those around me.
                         John Henry Newman (1801–1890)

33   Lord Jesus,
            take my mind and think through me,
            take my hands and bless through me,
            take my mouth and speak through me,
       above all, Lord Jesus,
            take my spirit and pray in me;
            so that it is you who move and have your being in me.
                         based on a prayer in a sixteenth-century Book of Hours

34   A PRAYER WITH A CANDLE
       My Lord and my God –
       thank you for drawing me to Yourself . . .
       Keep the burning of my desire for you

as clear and steady as the flame of this candle,
– a single, undivided focus of attention,
a steady offering of the will.
Let my whole being be filled with Your light
so that others may be drawn to You.
Let my whole being be cleansed by the flame of Your love
from all that is contrary to Your will for me ...
– my Lord and my God.

Margaret Dewey (abbreviated)

35   Lord, let me not live to be useless.

John Wesley (1703–1791)

36   Lord increase
My zest for living
My vision of glory
My hearing of your call
My grasp on reality
My response to your love
My sensitivity to others
My gentleness to creation
My taste for wonder
My love for you.

David Adam

37   The things, good Lord, that I pray for, give me the grace to
labour for.

St Thomas More (1478–1535)

38   Take my life, and let it be
Consecrated, Lord, to thee;
Take my moments and my days,
Let them flow in ceaseless praise.

Take my will, and make it thine:
It shall be no longer mine.
Take my heart: it is thine own;
It shall be thy royal throne.

Take my love; my Lord, I pour
At thy feet its treasure-store.
Take myself, and I will be
Ever, only, all for thee.

Frances R. Havergal (1836–1879)

39   Lord, give me grace
to follow your example.
Create in me the desire and will
to put the needs of others before my own.
Take me and all I have;
do with me whatever you will;
send me wherever you will;
use me as you will.
I surrender myself
and all I possess
absolutely and entirely,
unconditionally and for ever
to your control.

Edith Ventress

40   I place my hands in yours Lord
I place my hands in yours

I place my will in yours Lord
I place my will in yours

I place my days in yours Lord
I place my days in yours

I place my thoughts in yours Lord
I place my thoughts in yours

I place my heart in yours Lord
I place my heart in yours

I place my life in yours Lord
I place my life in yours

David Adam

41   Holy and intimate God,
      you are closer to us than we are to ourselves,
      yet beyond our farthest imagining:
      remind us of your presence
      as we walk the ways of daily life,
      and draw us beyond ourselves
      into adoration and praise of you;
      through Jesus, your beloved Son,
      our Brother and our Saviour.

                                              A.A.

42   Lord, I have time,
      I have plenty of time,
      All the time that you give me,
      The years of my life,
      The days of my years,
      The hours of my days,
      They are all mine.
      Mine to fill, quietly, calmly.
      But to fill completely, up to the brim,
      To offer them to you, that of their insipid water
      You may make a rich wine such as you made once in Cana of
      Galilee.

      I am not asking you tonight, Lord, for time to do this and then
      that,
      But your grace to do conscientiously, in the time that you give
      me, what you want me to do.

                                     Michel Quoist

43   Lord, you entered into the world and became flesh so that the
      love which abides with the world could still be seen and felt. By
      your grace, enable me to enter into your healing life with loving
      and caring action, as your Spirit shall lead.

                                        CARA

44   O Holy Spirit of God –
      Come into my heart and fill me:
      I open the window of my soul to let you in.
      I surrender my whole life to you.
      Come and possess me, fill me with light and truth.
      I offer to you the one thing I really possess,
      My capacity for being filled by you.
      Of myself I am an empty vessel.
      Fill me so that I may live the life of the Spirit,
      The life of Truth and Goodness,
      The life of Beauty and Love,
      The life of Wisdom and Strength.
      But, above all, make Christ to be formed in me,
      That I may dethrone self in my heart
      and make him King;
      So that he may be in me, and I in him,
      Today and for ever.
                          the late Bishop of Bloemfontein

45   Lord, make me an instrument of your peace.
      Where there is hatred, let me sow love;
      Where there is injury, pardon;
      Where there is doubt, faith;
      Where there is despair, hope;
      Where there is darkness, light;
      Where there is sadness, joy.
      O divine Master, grant that I may not so much seek
      To be consoled, as to console,
      To be understood, as to understand,
      To be loved, as to love;
      For it is in giving that we receive;
      It is in pardoning that we are pardoned;
      It is in dying that we are born to eternal life.
                          attributed to St Francis (1182–1226)

46   O Living God,
                    we who are partly living,
                        scarcely hoping,
                      and fitfully caring,

pray to you now
to make us fully alive.
Give us the vitality, awareness and commitment
that we see in Jesus Christ,
through the power of his death and resurrection.
We ask this in his Name.
John V. Taylor

47   Almighty God, you have made us for yourself, and our hearts
are restless till they find rest in you. Grant us purity of heart and
strength of purpose, that no selfish passion may hinder us from
knowing your will, and no weakness hinder us from doing it; but
that in your light we may see light, and in your service find our
perfect freedom; through Jesus Christ our Lord.
after St Augustine of Hippo (354–430)

48   Agreeing to lose everything for you, O Christ,
in order to take hold of you,
as you have already taken hold of us,
means abandoning ourselves to the living God.
Centring our life on you, Christ Jesus,
means daring to choose:
leaving ourselves behind so as no longer to walk
on two roads at the same time:
saying no to all that keeps us from following you,
and yes to all that brings us closer to you,
and through you, to those whom you entrust to us.
Brother Roger of Taizé

49   Lord, perfect in us all that is lacking of your gifts:
   of faith, to increase it,
   of hope, to strengthen it,
   of love, to rekindle it,
and make us fear one thing only,
that we should honour anything more than you,
our Father, our Saviour, and our Lord.
after Lancelot Andrewes (1555–1626)

50   O Almighty God, we humbly ask you to make us like trees
planted by the waterside, that we may bear fruits of good living
in due season. Forgive our past offences, sanctify us now, and
direct all that we should be in the future; for Christ's sake.

prayer from Nigeria

51   O God, help us to be masters of ourselves that we may become
the servants of others, and thus follow in the path of thy blessed
Son Jesus Christ our Lord.

Alec Paterson

52   O Lord God,
when thou givest to thy servants to endeavour any great matter,
grant us also to know that it is not the beginning,
but the continuing of the same unto the end,
until it be thoroughly finished, which yieldeth the true glory;
through him who for the finishing of thy work laid down his life,
our Redeemer, Jesus Christ.

after Sir Francis Drake (c.1540–1596)

53   God of work and rest and pleasure,
grant that what we do this week may be for us
an offering rather than a burden;
and for those we serve, may it be the help they need.

A New Zealand Prayer Book

54   Jesus, Son of God,
let your love shine through our eyes,
your Spirit inspire our words,
your wisdom fill our minds,
your mercy control our hands,
your will capture our hearts,
your joy pervade our being;
until we are changed into your likeness
from glory to glory.

Michael Perry

55   O God, you are the light of the minds that know you,
the life of the souls that love you,
and the strength of the wills that serve you:
Help us so to know you that we may truly love you,
and so to love you that we may fully serve you,
whom to serve is perfect freedom;
through Jesus Christ our Lord.

St Augustine of Hippo (354–430)

AT THE OFFERTORY IN A CHURCH SERVICE

56   We offer these gifts, O Lord, as a sign of thankfulness and a pledge of our love. Everything we possess comes from you. Take all that we are, and show us how to give with joy and share without fear.

A.A.

57   Great Giver of all good gifts, we offer you back
our talents, our time and all that we possess.
Transform them, along with our lives,
into means of your life-giving freedom for all.

Worship in an Indian Context

58   Lord, everything we have, all that we are, comes from you. Our gifts, our talents, all our possibilities belong to us only because they come direct from you. Help us not to belittle these gifts of yours, not to bury them, but rather use them to make you better known to the people of our neighbourhood and to the people of the world.

Colin Semper

PARAPHRASES OF THE LORD'S PRAYER

59   God, lover of us all,
      most holy one,
      help us to respond to you,
      to create what you want for us here on earth.
      Give us today enough for our needs;
      forgive our weak and deliberate offences,
      just as we must forgive others
      when they hurt us.
      Help us to resist evil
      and to do what is good;
      for we are yours,
      endowed with your power
      to make our world whole.
                              Lala Winkley

60   Father and Mother of us all,
      You are love through and through,
      and we bless You.
      Let Your new world come,
      let what You long for be always done,
      in everyone, everywhere – and in us.
      Be near enough to reach our need every day.
      Be gentle enough to forgive us
      the hurt we have done to You –
      as we are gentle and forgive in our turn.
      Never let us fall,
      but draw us away from evil and the dark.
      For we know the world that is coming is Yours,
      all Yours, in richness and beauty and splendour.
                              Simon Bailey

THE COST OF
DISCIPLESHIP

Abba, Father, take this cup away from me; nevertheless, not my will, but yours be done.

MARK 14:36

ꜩ꜡ ꜡ꜩ

61 Jesus, where are you taking me?
      Into joy.
      Into pain.
    I am afraid,
    but to do anything other than go with you
    would be to die inwardly;
    and to look for wholeness apart from you
    would be to lose my true self.
    So I come to you,
    protesting and confused,
    but loving you all the same.
    You will have to hold on to me
    as we walk together
    through this compelling and frightening landscape
    of the kingdom of God.
                              A.A.

62 Good Jesus, who bore the cross for me, what cross is it you will
    that I should bear for you? You know, Lord, that I am all weak-
    ness; teach me to bear my cross: bear it for me, bear it in me.
                              Edward Pusey (1800–1882)

63 It is the easy way
      to dwell on what we'd like to do
        but cannot,

to mourn what might have been
    but is not,
to weep for what was nearly done
    but not quite.
That way is wide
but is not your way;
    you fulfil
    your own desires,
you nurture
    what you love,
you treasure
    those you create.
Be Lord of my life, Sovereign God!
Jane Grayshon

64   O Heavenly Father,
I praise and thank you for all your goodness
and faithfulness throughout my life.
You have granted me many blessings.
Now let me accept tribulation from your hand.
You will not lay on me more than I can bear.
You make all things work together for good
For your children.
Dietrich Bonhoeffer (1906–1945)

65   O my God, stand by me against all the world's wisdom and reason. Not mine, but yours is the cause. I would prefer to have
peaceful days, and to be out of this turmoil. But yours, O Lord,
is this cause; it is righteous and eternal. Stand by me, O God, in
the name of your dear Son, Jesus Christ, who shall be my
Defence and Shelter, my Mighty Fortress, through the might and
strength of your Holy Spirit. God help me.
Martin Luther (1483–1546)

66   Jesus our brother,
you followed the necessary path
and were broken on our behalf.
May we neither cling to our pain

where it is futile,
nor refuse to embrace the cost
when it is required of us:
that in losing our selves for your sake,
we may be brought to new life.

Janet Morley

67　O Lord,
whatever the world may say,
may we only pay attention
to what you are saying to us,
and seek only your approval,
which far outweighs any honour or praise
that the world might bestow or withhold.

after General Gordon (1833–1885)

68　O God our Father, whose blessed Son, being falsely accused,
answered nothing; being reviled, reviled not again: Give us faith,
when others accuse us falsely, to go quietly on our way, com-
mitting ourselves to you, who judge righteously, after the pattern
of our Lord and Saviour Jesus Christ.

Eric Milner-White (1884–1963) and G. W. Briggs (1875–1959)

69　Let us embrace the way of the Crucified Jesus:
fountain of life,
source of hope,
deliverer from slavery,
maker of peace,
obedient to death,
pioneer of the narrow way,
burning flame of love,
source of all faithfulness,
sanctuary of justice,
elder brother,
Lamb slain from before the foundation of the world,
bodily presence of the fullness of God,
our life, our death, our resurrection.

Jim Cotter

70   Good God,
      may we confess your name to the end.
      May we emerge unsullied and glorious
      from the traps and dark powers of this world.
      As you have bound us together
      in love and peace,
      and as, together, we have persevered
      through times of hardship,
      may we also rejoice together
      in your heavenly kingdom.

St Cyprian of Carthage (c.200–258);
This was written in the year of his martyrdom, to encourage his fellow-Christians
under persecution.

LIFE IN GOD

In you, Lord, I live and move and have my being
BASED ON ACTS 17:28

71 and you held me and there were no words
and there was no time and you held me
and there was only wanting and
being held and being filled with wanting
and I was nothing but letting go
and being held
and there were no words and there
needed to be no words
and there was no terror only stillness
and I was wanting nothing and
it was fullness and it was like aching for God
and it was touch and warmth and
darkness and no time and no words and we flowed
and I flowed and I was not empty
and I was given up to the dark and
in the darkness I was not lost
and the wanting was like the fullness and I could
hardly hold it and I was held and
you were dark and warm and without time and
without words and you held me
                                    Janet Morley

72 O living God,
draw all the fragments of my life
into the bright mosaic of your love;
weave all the tangled threads of my desires
into the tapestry you are spreading,
like a rainbow,
on the loom of the world;

and help me celebrate
the many facets
and the dazzling colours
of your peace.

Julie M. Hulme

73   Nothing can comprehend you,
nothing can apprehend you.
You pass through me in waves.
The limitations of my body
cannot hold you.
I am confused but filled with joy.
You have taken hold of me
and healed me with your presence.

Ulrich Schaffer

74   God, of your goodness, give me yourself, for you are sufficient
for me. To be worthy of you I cannot ask for anything less. If I
were to ask less, I should always be in want, for in you alone
do I have all.

Julian of Norwich (c.1342–1413)

75   If every part of my life
is with you
and in you, Lord,
then everything is made good:
even the things I struggle not to resent,
even the draining and hurtful encounters.
Let every moment of my life be your moment,
whether or not I consciously remember you,
and make me more open
to the pulse of your life
and the breath of your love.

A.A.

76   Your kingdom is already growing in me.
       I meet you as you spread out in me,
       and shape the landscape of my life
       after your will.

                                    Ulrich Schaffer

77   Lord,
       you trust me,
       you free me,
       you love me,
       you fill me,
       you share your work with me,
       you are my life.

                                         A.A.

78   You yourself are my contemplation;
       you are my delight.
       You, for your own sake,
       I seek above all else.
       From you yourself
       I feed within me.
       You are the field
       in which I labour.
       You are the food
       for which I labour.
       You are my cause,
       you are my goal,
       you are my beginning,
       you are my end, without end.
       You are for me
       eternity.

                            after Isaac of Stella

79   Lord,
       I cannot fathom or hold you;
       I can only ask you
       to take hold of me.

I cannot grasp or contain you
in a formula or tradition;
I can only ask you to fill me with yourself,
and make me part
of the mystery of your presence
in the world.

A.A.

80   O Lord, I do not know what to ask of you. You alone know what
are my true needs. You love me more than I myself know how to
love. Help me to see my real needs, which are concealed from me.
I dare not ask for either a cross or a consolation; I can only wait
on you. My heart is open to you. Come to me and help me, for
your great mercy's sake ...
I put all my trust in you. I have no other desire than to fulfil your
will. Teach me how to pray; pray yourself in me.

Metropolitan Theodore Philaret of Moscow (1553–1633)

81   Lord, cleanse and sweeten the springs of my being,
that your freedom and light
may flow into my conscious mind
and into my hidden, unconscious self.

A.A.

82   It is well and good, Lord, if all things change, provided we are
rooted in you. If I go everywhere with you, my God, everywhere
things will happen for your sake; that is what I desire.

St John of the Cross (1542–1591)

83   Lord, you have searched me out and known me;
you know when I sit down, and when I rise up,
you discern my thoughts long before.
You know my journeys and the places where I rest;
you are acquainted with all my ways.
You are behind me and before me;
you have laid your hand upon me.
Such knowledge is too wonderful for me;
so great that I can hardly bear it.

Psalm 139:1–2, 5–6

84   Circle me O God
      Keep peace within
      Keep turmoil out.

      Circle me O God
      Keep calm within
      Keep storms without.

      Circle me O God
      Keep strength within
      Keep weakness out.

                              David Adam

85   My God,
      I pray that I may so know you and love you
      that I may rejoice in you.
      And if I may not do so fully in this life,
      let me go steadily on
      to the day when I come to fullness of life.
      Meanwhile let my mind meditate on your eternal goodness,
      let my tongue speak of it,
      let my heart live it,
      let my mouth speak it,
      let my soul hunger for it,
      and my whole being desire it,
      until I enter into your joy.

                              St Anselm (1033–1109)

86   God to surround me, God to encompass me;
      God in my words, God in my thought;
      God in my waking, God in my resting;
      God in my hoping, God in my doing;
      God in my heart, God in my soul;
      God in my weakness, God in my strength;
      God in my life, God in eternity;
      God in my life, God in eternity.

                              W. Mary Calvert

87   God be in my head, and in my understanding;
God be in my eyes, and in my looking;
God be in my mouth, and in my speaking;
God be in my heart, and in my thinking;
God be at my end and at my departing.

The Sarum Primer (1558)

88   I am not worthy, Master and Lord, that you should come beneath
the roof of my soul; yet since in your love towards all, you wish
to dwell in me, in boldness I come. You command; open the gates,
which you alone have made. And you will come in, and enlighten
my darkened reasoning. I believe that you will do this; for you
did not send away the harlot who came to you with tears, nor
cast out the repenting tax-collector, nor reject the thief who
acknowledged your kingdom. But you counted all of these as
members of your band of friends. You are blessed for evermore.

St John Chrysostom (c.347–407)

89   God,
to whom all hearts are open,
to whom all wills speak
and from whom no secret is hidden,
I beg you,
so to cleanse the intent of my heart
with the unutterable gift of your grace,
that I may perfectly love you
and worthily praise you.

The fourteenth-century author of The Cloud of Unknowing

90   O God, you are the unsearchable abyss of peace,
the ineffable sea of love,
and the fountain of blessings.
Water us with plenteous streams
from the riches of your grace;
and from the most sweet springs of your kindness,
makes us children of quietness and heirs of peace.

from the Syrian liturgy of St Clement of Alexandria (c.150–c.215)

91   Make us receptive and open,
      and may we accept your kingdom
      like children taking bread
      from the hands of their father.
      Let us live in peace,
      at home with you,
      all the days of our lives.
                            Huub Oosterhuis

92   Great and merciful God,
      your life is the source of the whole world's life;
      your mercy is our only hope;
      your eyes watch over all your creatures;
      you know the secrets of our hearts.
      By your life-giving Spirit, draw us into your presence,
      that we may worship in the true life of your Spirit,
      with lives moved by your love,
      through him who has led us to your heart of love,
      even Jesus Christ, our Lord.
                      The Church of South India

LOVE OF GOD

*Beloved, let us love one another, because love is from God;
everyone who loves is born of God and knows God.*
1 JOHN 4:7

93   O living flame of love,
that wounds my soul so tenderly
in its deepest centre;
since, by your grace, I can endure your touch,
perfect your work in me
according to your will.
St John of the Cross (1542–1591)

94   I love you, O my God, and my only desire is to love you until the last breath of my life. I love you, and I would rather die loving you than live without loving you. I love you, Lord, and the only grace I ask is to love you eternally. My God, if my tongue cannot say in every moment that I love you, I want my heart to repeat it to you as often as I draw breath.
Jean-Baptiste Vianney, Curé d'Ars (1786–1859)

95   Lord, you are my lover;
you are my flowing stream;
you are my sun;
make me your reflection.
after Mechtild of Magdeburg (1207–94)

96   O my Love, I cannot love thee, but that I must desire above all things to be like my Beloved. O give me grace to tread in thy steps and conform me to thy divine image, that the more I grow like thee, the more I may love thee, and the more I may be loved by thee.
Thomas Ken (1637–1711)

97   Lord, let the flame of your love
                set on fire my whole heart.
            May I wholly burn towards you,
                wholly love you,
                set aflame by you.
            St Augustine of Hippo (354–430)

98   At each beat of my heart I want, O my Beloved, to renew my offer-
      ing to you an infinite number of times, until the shadows have dis-
      appeared and I can tell you of my love face to face in eternity.
            St Thérèse of Lisieux (1873–97)

99   You know better than I how much I love you, Lord. You
      know it and I know it not, for nothing is more hidden from me
      than the depths of my own heart.
          I desire to love you; I fear that I do not love you enough. I
      beseech you to grant me the fullness of pure love.
          Behold my desire; you have given it to me. Behold in your
      creature what you have placed there. O God, you love me
      enough to inspire me to love you for ever; behold not my sins.
      Behold your mercy and my love.
            François Fénelon (1631–1715)

100   O Jesu, O Sacred Heart,
            burning with Divine Love
      send into my heart
          a spark of that fire
          which burneth in thee;
      excite in me a burning and a flaming spirit;
      impress upon me
          the seal of thy Love
          that I may worthily perform thy work.
            Gilbert Shaw (1886–1967)

101   Grant, Lord, that I may not for one moment admit willingly into
      my soul any thought contrary to your love.
            Edward Pusey (1800–1882)

102   Jesus, receive my heart, and bring me to your love. You are all
       my desire. Kindle fire within me, that I may enter your love, and
       see your face in bliss, in heaven with never an ending.
                              after Richard Rolle (1300–1349)

103   I am serene because I know thou lovest me.
       Because thou lovest me, naught can move me from my peace.
       Because thou lovest me, I am one to whom all good has come.
                              Ancient Celtic prayer from Scotland

104   Lord, grant me, I pray,
       in the name of Jesus Christ, the Son,
       that love which knows no fall,
       so that my lamp
       may feel his kindling touch
       and know no quenching;
       burning for me
       and giving light for others.
                              St Columbanus (c.543–615)

105   Eternal goodness,
       you want me to gaze into you
       and see that you love me.
       You love me freely,
       and you want me
       to love and serve my neighbours
       with the same love,
       offering them my prayers and my possessions,
       as far as in me lies.
       O God, come to my assistance!
                              St Catherine of Siena (1347–1380)

106   O Love, O God, who created me, in your love recreate me.
       O Love, who redeemed me, fill up in me whatever part of your
       love has fallen into neglect within me.
       O Love, O God, who first loved me, grant that with my whole
       heart, and with my whole soul, and with my whole strength, I
       may love you.
                              St Gertrude the Great (1256–c.1302)

107   Lord, you have taught us
       that all our doings without love are nothing worth.
       Send your Holy Spirit
       and pour into our hearts that most excellent gift of love,
       the true bond of peace and of all virtues,
       without which whoever lives is counted dead before you.
       Grant this for the sake of your only Son,
       Jesus Christ our Lord.
                       The Alternative Service Book *1980*

108   God our lover,
       in whose arms we are held,
       and by whose passion we are known:
       require of us also that love
       which is filled with longing,
       delights in the truth,
       and costs not less than everything,
       through Jesus Christ, Amen.
                                  Janet Morley

109   Great God, your love has called us here
       as we, by love, for love were made.
       Your living likeness still we bear,
       though marred, dishonoured, disobeyed.
           We come, with all our heart and mind,
           your call to hear, your love to find.
                                Brian A. Wren

110   May the power of your love, Lord Christ, fiery and sweet, so
       absorb our hearts as to withdraw them from undue attachment
       to all that is under heaven; grant that we may be ready to die
       for love of your love,
       as you died for love of our love.
                       after St Francis of Assisi (1182–1226)

111 Jesus, how sweet is the very thought of you! The sweetness of
your love surpasses the sweetness of honey. Nothing sweeter
than you can be described; no words can express the joy of your
love. Only those who have tasted your love for themselves can
comprehend it. Thank you for giving yourself to us.

St Bernard of Clairvaux (1091–1153)

112 O our Saviour! of ourselves we cannot love you, cannot follow
you, cannot become one with you,
  but you came down that we might love you,
  you ascended that we might follow you,
  you bound us close to you,
  that we might be held fast to you.
Since you have loved us, make us love you.
Since you found us when we were lost,
  be yourself the way,
  that we may find you
  and be found in you
  our only hope, and our everlasting joy.

Edward Pusey (1800–1882)

113 O God of love, we ask you to give us love;
Love in our thinking, love in our speaking,
Love in our doing,
And love in the hidden places of our souls;
Love of those with whom we find it hard to bear,
And love of those who find it hard to bear with us;
Love of those with whom we work,
And love of those with whom we take our ease;
That so at length we may be worthy to dwell with you,
Who are eternal love.

William Temple (1881–1944)

114   Lord Jesus Christ,
                   fill us, we pray, with your light
                that we may reflect your wondrous glory.
                      So fill us with your love
            that we may count nothing too small to do for you,
                      nothing too much to give,
                    and nothing too hard to bear.
                   St Ignatius Loyola (1491–1556)

115   O God, in whom nothing can live but as it lives in love: grant
      us the spirit of love, which does not want to be rewarded, hon-
      oured, or esteemed, but only to become the blessing and happi-
      ness of all who need it; this we pray in your name, for you
      yourself are Love, in time and eternity.
                   after William Law (1686–1761)

H U M I L I T Y

*You have heard the longing of the meek, O Lord; you will
strengthen their hearts, and turn your ear to their heart's
desire.*

PSALM 10:17

ᐃᑯ ᐃᑯᐤ

116   Save me, Lord, from the distraction
       of trying to impress others,
       and from the dangers of having done so.
       Help me to enjoy praise for work well done,
       and then to pass it on to you.
       Teach me to learn from criticism,
       and give me the wisdom
       not to put myself at the centre of the universe.

A.A.

117   O God, when I encounter the two imposters 'triumph' and
       'disaster',
       show me the truth once more.
       Give me the good sense
       to be neither puffed up with pride
       nor plunged into gloom.
       Pick me up and put me firmly
       on the narrow way that leads to freedom,
       and redeem both my mistakes and my successes
       in your abundant mercy.

A.A.

Rudyard Kipling (1865–1936) spoke of 'Triumph' and 'Disaster' equally as
'imposters', in the poem 'If–'.

118   Christ our companion,
       you came not to humiliate the sinner
       but to disturb the righteous.

ᐃ54

Welcome us when we are put to shame,
but challenge our smugness,
that we may truly turn from what is evil,
and be freed even from our virtues,
in your name.

Janet Morley

119   Suffer us, O Lord, never to think
       that we have knowledge enough to need no teaching,
           wisdom enough to need no correction,
           talents enough to need no grace,
           goodness enough to need no progress,
           humility enough to need no repentance,
           devotion enough to need no quickening,
           strength sufficient without your Spirit;
       lest standing still, we fall back for evermore.

Eric Milner-White (1884–1963)

120   Take away from our hearts, O Christ, all over-confidence and
       boasting, all high and vain thoughts, all desire to excuse ourselves
       for our sins, or to compare ourselves proudly with others; and
       grant us rather to take as Master and King you who chose to be
       crowned with thorns and to die in shame for us all, Jesus our Lord.

Charles Vaughan (1816–1897)

121   Eternal Father,
       whose Son Jesus
       was in the fullness of his power most gentle,
       and in his greatness most humble;
       bestow his mind and spirit upon us,
       who have no cause for pride;
       that clothed in true humility
       we may discern the way of true greatness.
       Hear our prayer through the same Jesus
       who is now Lord and Christ.

Paul Iles (adapted)

CALLING ON CHRIST

Lord, you know that I love you.
JOHN 21:15

122   Christ, I call upon your Name, for You are with me. I am never alone, never without help, never without a friend, for I dwell in You and You in me! 'Yea, though I walk through the valley of the shadow of death, I will fear no evil; for You are with me.'

David Adam

123   O Christ, you lived and breathed everything that matters.
Whatever the Spirit that was in you,
     let it be in me as well.
Whatever the energy
     that healed those who came into contact with you,
     let it flow through me as well.
Fill me with the vision, the tenderness and the passion
     that filled you.

A.A.

124   Behold, Lord, an empty vessel that needs to be filled. My Lord, fill it. I am weak in the faith; strengthen me. I am cold in love; warm me and make me fervent that my love may go out to my neighbour. I do not have a strong and firm faith; at times I doubt and am unable to trust you altogether. O Lord, help me and strengthen my faith and trust in you.

Martin Luther (1483–1546)

125   Jesus! my Shepherd, Brother, Friend,
     My Prophet, Priest, and King,
My Lord, my Life, my Way, my End,
     Accept the praise I bring.

Weak is the effort of my heart,
  And cold my warmest thought;
But when I see thee as thou art,
  I'll praise thee as I ought.

Till then I would thy love proclaim
  With every fleeting breath;
And may the music of thy name
  Refresh my soul in death.

John Newton (1725–1807)

126   Lord Jesus Christ,
      alive and at large in the world,
      help me to follow and find you there today,
      in the places where I work,
      meet people,
      spend money,
      and make plans.
      Take me as a disciple of your kingdom,
      to see through your eyes,
      and hear the questions you are asking,
      to welcome all others with your trust and truth,
      and to change the things that contradict God's love,
      by the power of the cross
      and the freedom of your Spirit.

John V. Taylor

127   O blessed Jesus, give me stillness of soul in Thee.
      Let Thy mighty calmness reign in me;
      Rule me, O King of gentleness, King of peace.
      Give me control, great power of self-control,
      Control over my words, thoughts and actions.
      From all irritability, want of meekness, want of gentleness, dear
      Lord, deliver me.
      By Thine own deep patience, give me patience.
      Make me in this and all things more and more like Thee.

St John of the Cross (1542–1591)

128   Thanks to be to thee, my Lord Jesus Christ,
          for all the benefits thou hast won for me,
          for all the pains and insults thou hast borne for me.
      O most merciful Redeemer, Friend and Brother,
          may I know thee more clearly,
          love thee more dearly,
          and follow thee more nearly,
          day by day.
                        St Richard of Chichester (1197–1253)

129   Christ be with me, Christ within me,
      Christ behind me, Christ before me,
      Christ beside me, Christ to win me,
      Christ to comfort and restore me.

      Christ beneath me, Christ above me,
      Christ in quiet, Christ in danger,
      Christ in hearts of all that love me,
      Christ in mouth of friend and stranger.
                        St Patrick (c.389–c.461)

130   Grant me, O most merciful Jesus, your grace ever to desire and to
      will what is most acceptable to you and most pleasing in your sight.

      Let your will be mine, and let my will ever follow yours, and
      fully accord with it.

      Let there be between you and me one single will, so that I may
      love what you love, and abhor what you hate; and let me not
      be able to will anything which you do not want, nor let me dis-
      like anything which you desire.
                        Thomas à Kempis (1380–1471)

131   O Christ you are a bright flame before me
      You are a guiding star above me
      You are the light and love I see in others' eyes.
      Keep me O Christ in a love that is tender
      Keep me O Christ in a love that is true
      Keep me O Christ in a love that is strong
      Tonight, tomorrow and always.
                        J. Philip Newell

132   Come, O Christ my Light, and illumine my darkness.
Come, my Life, and revive me from death.
Come, my Physician, and heal my wounds.
Come, Flame of divine love, and burn up the thorns of my sins,
kindling my heart with the flame of your love.
For you alone are my King and my Lord.
St Dimitrii of Rostov (seventeenth century)

133   O Lord Jesus Christ,
      stay beside me to defend me,
      within me to guide me,
      before me to lead me,
      behind me to guard me,
      and above me to bless me;
that with you and in you
I may live and move and have my being,
for ever and ever.
Source unknown

134   Love of Jesus, fill us,
Joy of Jesus, surprise us,
Peace of Jesus, flood us,
Light of Jesus, transform us,
Touch of Jesus, warm us,
Strength of Jesus, encourage us.
O Saviour, in your agony, forgive us,
in your wounds, hide us,
and in your risen life take us with you,
for your love's sake.
A.A.

135   O Christ, Saviour most sweet to us,
      kindle our lamps,
that they may shine continually in your house,
constantly receiving light from you,
the eternal Light,
so that our darkness may be driven from us.
St Columbanus (c.543–615)

136   Lift up our hearts, O Christ, above the false shows of things, above laziness and fear, above selfishness and covetousness, above whim and fashion, up to the everlasting Truth that you are; that we may live joyfully and freely, in the faith that you are our King and our Saviour, our Example and our Judge, and that, so long as we are loyal to you, all will ultimately be well.

Charles Kingsley (1819–1875)

137   O Christ, our Morning Star,
Splendour of Light Eternal,
shining with the glory of the rainbow,
come and waken us
from the greyness of our apathy
and renew in us your gift of hope.

The Venerable Bede (671–735)

138   O Lord, the help of the helpless,
    the hope of the hopeless,
    the saviour of the storm-tossed,
    the harbour of voyagers,
    the physician of the sick;
we pray to you.
O Lord, you know each of us and our petitions;
    you know each house and its needs;
receive us all into your kingdom;
make us children of light,
and bestow your peace and love upon us.

St Basil of Caesarea (c.330–379)

139   When our lives are empty, our hearts are cold and our spirits are low;
Christ of the Bethlehem stable, be born in us.

When we find temptation and the snare of power and pleasure hard to bear;
Christ of the desert wilderness, pray with us.

When we rejoice in health and happiness and life seems fair and good;
Christ of the roads of Galilee, walk with us.

When we seek our own interests and concerns before those of others;
Christ of the Temple cleansing, deal with us.

When our decisions are hard, our ways are stony and our hopes are dim;
Christ of Gethsemane, weep with us.

When we tread the paths of suffering and loss, of bitterness and despair;
Christ of the cross at Calvary, stay with us.

When our journey is ended and we bring our souls into your keeping;
Christ of the empty tomb, welcome us.

Alan Warren (adapted)

140   THE LIGHT OF CHRIST—A LITANY WITH CANDLES

Leader: *(holding up lighted candle)*
           The light and peace of Christ be with us all.

All: **The light and peace of Christ be with us all.**
           (This first candle is placed in a central position, with three unlit candles around it.)

1st person: I will light a light,
           The light of the Creator
           Who lit the world
           And breathed life into our souls.
           (lights a candle)

2nd person: I will light a light,
           The light of the Son
           Who saved the world
           And called on us to follow Him.
           (lights a candle)

3rd person: I will light a light,
The light of the Spirit
Who permeates the world
And remains a source of constant yearning.
(lights a candle)

Leader: As we light these candles, Lord,
We bend our knees and lay ourselves before you.
(people may kneel here if they wish)
Kindle in our hearts a flame of love,
Love to give warmth to our homes and dear ones,
Love to make happy our neighbours and communities,
Love to comfort our friends and forgive our foes,
Love to give light to our lives
And to lighten our way.

Leader: The light and peace of Christ be with us all.
All: The light and peace of Christ be with us all.

Brian Bell

FOR GUIDANCE AND DISCERNMENT

Teach me, O Lord, the way of your statutes; guide me in the path of your commandments, for my delight is in them.

PSALM 119:33, 35

∽⊙ ⊙∼

141 Lord, I am yours, I was born for you;
       what is your will for me?
     Let me be rich or beggared,
         exulting or lamenting
         comforted or lonely;
     since I am yours, yours only,
         what is your will for me?

St Teresa of Avila (1515–1582)

142 God,
       here I am.
     You alone fully know why.
     May I rest
     on that knowledge,
     and let it bear me
     where you will.

Sr Sheila, Community of All Hallows, Ditchingham

143 Jesus my Teacher, guide me along your way, and help me to piece together the jigsaw of life in your kingdom. When I make decisions, lead me to the heart of the matter, and when I face conflict, do not let my own panic drown out the still, small voice of your wisdom.

A.A.

144   My dearest Lord,
    be now a bright flame to enlighten me,
    a guiding star to lead me,
    a smooth path beneath my feet,
    and a kindly shepherd along my way,
    today and for evermore.
after St Columba (521–597)

145   Grant me grace, Lord, to be strong and wise in all things. Give me a generous love. Fill me with the spirit of intelligence and wisdom. Let me always be mindful of others. O perfect and eternal Light, enlighten me.
Alcuin of York (735–804)

146   Most high and glorious God,
come and enlighten the darkness
of my heart.
Give me right faith,
certain hope,
and perfect love,
that everything I do may be in fulfilment of your holy will;
through Jesus Christ my Lord.
St Francis of Assisi (1182–1226)

147   Show me your ways, O Lord,
    and teach me your paths.
Lead me in your truth, and guide me,
    for you are the God of my salvation,
    and my hope is in you all the day long.
Psalm 25:4–5

148   Eternal Godhead, O sea profound,
    what more could you give me than yourself?
You are the fire that never burns out;
You consume in your heat all the soul's self-love;
You are the flame that drives away the cold.
Give me your light that I may know all truth,
clothe me with yourself, eternal truth,

that I may live this mortal life with true obedience,
and in the light of your most holy faith.

St Catherine of Siena (1347–1380)

149 Grant me, O Lord, to know what is worth knowing,
to love what is worth loving,
to praise what delights you most,
to value what is precious to you,
and to reject whatever is evil in your eyes.
Give me true discernment,
so that I may judge rightly between things that differ.
Above all, may I search out and do
what is pleasing to you;
through Jesus Christ my Lord.

Thomas à Kempis (1380–1471)

150 O Creator past all telling,
you have so beautifully set out all parts of the universe;
you are the true fount of wisdom
and the noble origin of all things.
Be pleased to shed on the darkness of my mind
the beam and warmth of your light
to dispel my ignorance and sin.
Instruct my speech and touch my lips with graciousness;
make me keen to understand, quick to learn,
and able to remember;
and keep me finely tuned
to interpret your word,
for you are God for ever and ever.

St Thomas Aquinas (1225–1274)

151 As we plan and make decisions,
God be our way.
As we learn and ask questions,

we change,

Ruth Burgess

152   God our Father,
      gifts without measure flow from your goodness
      to bring us your peace.
      Our life is your gift.
      Guide our life's journey,
      for only your love makes us whole.

                                    The Roman Missal

153   God, give us grace to accept with serenity
      the things that cannot be changed,
      courage to change the things that should be changed,
      and the wisdom to distinguish the one from the other.

                         Reinhold Niebuhr (1892–1971)

154   Spirit of truth and judgement,
      who alone can exorcize
      the powers that grip our world:
      at the point of crisis
      give us your discernment,
      that we may accurately name what is evil,
      and know the way that leads to peace,
      through Jesus Christ.

                                    Janet Morley

155   O God, help us not to despise or oppose what we do not under-
      stand.

                         William Penn (1644–1718)

156   Lord Jesus Christ, you said that you are the Way, the Truth, and
      the Life; let us never stray from you, who are the Way; nor dis-
      trust you, who are the Truth; nor rest in any other but you, who
      are the Life, beyond whom there is nothing to be desired, either
      in heaven or on earth. We ask it for your name's sake.

                              Erasmus (1466–1536)

157   Almighty God, the fountain of all wisdom,
      you know our needs before we ask
      and our ignorance in asking;
      have compassion on our weakness,

and give us those things
which for our unworthiness we dare not
and for our blindness we cannot ask,
for the sake of your Son, Jesus Christ our Lord.

Ministry to the Sick: Authorized Alternative Services

158 O Lord, to be turned from you is to fall, to turn to you is to rise,
and to stand in your presence is to live for ever. Grant us in all
our duties your help, in all our perplexities your guidance, in all
our dangers your protection, and in all our sorrows your peace;
through Jesus Christ our Lord.

after St Augustine of Hippo (354–430)

159 Lord, you lead us by ways we do not know, through joy and sorrow, through victory and defeat, beyond our understanding.
Give us faith to see your guiding hand in all things; that being
neither lifted up by seeming success, nor cast down by seeming
failure, we may press forward wherever you lead, to the glory of
your name.

Eric Milner-White (1884–1963) and G. W. Briggs (1875–1959)

160 Eternal Light, shine into our hearts,
eternal Goodness, deliver us from evil,
eternal Power, be our support,
eternal Wisdom, scatter the darkness of our ignorance,
eternal Pity, have mercy upon us;
that with all our heart and mind and soul and strength
we may seek your face
and be brought by your infinite mercy to your holy presence;
through Jesus Christ our Lord.

Alcuin of York (735–804)

161 O Lord God,
who called your servants
to ventures of which we cannot see the ending,
by paths as yet untrodden,
through perils unknown:

Give us faith
to go out with a good courage,
not knowing where we are going,
but only that your hand is leading us,
and your love supporting us;
to the glory of your name.
Eric Milner-White (1884–1963) and G. W. Briggs (1875–1959)

162   O God, you are both the light and the guide of those who put
       their trust in you. Grant us in all our doubts and uncertainties
       the grace to ask what you would have us do; that the Spirit of
       wisdom may save us from all false choices, and that in your light
       we may see light; through Jesus Christ our Lord.
                          William Bright (1824–1901)

163   O God, the protector of all that trust in thee, without whom noth-
       ing is strong, nothing is holy: Increase and multiply upon us thy
       mercy; that, thou being our ruler and guide, we may so pass
       through things temporal, that we finally lose not the things eternal:
       Grant this, O heavenly Father, for Jesus Christ's sake, our Lord.
                     The Book of Common Prayer

SPEECH

164   Lord, guard my lips;
                          free me from
                  the clutter of unnecessary words,
                    the clamour of vengeful words,
                 and the cleverness of cynical words.
                      Teach me when to be silent,
        and when silence would mean cowardice or unkindness.
                  Let all my words be well used,
               coming from a quiet point within me
                        where you are,
                          the Word,
                     at the heart of my life.
                  A.A. (adapted from Psalm 141:3)

165   Lord give us wisdom before we speak,
          understanding while we listen,
          sensitivity towards those we meet,
          and the perspective of your kingdom.
                              John L. Bell

166   Set a watch, O Lord, upon our tongue:
          that we never speak the cruel word
               which is untrue;
          or, being true, is not the whole truth;
          or, being wholly true, is merciless;
               for the love of Jesus Christ our Lord.
          Eric Milner-White (1884–1963) and G. W. Briggs (1875–1959)

THE PILGRIMAGE OF LIFE

167   Christ our Guide,
          stay with us on our pilgrimage through life:
               when we falter, encourage us,
               when we stumble, steady us,
               and when we have fallen, pick us up.
          Help us to become, step by step, more truly ourselves,
          and remind us that you have travelled this way before us.
                              A.A.

USING THE BIBLE; JESUS THE WORD

Your word is a lantern to my feet, and a light to my path.
PSALM 119:105

෴ ෴

168   Thank you, Lord, for the gift of the Scriptures.
As I reflect on the Bible,
make me open to your wisdom,
receptive to your will
and courageous in my response;
in the love of Jesus,
Rabbi, Teacher, Friend.
A.A.

169   God of the living word,
give us the faith to receive your message,
the wisdom to know what it means,
and the courage to put it into practice.
A New Zealand Prayer Book

170   Father, we praise you for the gift of words: the words we hear and read, the words we speak and write. As we handle and use the Holy Scriptures, makes us more sensitive to what they say, more appreciative of the life and truth in these pages, and of the love and courage of those who wrote them; and open our ears to your voice, and our lives to yourself; through Jesus Christ our Lord.
Source unknown

171   Lord God,
you feed us with the living bread from heaven;
you renew our faith,

increase our hope,
and strengthen our love.

Teach us to hunger
for Christ who is the true and living bread,
and to live by every word
that comes from your mouth,
through Jesus Christ our Lord.

Westcott House (adapted)

172 God of revelation,
we thank you that you are not a silent God, isolated from
humanity, leaving us to guess and speculate about the things that
matter.
We pray for those who serve you by studying manuscripts and
clarifying texts: for scholars and preachers who wrestle with the
words of life for the building up of your Church;
for linguists, translators, and publishers who continue to serve
the cause of your Gospel by making the Bible available to more
and more people.

Lord, create in us a hunger for your Word,
a thankfulness for your Gospel, and a faithfulness to your commands; through Jesus Christ our Lord.

Patterns and Prayers for Christian Worship

173 O Lord Jesus,
let not your word become a judgement upon us,
lest we hear it and do not do it,
or believe it and do not obey it.

Thomas à Kempis (1380–1471)

174 God of truth, save us from a religion of mere words:
from repeating pious phrases which have lost their meaning;
from uttering empty prayers which have no soul;
from calling Jesus 'Lord, Lord', when we fail to own his
sovereignty.

We pray that the Gospel may come into our lives
    not in word only but also in the power of the Spirit,
and that our love may not be a matter of words or talk
    but be genuine and show itself in action.
Help us, our Father, to mean this our prayer
    as we ask it in the name of Christ our Lord.

Frank Colquhoun

175   Lord, thy word abideth,
    And our footsteps guideth;
    Who its truth believeth
    Light and joy receiveth.

O that we discerning
Its most holy learning,
Lord, may love and fear thee,
Evermore be near thee.

Sir Henry W. Baker (1821–1877)

176   O Lord, you have given us your word for a light to shine upon
    our path; inspire us to meditate on that word and to follow its
    teaching, that we may find in it the light that shines more and
    more until the perfect day; through Jesus Christ our Lord.

St Jerome (c.347–420)

See also:
    The Cost of Discipleship, 61–70
    Intercession – Offering Ourselves as Channels, 398–407
    Becoming a Full Church Member, 935–40
    Prayers for Good Friday, 790–811
    Pentecost Prayers, 838–59
Also:
    No. 570: 'Lord, may I ever speak . . .'
    No. 633: 'Each morning, Lord, I hold out my life to you'

part two

PRAISE AND THANKSGIVING

GENERAL AND SPECIFIC THANKSGIVINGS

Praise the Lord. Praise the Lord from heaven: O praise him in the heights.

PSALM 148:1

🙠 🙡

177   How can I tell of such love to me?
You made me in your image
and hold me in the palm of your hand,
your cords of love, strong and fragile as silk
bind me and hold me.
Rich cords, to family and friends,
music and laughter echoing in memories,
light dancing on the water, hills rejoicing.
Cords that found me hiding behind carefully built walls and led me out,
love that heard my heart break and despair and rescued me,
love that overcame my fears and doubts and released me.
The questions and burdens I carry you take,
to leave my hands free–to hold yours, and others,
free to follow your cords as they move and swirl in the breeze,
free to be caught up in the dance of your love,
finding myself in surrendering to you.
How can I tell of such love? How can I give to such love?
I am, here am I.
Catherine Hooper

178   As a needle turns to the north when it is touched by the magnet, so it is fitting, O Lord, that I, your servant, should turn to love and praise and serve you; seeing that out of love to me you were willing to endure such grievous pangs and sufferings.
Raymond Lull (1235–1315)

179   My Father, you have carried me through all my wanderings
         and loved me through my rebelliousness.
      I praise you.
      You have given me untold riches:
         friends to love,
         beauty to enjoy,
         quiet spaces.
      I praise you for life on this planet,
         for trust between people,
         and the unimaginable gift of the Gospel.
      Keep me thankful all my days,
      that, against all the odds,
      I may never lose sight
      of hope and delight.
                                    A.A.

180   Lord, you have given me so much; I ask for one more thing—
      a grateful heart.
                        after George Herbert (1593–1633)

181   It is good to give thanks to the Lord,
         to sing praises to your name, O Most High;
      to declare your steadfast love in the morning,
         and your faithfulness at night.
      For you have made me glad, O Lord, in all you have done,
         and I sing for joy at the works of your hands.
                              Psalm 92:1–2, 4

182   I will give thanks to the Lord with all my heart: his praise shall
      be continually in my mouth. O praise the Lord with me: let us
      exalt his name together.
                              Psalm 34:1, 3

183   Praise the Lord, O my soul, and all that is within me, praise his
      holy name;
      praise the Lord, O my soul, and forget not all his benefits.

For he forgives all your sins, and heals all your diseases;
he saves your life from destruction, and crowns you with mercy
and loving-kindness.

Psalm 103:1–4

184 I will give thanks to you, O Lord, among the people; I will sing
your praises among the nations.
For your mercy is greater than the heavens, and your faithfulness reaches to the clouds.

Psalm 108:3–4

185 Blessing and honour, thanksgiving and praise, more than I can
utter, more than I can understand, be yours, O most glorious
Trinity, Father, Son and Holy Spirit, by all angels, all people, all
creatures, now and for ever.

Lancelot Andrewes (1555–1626)

186 Praise to the Holiest in the height,
    And in the depth be praise,
In all his words most wonderful,
    Most sure in all his ways.

John Henry Newman (1801–1890)

187 Mighty God
we rejoice in your reckless and extravagant love
scattered among us
and found in the mud and thorns of life.

We rejoice
that your will for us and for the world
is not one of carefully apportioned judgement
or neatly wrapped rewards.

Praise be!
Your aim and desire for all your creation
is a cup full and overflowing with good wine,
a banquet for all to share,
a harvest of full and ripe grains,
a growing tree in which all can make their nest.

Your gifts, freely offered,
are life in all its fullness,
hope in abundance,
peace that passes understanding,
love that none can measure
from which nothing can separate us.

Terry Hinks

188   Praise to you, O faithful God!
You never fail those who trust in you,
but you allow them to share in your glory.
You fight for us against everything
that could attack or do us harm.
You are our shepherd,
and you free us from the snare.
You protect us who honour you, O God;
great is the sweetness that you give.

Notker (c.840–912)

189   You are holy, Lord, the only God,
and your deeds are wonderful.
You are love, you are wisdom.
You are humility, you are endurance.
You are rest, you are peace.
You are joy and gladness.
You are all our riches, and you suffice for us.
You are beauty, you are gentleness.
You are our protector,
You are our guardian and defender.
You are courage,
You are our haven and hope.
You are our faith, our great consolation.
You are our eternal life, great and wonderful Lord,
God almighty, merciful Saviour.

St Francis of Assisi (1182–1226) (abridged)

190 Eternal Father,
      through your Spirit delighting in the world,
      you created us from joy and for joy:
      grant us a deeper knowledge of the joy
      which is ours in Christ Jesus,
      that here our hearts may be glad,
      and in the world to come our joy may be full:
      for with the Son and the Holy Spirit,
      you are our God, now and for ever.

Raymond Hockley, 'The Order for Evening Prayer', York Minster

191 God our Creator, Father and Friend, we give thanks for the
      wonderful gift of life, with all its joys and responsibilities, its
      experiences and opportunities.
      We praise you for good health and daily food, for the shelter and
      care of our homes, and the love and loyalty of our friends.
      We bless you for work honestly done, for games well played, and
      for all the truth we have learned and the good we have been able
      to achieve.
      We thank you for the teaching and example of our Lord Jesus
      Christ, for the forgiveness and salvation we have received
      through him, for his presence with us always and for the serv-
      ice into which he has called us.
      Help us to express our thanks not only in our praises and
      prayers, but also through the lives we lead; through Jesus Christ
      our Lord.

                    Patterns and Prayers for Christian Worship

192 Gracious and heavenly Father, source of every blessing,
      giver of every good gift, we worship and adore you and bless
      your holy name.
      We praise you for the revelation of yourself in our Lord Jesus
      Christ and every glimpse we have of your nature.
      May our love and worship of you so fill our lives that we show
      you forth to others.
      We praise you for all the joys of life,

and the everyday blessings which we receive from you.
May we in turn be a source of blessing to all with whom we
come into contact.
We ask in Jesus' name.

The Mothers' Union Anthology of Public Prayers

193   Praise our God all you his servants,
honour him, you who fear God, both great and small.
Heaven and earth praise your glory, O Lord,
all creatures in heaven, on earth and under the earth;
let us praise and glorify him for ever.

St Francis of Assisi (1182–1226)

194   Great and wonderful are your deeds, O Lord God Almighty!
Just and true are your ways, O King of the nations!
Lord, who shall not fear and glorify your name?
For you alone are holy.
All nations will come and worship you.

Revelation 15:3–4

195   To God the Father who first loved us, and made us accepted in
the beloved Son;
to God the Son, who loved us and washed us from our sins in
his own Blood;
to God the Holy Spirit, who sheds abroad the love of God in
our hearts;
to the one true God be all love and all glory for time and
eternity.

Thomas Ken (1637–1711)

196   O God, for your love for us, warm and brooding,
which has brought us to birth and opened our eyes
to the wonder and beauty of creation,
We give you thanks.

For your love for us, compassionate and patient,
which has carried us through our pain,

wept beside us in our sin,
and waited with us in our confusion,
We give you thanks.

For your love for us, strong and challenging,
which has called us to risk for you,
asked for the best in us,
and shown us how to serve,
We give you thanks.

O God we come to celebrate
that your Holy Spirit is present deep within us,
and at the heart of all life.
Forgive us when we forget your gift of love
made known to us in Jesus,
and draw us into your presence.

Ali Newell

197 Living Love,
beginning and end,
giver of food and drink,
clothing and warmth,
love and hope:
life in all its goodness –
We praise and adore you.

Jesus, wisdom and word:
lover of outcasts,
friend of the poor,
one of us yet one with God,
crucified and risen:
life in the midst of death –
We praise and adore you.

Holy Spirit, storm and breath of love;
bridge-builder, eye-opener,
waker of the oppressed,
unseen and unexpected,
untameable energy of life –
We praise and adore you.

Holy Trinity, forever one,
whose nature is community;
source of all sharing,
in whom we love, and meet, and know our neighbour:
life in all its fullness,
making all things new:
We praise and adore you.

Brian A. Wren

198   LITANY OF ADORATION
Blessèd be God, the only God, three Persons in one eternity of
love:
Blessèd be God.
Blessèd be God, the lover of humankind, our Creator, Redeemer
and Sanctifier:
Blessèd be God.
Blessèd be God, the Fount of human love, by whom all our com-
mon life is made fruitful:
Blessèd be God.
Blessèd be God for all that He is:
Blessèd be God.
Blessèd be God for all that He has done:
Blessèd be God.
Blessèd in the fellowship of His Church and blessèd amid the
celestial host:
Blessèd be God.
Blessèd by the chorus of all people, and blessèd by the whisper
of each single soul:
Blessèd be God.
Blessèd from everlasting, blessèd now, and blessèd for ever.
Blessèd be God.

Ancient 'Agape' Liturgy

THANKSGIVING FOR HELP IN TROUBLE
199   Give thanks to the Lord, for he is good;
his loving-kindness endures for ever.

I was hard pressed, and almost fell,
  but the Lord helped me.
You are my God, and I will praise you.
  You are my God, I will extol you.
Psalm 118:1, 13, 28

200 I will praise you, O Lord, for you have drawn me up from the
  depths,
    and have not let my foes rejoice over me.
  O Lord my God, I cried to you for help,
    and you made me whole.
  You have turned my laments into dancing;
    you have taken off my sackcloth and clothed me with joy.
  So my heart will sing your praise and not be silent;
    O Lord my God, I will give thanks to you for evermore.
Psalm 30:1–2, 11–12

THE VARIETY OF THE HUMAN RACE

201 We thank you, Lord, that we are citizens of a world made up of
  different races. Your grace touches us all, whatever our race and
  colour. We rejoice in the richness of our cultures, our music and
  dance, our folklore and legends. We thank you for all these gifts.
  We delight in the joy they bring to our lives.
Women of Brazil (adapted)

MUSIC

202 We thank you, Lord, for music: for rich harmonies and com-
  pelling rhythms; for peaceful melodies and the great, stirring
  choruses. When we listen to music or share in making it, help us
  to do so with our full attention, so that our hearts as well as our
  heads may be open to the hints of glory that music can give;
  through Jesus Christ, our Lord.
A.A.

203   Let us make a joyful noise to the Lord,
          breaking forth into song and singing his praises.
       Lord, we praise you with joyful instruments,
          with harps, trumpets and pipes we make melody,
       for you are our King and our God.
                          based on Psalm 98:4–6

VISITING PLACES

204   A RETREAT OR QUIET DAY
       I thank you, Father, for my time at . . .
       For the beauty of the garden, and the labour of those who cultivate it.
       For the luxury of meals cooked for us, and for those who shoulder the heavy domestic burden.
       For the wise words I have heard, and the chance to see my life in true perspective.
       For the space to relax, and read, and think.
       For the quiet of the chapel, for burdens unloaded, and sin confessed and absolved.
       For the fellowship and inspiration of the Eucharist, and the chance to get deeper into prayer.
       Especially I praise you for the sense of joy and the intimations of Heaven to come.
       As I return to the busyness of the world, may I keep some of that peace and joy in my heart, so that I may radiate your love to others. Through your Son, Jesus Christ.
                          Mary Rose de Lisle

205   A PLACE OF PILGRIMAGE
       Thank you, Father, for this ancient place of prayer:
             for the faith that has blossomed here,
             and for worship in all seasons offered here;
             for the lives that have been touched here,
             and commitment stirred into life here.
       As we tread in the footsteps of our mothers and fathers in the faith,

bless us and all who come here,
and speak to us with the whisper of your love;
for you are a God of renewal and steadfastness,
now and for ever.

A.A.

206   HOLIDAYS

Thank you, Father, for the rhythm of rest and Sabbath at the
heart of creation. Bless those who are on holiday now; may they
be refreshed and re-created, and come home with new vision,
energy and contentment.

A.A.

PRAISE FOR CREATION

Lord, how manifold are your works; in wisdom have you made them all; the earth is full of your riches, and all the world sings your praise.

BASED ON PSALM 104:24, 33

207   I open my eyes, O God, to the glory and sunshine in your creation, and I open my heart to receive the full impact of your love.
May your radiant fire burn away all that is rotten in me.
Let me breathe in the fresh air of life on which I depend in the miracle of existence.
May the wind of your Spirit blow through me and clear away the cobwebs and the rubbish.
I surrender my whole being to the wind and sun of your love.

A.A.

208   Lord of life,
your life embraces me on
every side;
I open my arms to greet you.

God, grant me a clearer vision
of the many-splendoured thing,
your presence in and through all things,
that I may be one with your mind of love.

Richard Harries

209   Your Spirit, Lord, is around me
in the air I breathe;
your glory touches me
in the light that I see
and the fruitfulness of the earth
and the joy of its creatures.

You have written for me your revelation,
as you have granted me my daily bread;
teach me how to receive it.

based on words of John Ruskin (1819–1900)

210   God of delight, Source of all joy,
     thank you for making me part of the web of life,
     depending on the rhythms and fruits of the earth
               for my existence.
       Help me to be wholly present to you,
               now, in this place,
          where my feet are on the ground,
     and where I am surrounded by creation's gifts,
               from concrete to clouds,
          if I have the wit to notice them!
                    A.A.

211 I thank you, O God, for the pleasures you have given me
     through my senses; for the glory of thunder, for the mystery of
     music, the singing of birds and the laughter of children. I thank
     you for the delights of colour, the awe of the sunset, the wild
     roses in the hedgerows, the smile of friendship. I thank you for
     the sweetness of flowers and the scent of hay. Truly, O Lord, the
     earth is full of your riches!

          Edward King (1829–1910) (adapted)

212 Glory be to God for dappled things –
          For skies of couple-colour as a brinded cow;
          For rose-moles in all stipple upon trout that swim;
     Fresh-firecoal chestnut-falls; finches' wings;
          Landscape plotted and pieced – fold, fallow, and plough;
          And all trades, their gear and tackle and trim.

All things counter, original, spare, strange;
     Whatever is fickle, freckled (who knows how?)
          With swift, slow; sweet, sour; adazzle, dim;
He fathers-forth whose beauty is past change:
                    Praise him.

          Gerard Manley Hopkins (1844–1889)

213   Blessed are you, Lord God, our light and our salvation;
           to you be glory and praise for ever!
       From the beginning you have created all things
           and all your works echo the silent music of your praise.
       In the fullness of time you made us in your image,
           the crown of all creation.
       You give us breath and speech, that with all the powers of
       heaven,
           we may find a voice to sing your praise.
                         Patterns for Worship

214   Creator God, we worship you. In the beginning you said, 'Let
       there be light'; and the light shone, piercing the darkness.
       You have made the vast universe and amidst its movements and
       glories your Spirit is at work.
       Scattering the stars and moulding the hills, you have made a
       world full of beauty.
       You have made humankind in your own image, stewards of the
       earth, partners in creation.
       We are here because of you: that we exist is your doing. You are our
       God, our parent giving us life, lavishing gifts upon your children.
       The distances of space praise you. The depths of our being
       acknowledge your creating power.
       Creator God, we praise you.
                 Patterns and Prayers for Christian Worship

215   Praise the Lord!
       Praise him, sun and moon:
           praise him, all you shining stars,
           praise him, you highest heavens!
       Let them praise the name of the Lord,
           for he commanded and they were created.
       Praise the Lord from the earth,
           you sea creatures and all deeps,
       fire and hail, snow and frost,
           stormy wind fulfilling his will!
       Mountains and all hills,
           fruit trees and all cedars!

Wild animals and all cattle,
    creeping things and flying birds!
Let them praise the name of the Lord,
    for his name alone is exalted.
Psalm 148:1, 3–5, 7–10, 13

216   All beings pay you homage,
        those that think and those that cannot.
The universal desire, the groaning of all creation,
    aspires towards you.
Towards you all beings that can read your universe
    raise a hymn of silence.
The movement of the universe surges towards you;
    of all beings you are the goal,
you who are beyond all things.
St Gregory of Nazianzus (c.330–89) (Psalm 103:22, Romans 8:22)

217   You are to be praised, O God of Zion,
        and to you shall we make our pledge.
By your strength you established the mountains,
    and you are the hope of the ends of the earth.
You visit the earth and water it;
    you make it richly fertile, providing grain for the people.
You crown the year with your bounty,
    the pastures overflow and the hills are clothed with joy!
The valleys stand so thick with corn,
    they shout for joy and sing.
Psalm 65:1, 6, 9–13

218   For the beauty of the earth,
        For the beauty of the skies,
For the love which from our birth
    Over and around us lies,
Lord of all, to thee we raise
This our grateful hymn of praise.

For the beauty of each hour
    Of the day and of the night,

Hill and vale, and tree and flower,
    Sun and moon and stars of light,
Lord of all, to thee we raise
This our grateful hymn of praise.
Folliott S. Pierpoint (1835–1917) (adapted)

219   Worship and praise belong to you, God our maker.
Where nothing was you wove the web of being,
and still you draw the universe to its fulfilment.
Dawn and evening celebrate your glory
till time shall be no more.

In Christ your Son,
the life of heaven and earth were joined,
sealing the promise of a new creation,
given, yet still to come.

Taught by your Spirit,
we who bear your threefold likeness
look for the City of Peace
in whose light we are transfigured
and the earth transformed.
Scottish Liturgy

220   CANTICLE OF THE SUN
Most high, most powerful, good Lord, to you belong praise, glory, honour and all blessing!
Praised be my Lord God with all his creatures, and especially our brother the sun, who brings us the day and brings us the light; fair is he and shines with a great splendour.
O Lord, he signifies you.
Praised be my Lord for our sister the moon, and for the stars, which he has set clear and lovely in the heavens.
Praised be my Lord for our brother the wind, and for air and cloud, calms and all weather, by which you uphold life in all creatures.
Praised be my Lord for our sister water, who is very serviceable unto us and humble and precious and pure.

Praised be my Lord for our brother fire, through whom you give light in the darkness; and he is bright and pleasant and very mighty and strong.

Praised be my Lord for our mother the earth, who sustains us and keeps us, and brings forth various fruits and flowers of many colours.

Praise and bless the Lord, and give thanks unto him, and serve him with great humility.

St Francis of Assisi (1182–1226)

221 For the earth in all its richness,
     We praise you, Lord.
     For rocks, mountains and islands, signs of your strength and power,
     We praise you, Lord.
     For fossils, shells, and tiny, intricate creatures, signs of your delight in creation,
     We praise you, Lord.
     For fruits and nuts, berries, beans and blossoms, signs of your bounty towards us,
     We praise you, Lord.
     For wind and clouds, stars and galaxies, signs of your infinite mystery,
     We praise you, Lord.
     For birds and fish, reptiles and all animals that walk on land, signs that you trust us not to abuse earth's creatures,
     We praise you, Lord.
     For varieties of language and differences in cultures, signs of the wealth of gifts that we share,
     We praise you, Lord.
     For similarities between peoples and our dependence on each other, signs that we are all made in your image,
     We praise you, Lord.
     Give us generous eyes, thankful hearts and open hands, Creator God, whom we praise with all our hearts.

A.A.

222   Loving God, we praise you
      for giving to the world
      fish, birds and animals
      and trusting us to name them

      Whales that sing beneath the waves
      jellyfish and crabs
      sticklebacks and sharks
      friendly dolphins and porpoise schools
      rainbow trout and brilliant neon
      halibut and lemon sole
      carp and cod and coelacanth*
      Living God you made them
      and these are their names

      Thrushes singing
      swallows skimming
      herons fishing
      buzzards hovering
      skuas diving
      puffins shuffling
      robins chatting
      Creating God you made them
      and these are their names

      Elephants and midges
      gorillas and gerbils
      badgers and hedgehogs
      cows, pigs and sheep
      kangaroos and kittens
      lions and lemurs
      crocodiles and monkeys
      Enlivening God you made them
      and these are their names
      Loving God we pray now for the unity of the breathing world
      that we and all your creatures may live together in harmony and
      peace in the name of Jesus

                              Tony Burnham
      *Pronounced see-lar-canth – these are very rare, now mostly extinct fishes.

See also:
      Prayers for Harvest, 876–87
Also:
      No. 813: 'I thank you God'

part three

In Times of Difficulty

Trouble and Conflict

Why are you so full of heaviness, my soul, and why so unquiet within me? O put your trust in God, for I will praise him yet, who is my deliverer and my God.

PSALM 42:11

223 Heart of my shattered heart,
who will soothe the buried lament?
Who will pour oil on the biting pang
that never dies?
Christ, do you hear the words held back?
You are there, a love most healing.

Brother Roger of Taizé

224 Lord,
I am tearing the heart of my soul in two.
I need you to come
and lie there yourself
in the wounds of my soul.

Mechtild of Magdeburg (1207–1294)

225   I will face this pain.
I will accept its full impact
silently
turning my gaze
onto the crucified Christ
who is in this hell with me.
Even here
I am held in the love of Jesus
who is both Love-in-death
and Love-Risen.

A.A.

226   O Father God,
      I cannot fight this darkness by beating it with my hands.
      Help me to take the light of Christ right into it.
                              Prayer from Africa

227   Lord,
      through weariness and hurt,
      through disaster on the news,
      though headaches and depression,
      I am still yours.
      I do not understand,
      but I believe that you are here
      in the dark places of human life,
      and that nothing
      can take us out of your hands.
                              A.A.

228   From the depths of my despair I call to you,
          O Lord, hear my voice.
      I look for the Lord, my soul waits for him,
          in his word is all my trust.
      My soul waits for the Lord,
          more than those who watch for the morning.
      O Israel, trust in the Lord!
          for with him is steadfast love,
          and great is his power to save and redeem.
                          Psalm 130:1–2, 5–7

229   Here I am, Lord,
          wounded
          worried
          divided against myself.
      Here I am
          naked
          numb
          exposed to you.

Here I am
    held
    healed
    loved
passive in the arms of my God.

A.A.

230   Jesus, lover of my soul,
            Let me to thy bosom fly,
        While the gathering waters roll,
            While the tempest still is high:
        Hide me, O my Saviour, hide,
            Till the storm of life is past;
        Safe into the haven guide,
            O receive my soul at last.

        Other refuge have I none;
            Hangs my helpless soul on thee;
        Leave, ah, leave me not alone,
            Still support and comfort me.
        All my trust on thee is stayed,
            All my help from thee I bring;
        Cover my defenceless head
            With the shadow of thy wing.

Charles Wesley (1707–1788)

231   Dear Lord and Saviour, Jesus Christ,
        I hold up all my weakness to your strength,
        my failure to your faithfulness,
        my sinfulness to your perfection,
        my loneliness to your compassion,
        my little pains to your great agony on the Cross.
            I pray that you will cleanse me, strengthen me, and hide me,
        so that, in all ways, my life may be lived
        as you would have it lived,
        without cowardice
        and for you alone.

Mother Janet Stuart (1857–1914)

232   Calm my troubled heart; give me peace.
O Lord, calm the waves of this heart, calm its tempests!
Calm thyself, O my soul, so that the divine can act in thee!
Calm thyself, O my soul, so that God is able to repose in thee,
    so that his peace may cover thee!
Yes, Father in heaven, often have we found that the world can-
not give us peace, but make us feel that thou art able to give
peace; let us know the truth of thy promise: that the whole world
may not be able to take away thy peace.

Søren Kierkegaard (1813–1855)

233   Today has been a restless day,
things going wrong in all directions,
and my anger rising–at others,
at circumstances, at myself.

God, you are in the midst of this.
I sense your presence
prowling like a tiger,
pushing me, pursuing me,
restless yourself until I change.

I am ready to let rip,
to hurl stones into oceans,
to pound my fists into a brick wall.
I am ready to shout,
to rip sheets into shreds,
to curse the darkness,
to bury my head into warm flesh and sob.

I am afraid, God;
there is no one here but you and me,
my friends are out or busy or far away.
Do I trust you enough to give you my anger, my loneliness?
Do I believe you enough to reach through the emptiness
and grasp for your hand?

Credo.
God, I love you.
I can say no other words.

Ruth Burgess

234 Lord, this is what went wrong . . .
I give it all to you, every detail, every barb, every frustration,
the major things and the petty things.
May the pain I am feeling be for healing, and not a spring of
bitterness.
May my hurts be Christ-centred, and for those involved, rather
than self-centred and against them.

A.A.

235 anoint the wounds
of my spirit
with the balm
of forgiveness
pour the oil
of your calm
on the waters
of my heart

take the squeal
of frustration
from the wheels
of my passion
that the power
of your tenderness
may smooth
the way I love

that the tedium
of giving
in the risk
of surrender
and the reaching
out naked
to a world
that must wound

may be kindled
fresh daily

to a blaze
of compassion
that the grain
may fall gladly
to burst in the ground
—and the harvest abound.

Ralph Wright OSB

236   Lead kindly light, amid the encircling gloom,
Lead Thou me on;
The night is dark, and I am far from home;
Lead thou me on.
Keep thou my feet; I do not ask to see
The distant scene; one step enough for me.

John Henry Newman (1801–1890)

237   As the beautiful, dew-covered rose
      rises from amongst its thorns,
so may my heart be so full of love for you, my God,
      that I may rise above the storms and evils that assail me,
and stand fast in trust and freedom of spirit.

after Hadewijch of Brabant (first half of thirteenth century)

238   Be not far from me, for trouble is near, and there is none to help.
I am poured out like water, and all my bones are out of joint.
My heart is like wax, and my strength is dried up like a potsherd;
I can count all my bones, they stare and gloat over me.
But be not far from me, O Lord;
You are my helper, hasten to my aid.
Deliver my soul from the sword,
my life from the power of the dog.

Psalm 22:11, 14–15, 17, 19–20

239   Lord, I know
that I am not at my best
when I am most exuberant and most impetuous,
but when I am trying to pull as steadily and bravely as I can

in the direction you have sent me.
Stay with me
when I am swamped by weariness and seeming impossibilities.
Turn my face gently towards you,
keep my heart loving
and my will determined to fight on to the end.
based on a meditation by Mother Janet Stuart (1857–1914)

240 O Lord, hear my voice when I cry unto you;
     have mercy on me and answer me.
Do not hide your face from me;
     nor thrust me aside in displeasure:
For you are my helper: cast me not away;
     do not forsake me, O God of my salvation.
Psalm 27:7, 9

241   I know
that when the stress has grown too strong,
     you will be there.

     I know
that when the waiting seems so long,
     you hear my prayer.

     I know
that through the crash of falling worlds
     you're holding me.

     I know
that life and death are yours
     eternally.
Mother Janet Stuart (1857–1914)

242 O God,
Early in the morning I cry unto you.
Help me to pray
And to think only of you.
I cannot pray alone.
In me there is darkness

But with you there is light.
I am lonely but you do not leave me.
I am feeble in heart but you do not leave me.
I am restless but with you there is peace.
In me there is bitterness, but with you there is patience.
Your ways are past understanding, but
You know the way for me.

Dietrich Bonhoeffer (1906–1945)

243 Lord Jesus, kind heart,
Through the storms of the day
  Guide me to the shore.
Lord Jesus, kind heart,
When darkness comes over me,
  Give me your light.
Lord Jesus, kind heart,
I am weary with travelling,
  Let me rest in you.

W. Mary Calvert

244 O Love that wilt not let me go,
  I rest my weary soul in thee:
I give thee back the life I owe,
That in thine ocean depths its flow
  May richer, fuller be.

O light that followest all my way,
  I yield my flickering torch to thee:
My heart restores its borrowed ray,
That, in thy sunshine's blaze, its day
  May brighter, fairer be.

George Matheson (1842–1906)

245 Grant, O God, that amidst all the discouragements, difficulties,
dangers, distress and darkness of this mortal life, I may depend
upon your mercy and on this build my hopes, as on a sure foundation. Let your infinite mercy in Christ Jesus deliver me from
despair, both now and at the hour of death.

Thomas Wilson (1663–1755)

246   I have no wit, no words, no tears;
My heart within me like a stone
Is numbed too much for hopes or fears.
Look right, look left, I dwell alone;
I lift mine eyes, but dimmed with grief
No everlasting hills I see;
My life is in the falling leaf.
O Jesus, quicken me.

My life is like a faded leaf,
My harvest dwindled to a husk:
Truly my life is void and brief
And tedious in the barren dusk:
My life is like a frozen thing,
No bud nor greenness can I see,
Yet rise it shall–the sap of Spring,
O Jesus, rise in me.

Christina Rossetti (1830–1894)

247   O Jesus, I have promised
To serve thee to the end,
Be thou for ever near me
My Master and my Friend.
I shall not fear the battle
If thou art by my side,
Nor wander from the pathway
If thou wilt be my guide.

John E. Bode (1816–1874)

248   Abide with me; fast falls the eventide;
The darkness deepens; Lord, with me abide;
   When other helpers fail, and comforts flee,
   Help of the helpless, O abide with me.

I need thy presence every passing hour;
What but thy grace can foil the tempter's power?
   Who like thyself my guide and stay can be?
   Through cloud and sunshine, Lord, abide with me.

Henry Francis Lyte (1793–1847)

249　　God our Mother,
Living Water,
River of Mercy,
Source of Life,
in whom we live
and move
and have our being,
who quenches our thirst,
refreshes our weariness,
bathes
and washes
and cleanses
our wounds,
be for us always
a fountain of life,
and for all the world
a river of hope
springing up in the midst
of the deserts of despair.

Miriam Therese Winter

250　　May we long
not for the smoothness of sand
which looks good, and feels flat,
and is easy to walk on
but will not withstand a storm.

May we build our hopes
on you.
Though you may not prevent the storms,
you keep us firm
within them.

So even if we're battered,
we cannot fall
except deeper into a crevice
in the rock;
deeper into you.

Jane Grayshon

251 Creator God, you know what we need without our words.
Hear our prayers and hear also our silence.
Give us strength,
and grant us those things we cannot or dare not voice.
We make all our prayers through our brother Jesus. Amen.
Oxford Women's Liturgy

252 Lord you are a present help in trouble.
Come revive
Redeem
Restore
In our darkness come as light
In our sadness come as joy
In our troubles come as peace
In our weakness come as strength
Come Lord to our aid
Revive
Redeem
Restore us
O Lord
Open our eyes to your Presence
Open our minds to your grace
Open our lips to your praises
Open our hearts to your love
Open our lives to your healing
And be found among us.
David Adam

253 Grant us, Jesus, that tender, indestructible love
which asks forgiveness for its executioners
and gives hope to the thief on the cross.
Keep us compassionate when the way is hard,
and gentle with those who oppose us.
A New Zealand Prayer Book

254   Lord, give us grace
         to hold to you
      when all is weariness and fear,
      and sin abounds, within, without,
      when that which I would do I cannot do,
      and that I do I would not do,
      when love itself is tested by the doubt
      that love is false or dead within the soul;
      when every act brings new confusion, new distress,
         new opportunities, new misunderstandings,
      and every thought new accusation.

   Lord, give us grace
      that we may know
      that in the darkness pressing round
      it is the mist of sin that hides your face,
      that you are there
      and you know we love you still.
                    Gilbert Shaw (1886–1967)

255   Cleanse the eye of our perception, O God, and purify our hearts,
      that we may will one thing, that your way indeed be followed
      through and beyond the perplexities we cannot escape.
                    Jim Cotter

256   When all we are and everything we do
      is called into question,
      grant us dignity and direction,
      grant us patience;
      Jesus, be there.
                    A New Zealand Prayer Book *(adapted)*

257   Jesus left his home in Nazareth and went into the desert;
      –help us when we are alone to use our solitude creatively and
      fruitfully.
      Jesus reached out to the poor and to the outcast;

–make us aware of the needs of our neighbours where we live and where we work.

When we find ourselves burdened by hectic demands on our time;

–may the solitude of our dwelling place be a solace and comfort.

When we experience feelings of loneliness and restlessness;

–transform our emptiness into the fullness of your presence and quiet our minds so that we may know your companionship.

When we have no one to share our joys and sorrows;

–enable us to unite this form of poverty with all those who find themselves alone or abandoned. May this emptiness know your creative power.

The Woman's Prayer Companion

WHEN BUSY AND OVER-TIRED

I trust in you, O Lord. I say, 'You are my God.'
My times are in your hand; save me in your steadfast love.

PSALM 31:14–15

ぐ◌ ◌ゝ

258   Lord, when I am feeling tired and strained, help me not to take
it out on other people.

A.A.

259   Even if my old familiar ways of praying are taken away from me,
I am never taken away from you, Lord,
for you are here, reaching out to me,
loving me now.

Even when I am denied a space to be quiet with you,
there is still space inside me, Lord,
an inner room where you are waiting for me,
and which I can enter at any moment.

Even though I feel miserable and worthless,
I am still precious in your eyes
because I am your child,
and you are waiting to open your arms and embrace me.

A.A.

260   Lord, I am poured out,
I come to you for renewal.
Lord, I am weary,
I come to you for refreshment.
Lord I am worn,
I come to you for restoration.
Lord I am lost,

I come to you for guidance.
Lord I am troubled,
I come to you for peace.
Lord, I am lonely,
I come to you for love.
Come, Lord,
Come revive me
Come re-shape me
Come mould me in your image.
Re-cast me in the furnace of your love.

David Adam

261   O Living God,
       when I am tired and cross and despairing,
       distracted by many thoughts,
       eaten up by multiple demands,
       and hungry for your peace;
       help me to offer again
       the five loaves and two fishes
       that you have given me,
       and so discover again
       the miracle of the strength
       that comes in sharing everything
       when we have nothing.

Julie M. Hulme

262   Lord, you put twenty-four hours in a day, and gave me a body
       which gets tired and can only do so much. Show me which tasks
       you want me to do, and help me to live prayerfully as I do them.
       Sharpen my senses, that I may truly
           see what I am looking at,
           taste what I am eating,
           listen to what I am hearing,
           face what I am suffering,
           celebrate the ways I am loved,
           and offer to you whatever I am doing,
       so that the water of the present moment
           may be turned into wine.

A.A.

263 Good Jesus, strength of the weary, rest of the restless, by the
     weariness and unrest of your sacred cross, come to me who am
     weary that I may rest in you.

                              Edward Pusey (1800–1882)

264 'My time', we say.
             How presumptuous!
     It's not ours:
             we didn't make it,
             we can't stop it;
             no one can preserve it.
     We can't hold the present moment,
             it slips through our fingers.
     We can't freeze it,
             or bottle it,
             to await our pleasure.
     We can't even define it:
             'animal, vegetable or mineral'!
     Does it exist?
     If it does,
             whose is it?

     God, teach us to value it,
             to love it,
             to relax in its embrace,
     and always to remember
             that it's not ours.

     It's yours.

                              Michael Forster

265 God who is with us
     at our beginning and ending,
     be with us now.
     Help us to find you
     in the chaos of our lives.
     Let your light shine in our darkness
     so that we may be guided
     to walk in your ways all the days of our life.

                              Ulla Monberg

266   God of all time,
      God beyond and behind time,
      may we know what is too late
      and what is too soon.
      May we always recognize
      the right time
      in the light of
      your timeless love.

                    Kate McIlhagga

FEAR, ANXIETY AND DOUBT

Hear my prayer, O God, and do not hide yourself from my petition; the terrors of death and trembling have come upon me, and horror overwhelms me.

PSALM 55:1, 5

৸৹ ৻৶

267   Lord, I believe, help me in my unbelief.
Mark 9:24

268   Dear God, be good to me;
the sea is so large,
and my boat is so small.
Traditional prayer of a Breton fisherman

269   O God, who am I now?
Once, I was secure
   in familiar territory
   in my sense of belonging,
unquestioning of
   the norms of my culture
   the assumptions built into my language
   the values shared by my society.

But now you have called me out and away from home,
and I do not know where you are leading.
I am empty, unsure uncomfortable.
I have only a beckoning star to follow.

Journeying God,
pitch your tent with mine
so that I may not become deterred
by hardship, strangeness, doubt.

Show me the movement I must make
   toward a wealth not dependent on possessions
   toward a wisdom not based on books
   toward a strength not bolstered by might
   toward a God not confined to heaven
but scandalously earthed, poor, unrecognized ...
Help me to find myself
as I walk in others' shoes.

Kate Compston

270   To you alone, O Jesus, I must cling;
running to your arms, dear Lord,
there let me hide, safe from all fears,
loving you with the tenderness of a child.

after St Thérèse of Lisieux (1873–97)

271   When I feel threatened
or believe myself to be a failure,
give me courage to enter my still centre,
the place of buried treasure
and sunshine
and solitude,
where you are, Lord,
and where it no longer matters
who approves of me
or how successful I am
because you are there,
and, in your presence,
I rediscover the confidence
to be me.

A.A.

272   The Lord is my light and my salvation; whom shall I fear?
the Lord is the stronghold of my life; of whom shall I be
afraid?
Even if an army encamp against me, I shall not be afraid;
and if war should rise against me, yet will I trust.

One thing I have asked of the Lord, which I will seek:
that I may dwell in the house of the Lord for ever.
For he will hide me in his shelter in the day of trouble,
and set me high upon a rock.

Psalm 27:1, 3–5

273   Lord of life
Why do I anticipate the worst
When time and time again
The worst never happens?
Even when it does, life goes on
And every day comes to an end.
Lord help me to overcome my fears
In this brief moment of reflection.
Calm my mind
Help me to relax
Let your comforting Spirit
Enter into me
And fill me with peace.

Frank Topping

274   To you, O Lord, I come for refuge,
do not let me be put to shame, deliver me in your
righteousness.
Incline your ear to me, make haste to help me,
for you are my strong rock and my fortress.
Into your hand I commit my spirit,
for you have redeemed me, O Lord, faithful God.

Psalm 31:1–2, 5

275   Lift me, Lord,
Out of fear into hope
Out of frailty into strength
Out of foolishness into sense.

Lift me, Lord.
You came down to lift us
You descended to hell to lift us to heaven

You entered death to raise us to life.
Come, Lord, raise me up, I pray you.

David Adam

276   Lord, I know that, however fearful I may be,
nothing can separate me from your love:
neither death, nor life,
angels, nor principalities,
things present, nor things to come,
evil powers, heights, depths,
nor anything else in all creation –
nothing at all!

based on Romans 8:31–9

277   Whether I fly with angels, fall with dust,
        Thy hands made both, and I am there:
        Thy power and love, my love and trust
        Make one place everywhere.

George Herbert (1593–1633)

278   In the hour of my fear I will put my trust in you;
        In God, whose word I praise, in God I trust and will fear not;
        what can flesh do to me?

Psalm 56:3–4

279   O God, you know we are often filled with fear and foreboding.
Give us courage and deepen our trust.
You are a rock which nothing can shatter.
On you we can place the whole weight of our lives.

Richard Harries

280   Lord our God, Father of all,
you guard us under the shadow of your wings
and search into the depths of our hearts.
Remove the blindness that cannot know you
and relieve the fear that would hide us from your sight.
We ask this through Christ our Lord.

The Liturgy of the Hours

281   Forgive us Lord,
         when we want proofs for our faith,
         and demand absolute certainty
         before we will commit ourselves to you.
         Strengthen our trust in you,
         so that we, who have not seen you,
         may still believe;
         and in believing may be blessed
         with the fullness of joy,
         now and always.
                          A.A. (based on John 20:24–29)

282   FEAR OF DEMENTIA
         If one day I should lose my mind,
         Lord, let me still be yours,
         even if I cease to understand
         what being 'yours' may mean.
         I fear the indignity of people saying, 'Poor soul,
         she's not the person that she used to be.'
         Lord, if this should happen,
         let my condition be
         an offering for the millions of others
         who have faced inner confusion and the loss of self.
         O God, even my fear of 'going mad'
         is outstripped by your love
         into eternity.

         So help me to forget about tomorrow,
         and concentrate on living in today.
                                    A.A.

INNER DARKNESS

Though I walk through the valley of the shadow of death, I will fear no evil, for you are with me, your rod and your staff comfort me.

PSALM 23:4

283   LORD OF HEALING
Lord of my darkest place:
Let in your light.

Lord of my greatest fear:
Let in your peace.

Lord of my most bitter shame:
Let in your word of grace.

Lord of my oldest grudge:
Let in your forgiveness.

Lord of my deepest anger:
Let it out.

Lord of my loneliest moment:
Let in your presence.

Lord of my truest self – my all:
Let in your wholeness.

Alison Pepper

284   How long will you be absent? For ever? Oh Lord! have you forgotten to be gracious, and have you shut up your loving kindness in displeasure? Will you be no more entreated? Is your mercy clean gone for ever, and your promise come utterly to an end for ever? Why do you wait for so long? Shall I despair of your mercy? Oh, God! Far be that from me; for you know better than I what is good for me. Therefore do with me in all things what you will.

Lady Jane Grey (1537–1554) (based on Psalm 89:46)

285   Now my life is hidden with Christ in God;
                         I am yours, Lord,
                        for better, for worse,
                 in times when I feel well and alive,
             and in the bleak landscape of my darkness;
                            in it all
                         I am yours.
                    A.A. (based on Colossians 3:3)

286   God,
      here I will stand
      to fulfil
      what your faith in me
      expects.
      I will take the desert upon myself,
      the absence of your answers,
      your multifaceted, eloquent silence,
      to allow the fruit of solitude
      to ripen in me
      as nourishment for others.

      I will not run away,
      even when I become afraid
      of the endless sand, of the senselessness,
      you silent one,
      because you are never far.
                              Ulrich Schaffer

287   Lord, life is empty, miserable and dreary;
      free me from this self-imprisonment.
      I feel worthless, yet I do matter to you.
      You love me.
      Help me to find freedom in that.

      I am heavy and lifeless,
      in the darkness with you –
      yet you are more than darkness.

This depression is like a huge wave:
help me to ride on it
rather than being engulfed by it.
No matter how awful I feel,
remind me that you are always loving me.

This is hard work, God.
Much easier to slump back
into a cushion of misery.
Give me strength
for the effort of each moment as it comes –
for this moment.

A.A.

288   Spirit of comfort and longing,
      enfold my fear,
      unclothe me of my pride,
      unweave my thoughts,
      uncomplicate my heart,
      and give me surrender:
      that I may tell my wounds,
      lay down my work,
      and greet the dark.

Janet Morley

289   O Lord, everything fills me with fear and apprehension. Even the
      smallest commitment has become a huge ordeal in my eyes. I
      cannot see any hope or purpose in my life. Teach me to go on
      praying, though my faith seems lost and there is no apparent
      response. Give me the strength to face one day at a time, and to
      know that, somehow, you will carry me through. Do not let me
      become so obsessed with myself that I fail to respond to the
      needs of others. As I echo the words of Jesus, 'Let this cup pass
      from me,' let me, like him, accept your will – and give me a little
      of his courage.

Mary Rose de Lisle

290   O my Lord, I am in a dry land, all dried up and cracked by the violence of the north wind and the cold; but as you see, I ask for nothing more; you will send me both dew and warmth when it pleases you.

St Jane de Chantal (1572–1641)

291   You meet me in gentleness.
You come close.
You take my coldness
and warm me from the inside.
As my cold heart melts, Lord,
let your streams flow through me
that I may play my part
in the renewing of the earth.

based on words by Ulrich Schaffer

292   Lord, come as sweet, healing oil
into my weary mind,
my bruised heart
and my dried-up soul.

A.A

293   Lord, even if you take from me all I ever received from you, yet, by your grace, leave me the gift of being true to you in my distress. I desire this more than anything else, even more than a place in your heavenly kingdom

after Mechtild of Magdeburg (1207–1294)

294   Thou mastering me
        God! giver of breath and bread;
World's strand, sway of the sea;
        Lord of living and dead;
Thou hast bound bones and veins in me, fastened me flesh,
And after it almost unmade, what with dread,
        Thy doing: and dost thou touch me afresh?
Over again I feel thy finger and find thee.

Gerard Manley Hopkins (1844–1889)

295   Broken in pieces all asunder,
          Lord, hunt me not,
          A thing forgot,
My thoughts are all a case of knives,
      Wounding my heart
      With scattered smart.

Oh help, my God! let not their plot
          Kill them and me,
          And also thee,
Who art my life: dissolve the knot,
     As the sun scatters by his light
     All the rebellions of the night.

Then shall those powers, which work for grief,
          Enter thy pay,
          And day by day
Labour thy praise, and my relief;
     With care and courage building me,
     Till I reach heaven, and, much more, thee.
             George Herbert (1593–1633)

296   My God, I can do no more!
     Be for me the one who can!
             Madame Acarie (1566–1618)

297   Lord, where can I escape from your spirit:
     or where can I flee from your presence?
If I ascend to heaven you are there:
     if I make my bed in the grave, you are there also.
If I spread out my wings towards the morning
     and dwell in the farthest parts of the sea,
even there your hand shall lead me,
     and your right hand shall hold me fast.
             Psalm 139:7–10

298   Lord, at the moment you do not seem real to me. My prayers are
lifeless, and my spirit feels numb. Help me to persevere when
faith seems absent, in the certainty that you are with me in the

darkness and your light is at the end of the tunnel. Renew my bruised spirit with your love, and help me to rest in you. In the name of Jesus, my Saviour.

Mary Rose de Lisle

299   O Lord, how hard it is to accept your way. You come to me as a small, powerless child born away from home. You live for me as a stranger in your own land. You die for me as a criminal outside the walls of the city, rejected by your own people, misunderstood by your friends, and feeling abandoned by your God.

I am trying to overcome the feelings of alienation and separation which continue to assail me. But I wonder now if my deep sense of homelessness does not bring me closer to you than my occasional feelings of belonging.

I do not have to run away from those experiences that are closest to yours. Every time I feel this way I have an occasion to be grateful and to embrace you better and taste more fully your joy and peace.

Come, Lord Jesus, and be with me where I feel poorest. I trust that this is the place where you will find your manger and bring your light. Come, Lord Jesus, come.

Henri Nouwen

300   Father in heaven! You speak to us in many ways. Even when you are silent, you still speak to us, in order to examine us, to try us, and so that the hour of our understanding may be more profound.

Oh, in the time of silence, when I remain alone and abandoned because I do not hear your voice, it seems as if the separation must last for ever. Father in heaven! It is only a moment of silence in the intimacy of a conversation. Bless then this silence, and let me not forget that you are silent through love, and that you speak through love, so that in your silence and in your word you are still the same Father, and that you guide and instruct even by your silence.

Søren Kierkegaard (1813–1855)

301 Lord, I am continually with you;
    you hold me by my right hand.
You guide me with your counsel,
    and afterwards you will receive me into your glory.
Whom have I in heaven but you?
    And there is nothing on earth that I desire other than you.
My flesh and my heart fail;
    but God is the strength of my heart,
    and my inheritance for ever.
                    Psalm 73:23–6

302 Deliver us from the long drought of the mind;
    Let leaves from the deciduous cross fall on us
    Washing us clean,
    Turning our autumn to gold
    by the affluence of their fountain.
                    R. S. Thomas
This could be made into a personal prayer by substituting the word 'me' for 'us'.

303 When on life a darkness falls,
    when the mist flows chilling,
    paths and signposts lost in doubt,
    loveless, unfulfilling,
    reach us, Jesus, from your cross,
    though we feel forsaken;
    keep us through the aching night
    till new dawns awaken.
                    Brian A. Wren

304 In darkness and in light,
    in trouble and joy,
    help us, heavenly Father,
        to trust your love,
        to serve your purpose
        and to praise your name,
    through Jesus Christ our Lord.
                    The Daily Office Revised *(adapted)*

WHEN TEMPTED

Incline my heart to your commands, and not to selfish gain;
Turn away my eyes from looking at vain things; as I walk in
your way, give me life.

PSALM 119:36–7

305   When I want to run – hold me.
      When I want to turn away – turn me round.
      When I want to hide – race me to my hiding place and win.
      When I want to hurt others – deflect my aim.
      When I want to hurt myself – love me.
      When I cry – grab me quickly
          and rock me safely
          in your strong arms.

Ruth Burgess

306   Stay at the centre of my soul, O God:
          be in my longing and my hurting;
          be in my hoping and my emptiness;
          be in my eyes and lips and heart,
      so that my desire to be true to you
      and to myself
      may prevail over everything else.

A.A.

307   Hear me and help me, O Lord,
      for I am poor and needy;
      teach me your way,
      that I may walk in your truth
      with an undivided heart.

Psalm 86:1, 11

308   The dearest idol I have known,
      Whate'er that idol be,
      Help me to tear it from thy throne,
      And worship only Thee.
                    William Cowper (1731–1800)

309   Fix the centre of my heart in yourself, O Lord, for only thus will
      I resist temptation and live according to your will.
                    after Meister Eckhart (1260–1327)

310   Eternal and most glorious God,
      suffer me not so to undervalue myself
            as to give away my soul,
            thy soul,
            thy dear and precious soul,
            for nothing;
      and all the world is nothing,
            if the soul be given for it.
      Preserve therefore my soul, O Lord,
            because it belongs to thee,
      and preserve my body
            because it belongs to my soul.
                    John Donne (1573–1631)

311   Most loving Lord, give me a steadfast heart, which no unworthy
      thought can drag downwards; an unconquered heart, which no
      hardship can wear out; an upright heart, which no worthless pur-
      pose can ensnare. Give me also, O Lord my God, understanding
      to know you, diligence to seek you, and a faithfulness that will
      finally embrace you; through Jesus Christ, my Lord.
                    St Thomas Aquinas (1255–1274)

312   Be thou my guardian and my guide,
            And hear me when I call;
      Let not my slippery footsteps slide,
            And hold me lest I fall.

And if I tempted am to sin,
   And outward things are strong,
Do thou, O Lord, keep watch within,
   And save my soul from wrong.

Isaac Williams (1802–1865)

313   Dear Lord and Father of mankind,
       Forgive our foolish ways!
     Re-clothe us in our rightful minds,
     In purer lives thy service find,
       In deeper reverence praise.

Breathe through the heats of our desire
     Thy coolness and thy balm;
Let sense be dumb, let flesh retire;
Speak through the earthquake, wind, and fire,
     O still small voice of calm!

John Greenleaf Whittier (1807–92)

BEING ILL

*Heal me, O Lord, and I shall be healed; save me and I shall
be saved; for you are my praise.*

JEREMIAH 17:14

314 I hate being ill,
I hate the helplessness,
I hate the vulnerability,
I hate myself for being like this,
I hate you for letting this happen to me.

Soothe me down, God.
Help me to hear your voice in the midst of my anger.
Help me to trust the caress of your fingers.
Help me not to push you away when you come near.
Help me to let go into your love.

Ruth Burgess

315 Jesus, I am afraid. I do not know what is going to happen to me;
I dislike not being in control. I am afraid of the loss of con-
sciousness that the anaesthetic will bring. I worry that I will be
a burden to others after the operation, and that I will not be so
active again. Lord, help me to trust you.

Michael Hollings and Etta Gullick (abbreviated)

316 Take, Lord, my heart, my life,
a vessel broken by ill-health,
shattered by loss,
emptied of ambitions and strivings.
Fill it with your love,
your joy, your grace, so full
that out of the cracks of pain,

the gashes of frustration,
the holes of despair,
may seep,
cleansing those wounds,
hope, comfort, healing,
to those for whom I pray,
and those you love, beyond my prayers.

Anne Lepine

317 Today, I feel isolated.
Like an island in the middle of a great ocean.
No one really understands my feelings, and I hesitate to burden others with my troubles.
'If only' things could change.
Living Jesus, please continue to love me through this illness and gloom.
Penetrate my loneliness with your divine presence.

Ann Shepherdson

318 Lord, this is unbearable. Even though I'm grateful for all the help from people rallying round, I hate the fact that I need them. Help me to receive as well as to give. Teach me to use this illness positively, as a chance to let go of my desire always to be organized, competent and in control. Set my spirit free—I know I am valuable to you, even when I'm stuck here!

A.A.

319 Lord, hang on to me, because I don't feel well enough to hang on to you.

A.A.

320 Lord, I trust you; use me, whatever and wherever I am. If I am sick, may my sickness serve you; if I am perplexed, may my perplexity serve you; if I am sorrowful, may my sorrow serve you. Lord, you know what you are about. I trust you. Thanks be to God.

John Henry Newman (1801–1890) (adapted)

321   Lord, you gave me health, and I forgot you.
      Now it has been taken away, and I come back to you.
      All is yours; you are my Lord.
      I offer you everything: comforts, success, health;
      take all the things that possess me,
      so that I may be wholly yours.

                    after François Fénelon (1631–1715)

322   Lord, grant me the gift of patience when I am well, so that I may
      use it when I am sick. When I am healthy, and relying on myself
      alone, I often discover how weak I am. Help me, when I am ill,
      to find the strength which comes from depending solely on you.

                    after Thomas Fuller (1608–1661)

See also:
      Prayers about Difficult Relationships, 375–88
      Prayers for Lent, 768–77
      Prayers for Healing, 555–63

Also:
      No. 316: 'Take Lord, my heart, my life.'
      No. 6: 'Lord, this moment is yours'

part four

PRAYERS FOR FORGIVENESS

God, be merciful unto me, a sinner.
LUKE 18:13

⌘ ⌘

323 My sins, Lord, are dulling my conscience.
   I get used to evil very quickly:
   A little self-indulgence here,
   A small unfaithfulness there,
   An unwise action farther on,
   And my vision becomes obscured;
   I no longer see stumbling-blocks, I no longer see other people on
   my road.

   Lord, I beseech you, keep me young in my efforts,
   Spare me the bondage of habit, which lulls to sleep and kills.
   Michel Quoist

324   Lord, you know well that I love you;
      have pity on me, for I am nothing but a sinner.
   St Thérèse of Lisieux (1873–1897)

325 O Lord Your tenderness
   Melting all my bitterness,
   O Lord, I receive Your love.
   O Lord, Your loveliness
   Changing all my ugliness,
   O Lord, I receive Your love,
   O Lord, I receive Your love.
   Graham Kendrick

326   How could I ever imagine,
      that I would cope without praying?
      How could I keep going
      unless I knew
      that I could return my heart to you
      and soak my darkness in your light?

Pour your mercy into my madness
and your Spirit into my will,
and make me know
in my heart as well as my head
that only in you
am I found, forgiven and free.

A.A.

327   Batter my heart, three-person'd God, for you
as yet but knock! Breathe, shine and seek to mend;
that I may rise and stand, o'erthrow me, and bend
your force to break, blow, burn and make me new.
I, like an usurp'd town, to another due
labour to admit you, but O, to no end!
Take me to you, imprison me, for I
except you enthral me, never shall be free,
nor ever chaste, except you ravish me.

John Donne (1573–1631)

328   Out of the depths I cry to you, O Lord,
Lord, hear my voice!
If you should keep account of our sins,
Lord, who could stand?
But there is forgiveness with you,
so that you may be revered.
I wait for the Lord, my soul waits for him,
and in his word is my hope.

Psalm 130:1–5

329   God of grace, I turn my face
To you, I cannot hide;
My nakedness, my shame, my guilt,
Are all before Your eyes.

Strivings and all anguished dreams
In rags lie at my feet,
And only grace provides the way
For me to stand complete.

And your grace clothes me in righteousness,
And Your mercy covers me in love.
Your life adorns and beautifies,
I stand complete in You.

Chris Bowater

330   O God, save me from this frivolous self which misuses your
      creation;
      this masterful self which manipulates your creation;
      this greedy self which exploits your creation;
      this self which throws the thick shadow of its own purposes and
      desires in every direction,
      so that I cannot see what it is that you, my Lord and my God,
      are showing to me.
      Teach me to stand out of my own light,
      and let your daylight shine.

based on words by Austin Farrer (1906–1968)

331   Have mercy on me, O life-giver, through your goodness.
      In your great tenderness soothe away my faults.
      Cleanse me of my guilt,
      do not hold my failures against me.
      For I have come to see that I fail you,
      when I have not acknowledged with my whole being
      that I am made truly in your image;
      in not walking in your ways I have sinned against you.
      You are love and truth itself
      and seek sincerity of heart;
      teach me the secrets of wisdom.
      Cleanse me from all that prevents me
      from listening to your word.

Ianthe Pratt (based on Psalm 51:1–7)

332   O think me worth thine anger, punish me,
      burn off my rusts and my deformity,
      restore thine image so much, by thy grace,
      that thou mayest know me, and I'll turn my face.

John Donne (1573–1631)

333   O God, my God and my all,
      without thee I am nothing, less than nothing,
      a rebel to thy love,
      a despiser of thy grace.
   O God, have pity upon me a sinner;
      grant me a new vision of thy love
         and of thy will for me:
      give me stillness in my soul that I may know thee and love
         thee, and grant me strength to do thy will,
   O God, my all.

Gilbert Shaw (1886–1967)

334   Have mercy on me, O God, according to your steadfast goodness;
      in your abundant mercy blot out my offences.
   Wash me thoroughly from my wickedness,
      and cleanse me from my sin.
   For I acknowledge my rebelliousness,
      and my sin is always before me.
   Against you only have I sinned,
      and done what is evil in your eyes.
   Purge me with hyssop and I shall be clean;
      wash me and I shall be whiter than snow.
   Create in me a clean heart, O God,
      and renew a right spirit within me.

Psalm 51:1–4a, 7, 10

335   O God, you desire truth in the inmost heart; forgive me my sins against truth – the untruth within me, the half-lies, the evasions, the exaggerations, the lying silences, the self-deceits, the masks I wear before the world. Let me stand naked before you, and see myself as I really am. Then, grant me truth in the inward parts and keep me in truth always.

George Appleton (1902–93) (adapted)

336   Rock of ages, cleft for me,
   Let me hide myself in thee;
   Let the water and the blood,

From thy riven side which flowed,
Be of sin the double cure:
Cleanse me from its guilt and power.

Nothing in my hand I bring,
Simply to thy Cross I cling;
Naked, come to thee for dress;
Helpless, look to thee for grace;
Foul, I to the fountain fly;
Wash me, Saviour, or I die.

Augustus M. Toplady (1740–1778)

337 My failure to be true even to my own accepted standards:
My self-deception in face of temptation:
My choosing of the worse when I know the better:
    O Lord, forgive.

My failure to apply to myself the standards of conduct I demand
of others:
My blindness to the suffering of others and my slowness to be
taught by my own:
My complacence towards wrongs that do not touch my own
case and my over-sensitiveness to those that do:
My slowness to see the good in my fellows and to see the evil in
myself:
My hardness of heart towards my neighbours' faults and my
readiness to make allowance for my own:
    O Lord, forgive.

John Baillie (1886–1960)

338 Forgive me my sins, O Lord; the sins of my present and the sins
of my past, the sins of my soul and the sins of my body, the sins
which I have done to please myself and the sins which I have
done to please others. Forgive me my casual sins and my deliberate sins, and those which I have laboured so to hide that I have
hidden them even from myself. Forgive me, O Lord, forgive all
my sins, for Jesus' sake.

Thomas Wilson (1663–1775)

339   Christ our friend,
      you ask for our love
      in spite of our betrayal.
      Give us courage to embrace forgiveness,
      know you again,
      and trust ourselves in you.

                              Janet Morley

340   O God, bring new life
      where we are worn and tired;
      new love
      where we have turned hard-hearted;
      forgiveness
      where we have wounded;
      and the joy and freedom of your Holy Spirit
      where we are the prisoners of our selves.

                  John L. Bell (extract from a longer prayer)

341   O God, we bring you our failure,
          our hunger, our disappointment, our despair,
          our greed, our aloofness, our loneliness.
      When we cling to others in desperation
          or turn from them in fear
          strengthen us in love.
      Teach us, women and men,
          to use our power with care.

      We turn to you, O God,
          we renounce evil,
          we claim your love,
          we choose to be made whole.

                          The St Hilda Community

342   We need your healing, merciful God;
      give us true repentance.
      Some sins are plain to us;
      some escape us,
      some we cannot face.

Forgive us;
set us free to hear your word to us;
set us free to serve you.

A New Zealand Prayer Book

343   Lord our God,
in our sin we have avoided your call.
Our love for you is like the mist,
disappearing in the heat of the sun.
Have mercy on us.
Bind up our wounds
and bring us back to the foot of the cross,
through Jesus Christ our Lord.

Patterns for Worship

344   Holy God,
holy and strange,
holy and intimate,
have mercy on us.

Janet Morley

345   From the cowardice that dare not face new truth,
From the laziness that is contented with half truth,
From the arrogance that thinks it knows all truth,
Good Lord, deliver us.

Prayer from Kenya

346   God help us to find our confession;
The truth within us which is hidden from our mind;
The beauty or the ugliness we see elsewhere
But never in ourselves;
The stowaway which has been smuggled
Into the dark side of the heart,
Which puts the heart off balance and causes it pain,
Which wearies and confuses us,
Which tips us in false directions and inclines us to destruction,
The load which is not carried squarely

Because it is carried in ignorance
God help us to find our confession.
Help us across the boundary of our understanding.
Lead us into the darkness that we may find what lies concealed;
That we may confess it towards the light;
That we may carry our truth in the centre of our heart;
That we may carry our cross wisely
And bring harmony into our life and our world.

Michael Leunig

347   Lord and Master of our lives,
take from us the spirit
    of laziness,
    half-heartedness,
    selfish ambition
    and idle talk.
Give us rather the spirit
    of integrity,
    purity of heart,
    humility,
    faithfulness
    and love.
Lord and King,
help us to see our own errors,
and not to judge our neighbours;
for your mercy's sake.

Orthodox Liturgy for Lent (adapted)

348   Lord, forgive us, for we are fragmented people. We go in many
directions at once. We seek opposite goals; we serve contradic-
tory causes. We preach justice: we walk in injustice. We shout
peace: we practise violence. We pray for life: we trade in death.
Through your compassion have mercy on us and make us whole.
May your thoughts become our thoughts, and our ways your
ways, through Jesus Christ.

National Council of Churches of the Philippines (adapted)

349 We grieve and confess
     that we hurt and have been hurt,
     to the third and fourth generations,
     that we are so afraid of pain
     that we shield ourselves from being vulnerable to others,
     and refuse to be open and trusting as a child . . .

     O God of Wholeness, we rest in you . . .
     You listen with us to the sound of running water,
     you sit with us under the shade of the trees of our healing,
     you walk once more with us in the garden in the cool of the day,
     the oil of your anointing penetrates the cells of our being,
     the warmth of your hands steadies us and gives us courage.
     O God of Wholeness, we rest in you . . .
                          Jim Cotter

350 O Lord God, our Father most loving, we would not, even if we
     could, conceal anything from you, but rejoice rather that you
     know us as we are and see every desire and every motive of our
     hearts. Help us, Lord, to strip off every mask and veil when we
     come into your presence, and to spread before you every thought
     and every secret of our being, that they may be forgiven, purified,
     amended, and blessed by you; through Jesus Christ our Lord.
                     Charles Vaughan (1816–97)

     *The following three prayers of confession may be followed by an
     affirmation of forgiveness, e.g., No. 354.*

351 Father eternal, giver of light and grace,
     we have sinned against you and against our neighbour,
     in what we have thought,
     in what we have said and done,
     through ignorance, through weakness,
     through our own deliberate fault.
     We have wounded your love,
     and marred your image in us.
     We are sorry and ashamed,
     and repent of all our sins.

For the sake of your Son Jesus Christ, who died for us,
forgive us all that is past;
and lead us out from darkness
to walk as children of light.
> The Alternative Service Book *1980 (adapted)*

352   Father,
we have sinned against heaven and against you.
We are not worthy to be called your children.
We turn to you again.
Have mercy on us,
bring us back to yourself
as those who once were dead
but now have life through Christ our Lord.
> Patterns for Worship

353   Almighty and merciful God,
we have sinned against you,
in thought, word and deed.
We have not loved you with all our heart.
We have not loved others
as our Saviour Christ loves us.
We are truly sorry.
In your mercy forgive what we have been,
help us to amend what we are,
and direct what we shall be;
that we may delight in your will
and walk in your ways,
through Jesus Christ our Saviour.
> A New Zealand Prayer Book

354   ANNOUNCEMENT OF FORGIVENESS
The Saviour of the world, Refuge of the repentant,
forgives and strengthens all who truly seek his grace.
He accepts you as his sons and daughters,
and sets you free from the bondage of your past.
For Christ died and rose to new life
that we might all share his wholeness and abundant life.
> Worship in an Indian Context

355   Grant, we beseech thee, merciful Lord, to thy faithful people pardon and peace; that they may be cleansed from all their sins, and serve thee with a quiet mind, through Jesus Christ our Lord.
      The Book of Common Prayer

356   If we have worshipped you as a relic from the past, a theological concept, a religious novelty, but not as a living God:
      Lord forgive us.

      If we have confused your will with our understanding of it, if we have preferred divergence to unity:
      Lord forgive us.

      If we have heard stories of struggle, with no intention of sharing the burden or pain:
      Lord forgive us.

      If we have identified the misuse of power, but failed to prophesy against it, and refused to empower the weak:
      Lord forgive us.

      If we have sung songs in praise of your creation, while defiling the goodness of the earth:
      Lord forgive us.

      The Lord says: I will bring my people back to me.
      I will love them with all my heart. No longer am I angry with them. I will be to the people like rain in a dry land.
      This is the promise of God.
      Amen. Thanks be to God.
      Worship Resources, World Conference on Mission and Evangelism

357   Our insensitivity to the needs of others,
              O Lord, forgive.
      Our prejudice and fear that prevent us from loving,
              O Lord, forgive.
      The narrowness of our vision and our shrinking from your demands,
              O Lord, forgive.

Our resentment against those who have hurt us,
   O Lord, forgive.
Our desire to do your work in our way,
   O Lord, forgive.
Our impatience with those who are different from us,
   O Lord, forgive.
Our failure to listen properly to other points of view,
   O Lord, forgive.
Our fear of coming out of the fortress of our own souls into
fuller life and deeper love,
   O Lord, forgive.
   Source unknown

358   THE COVENTRY LITANY OF RECONCILIATION
All have sinned and fallen short of the glory of God.
(The Letter to the Romans)
The hatred which divides nation from nation, race from race,
class from class,
   Father, forgive.
The covetous desires of people and nations to possess what is not
their own,
   Father, forgive.
The greed which exploits the work of human hands and lays
waste the earth,
   Father, forgive.
Our envy of the welfare and happiness of others,
   Father, forgive.
Our indifference to the plight of the imprisoned, the homeless,
the refugee,
   Father, forgive.
The lust which dishonours the bodies of men, women and children,
   Father, forgive.
The pride which leads us to trust in ourselves, not in God,
   Father, forgive.
Be kind to one another, tenderhearted, forgiving one another, as
God in Christ forgave you.
(The Letter to the Ephesians)
   Coventry Cathedral

See also:

Special confessions for Christmas, 733
Harvest, 881–3
Concerning the Hungry, 447

Also:

No. 800: 'Lord Jesus, forgive us for failing you'

part five

PERSONAL
RELATIONSHIPS

HOUSEHOLDS, FAMILIES AND FRIENDSHIP

Be kind to one another, tenderhearted, forgiving one another,
as God in Christ has forgiven you.

EPHESIANS 4:32

ৎ৩ ৩৵

359   Gentle God,
grant that at home
where we are most truly ourselves,
where we are known at our best and worst,
we may learn to forgive and be forgiven.

A New Zealand Prayer Book

360   Give us a sense of humour, Lord,
    and also things to laugh about.
Give us the grace to take a joke against ourselves
    and to see the funny side of life.
Save us from annoyance, bad temper,
    or resentfulness against our friends.
Help us to laugh even in the face of trouble;
    and fill our minds with the love of Jesus,
for his name's sake.

Frank Colquhoun

361   O God, we pray for our family life,
that we all may grow together
in awareness of your love,
that our lives together may reflect
your brightness and your goodness.

Worship in an Indian Context

362   O God, the Spirit of truth,
      help us to be truthful with one another.
      O God, the Spirit of gentleness,
      help us to be gentle with one another.
      O God, who knows what is in our hearts
      more clearly than we do ourselves,
      help us to hear one another.
      O God, lead us in the way
      of truth and love.

                    Richard Harries

363   O Lord, bless this household;
           grant us health and peacefulness,
                    fun and friendship,
              a warm and welcoming spirit,
        and the gentleness that quickly forgives,
                    now and always.

                    A.A.

364   O God, make the door of this house wide enough to receive all
      who need human love and friendship,
      but narrow enough to shut out all envy, pride, and malice.
      Make its threshold smooth enough to be no stumbling-block to
      children, nor to straying feet,
      but strong enough to turn away the power of evil.
      God, make the door of this house a gateway to your eternal
      kingdom.
      Grant this through Christ our Lord.

                Thomas Ken (1637–1711) (adapted)
      This prayer was originally placed at the door of a Christian hospital.

365   Gentle God, we thank you for the love and friendship sur-
      rounding ... in their new home.
      May this be a place of rest, laughter and forgiveness.
      Bless the working, the relaxing,
          the loving and the sharing that will happen here;
      and may the spirit of Christ rest on ... in all that they are and
      all that they do.

                    A.A.

366   BLESSING
Peace to this house from God our heavenly Father.
Peace to this house from his Son who is our peace.
Peace to this house from the Holy Spirit the Life-giver.
And the peace of the Lord be always with you.

Traditional

367   ONE-PARENT FAMILIES
Lord God, we offer to you the children living with only one
parent.
Help them to feel your love, and be with them in their times of
confusion and loneliness.
Give strength, patience and wisdom to the parents trying to be
both father and mother to the children, at the same time as they
face up to their own needs.
Help us in the family of the Church to be open and caring with these
as with all the families we know, through Jesus Christ our Lord.

Christine McMullen

368   SEPARATION FROM THOSE WE LOVE
O God,
protect those whom we love and who are separated from us.
Guide them when they are uncertain,
comfort them when they are lonely or afraid,
and bless them with the warmth of your presence.
Thank you that neither space nor time
can cut us off from the love we have in each other
and in you.

A.A.

369   GRANDPARENTS
Lord, make me a good grandparent.
Help me to be there when I'm needed,
        and not to interfere.
Show me how to encourage but not criticize,

support, and not judge.
Give me tact, warmth and a grateful heart
for this wonderful gift
of a child of my child.

Maria Hodges

MARRIAGE AND COMMITMENT

370   God of love and trust,
      bless our hopes, our risk-taking and our commitment;
      make us sensitive and forgiving,
      and give us the wisdom
      to allow each other freedom and space.
      Let our love be for the world around us
      as well as for each other,
      and keep us centred on you.

A.A.

371   Father, we pray for those soon to be married; may their joys and
      hopes be realized. Be with them as they make their plans and give
      them patience and understanding when things are difficult. In
      their growing love for each other may they come to know you
      as the source of all love, and may your presence and peace abide
      in their homes.

The Mothers' Union Prayer Book *(adapted)*

372   O God, your Son Jesus began his ministry at a wedding cele-
      bration. May the joy that is experienced as two people begin a
      life together continue to grow and deepen through all that life
      has to offer along the way. May Jesus continue to transform the
      water of their every day to the wine of new vision, so what seems
      ordinary becomes transformed by love. May couples grow old
      together knowing the best wine is saved till last and that Jesus
      is the abiding guest and their companion on the way. We ask this
      in Jesus' name.

Woman's Prayer Companion

373   Gracious God, always faithful in your love for us, we rejoice in
       your presence.
       You create love and out of loneliness unite us in one human
       family.
       You offer your word and lead us in your light.
       You open your loving arms and embrace us with strength.
       May the presence of Christ fill our hearts with new joy
       and make new the lives of ... and ... whose marriage we cele-
       brate.
       Bless all creation through the sign of your love given in their love
       for each other.
       May the power of your Holy Spirit sustain them and us, in the
       love that knows no end.
                        The Book of Worship *(adapted)*

374   WEDDING ANNIVERSARIES
       We pray for ... and ... who are celebrating their wedding
       anniversary, that they may give thanks to you, heavenly Father,
       for all the love which binds them together as husband and wife.
       May they remember with grateful hearts your gifts of home,
       family and friends. Help them to rejoice in their shared memo-
       ries of joy and laughter, sadness and disappointment.
       May they praise you for the past, thank you for the present, and
       trust you for the future.
                 The Mothers' Union Prayer Book *(adapted)*

DIFFICULTIES IN RELATIONSHIPS

Put on then, as God's chosen ones, compassion, kindness,
humility, gentleness and patience, bearing with one another,
and forgiving each other, as the Lord has forgiven you.

COLOSSIANS 3:12–1

৵ ৩৵

375 Lord, pick me up and put me together again. Sometimes things become unbearable, and being with ... brings out the worst in me. Help me. Forgive me my resentment and sharp reactions. Free me from endless churning over arguments in my mind. Stay at my centre, Lord, and let nothing take from me that inner point of sanity, where I am known by you and not condemned.

A.A.

376 O God, I know that my temper is far too quick.

I know only too well how liable I am to flare up, and to say things for which afterwards am heartily sorry.

I know only too well that sometimes in anger I do things which in my calmer moments I would never have done.

I know that my temper upsets things at home; that it makes me difficult to work with; that far too often it makes me a cause and source of trouble.

O God, help me. Help me to think before I speak. When I feel that I am going to blaze out, help me to keep quiet just for a moment or two, until I get a grip of myself again.
Help me to remember that you are listening to everything I say, and seeing everything I do.
O God, control me and my temper too.

This I ask for your love's sake.

William Barclay (1907–1978)

377   Almighty God,
      have mercy on . . . and . . . ,
      and on all who bear me evil will and would harm me,
      and forgive their faults and mine together,
      by such easy, tender, merciful means as your infinite wisdom can
      best devise;
      amend and redress and make us saved souls in heaven together,
      where we may ever live and love
      together with you and your blessed saints,
      O glorious Trinity,
      through the bitter passion of our sweet Saviour.
                              St Thomas More (1478–1535)

378   Merciful God, prone as we are to blame others and to hate our-
      selves, take from our eyes the dust that blinds us, that we may
      treat one another by the light of your compassion, and in the
      Spirit of Jesus Christ who is the Light of the world.
                              Jim Cotter

379   Dear Father in heaven
      let us be peacemakers:
      more ready to call people friends than enemies
      more ready to trust than to mistrust
      more ready to love than to hate
      more ready to respect than despise
      more ready to serve than be served
      more ready to absorb evil than to pass it on.
      Dear Father in heaven,
      let us be more like Christ.
            The Mother's Union Anthology of Public Prayers

380   God our Mother and Father, we come to you as children. Be with
      us as we learn to see one another with new eyes, hear one
      another with new hearts, and treat one another in a new way.
                  Corrymeela Community, Northern Ireland

381   Give us, we pray you, gentle God,
      a mind forgetful of past injury,
      a will to seek the good of others
      and a heart of love.

                  A New Zealand Prayer Book

382   Almighty God, Creator and Father of all, help us to love and care
      for those we find hard to like. Teach us to understand and
      befriend all who have been so hurt by life that they can only
      express themselves in hurtful ways; through Jesus Christ our
      Lord, whose healing power brought wholeness of life to all who
      came to him.

                  Rachel Stowe

383   Lord, help us to listen to each other,
          to be gentle with one another,
          to forgive each other
          and to be willing to laugh at ourselves.

                  A.A.

384   Despite our hopes and efforts, Lord, we fail and things go
      wrong.
      We offer you the mistakes we have made in ourselves and in our
      marriages and families.
      We pray for people who are suffering now either from their own
      mistakes or from the mistakes of others:
      for children separated from one parent and cut off from grand-
      parents;
      for parents who see their children for only part of the week;
      for families who have many problems and lack hope;
      for husbands and wives who no longer find joy in each other,
      who feel wounded and disillusioned, as their marriage breaks up;
      for families who face death, illness, or disablement, and feel they
      cannot cope;
      for the unemployed who feel hopeless and unwanted.
      We hold them before you, Lord, for your healing love.

                  Christine McMullen

A BROKEN RELATIONSHIP

385   Lord, take away this cup of bitterness. Break my anger, as my heart has been broken.
In the darkness of my hurt, let there be hope. And, one day, perhaps, let there be love again.

Jane Robson

386   Eternal friend, for whom a thousand years are but a day, watch with me now as I begin all over again. The months (and years) with . . . , all that hope and happiness, have fallen from my life like wasted time. And I feel older, not wiser. Give me comfort and the courage to go forward without denying the past, to learn from what I have lost without being crushed by it.

Jane Robson

DIFFICULTIES IN MARRIAGE

387   O God, our Father, whose Son blessed the marriage at Cana by his presence, hear our prayer for all who seek to counsel those whose marriages are at risk. Give them sympathy, understanding and insight, that, by your grace, hurts may be healed, faults forgiven and misunderstandings removed. We ask this in the name of Jesus our Saviour.

Llewellyn Cumings (abridged)

FOR THE SEPARATED AND DIVORCED

388   O Lord, we pray for those who, full of confidence and love, once chose a partner for life, and are now alone after final separation.
May they receive the gift of time, so that hurt and bitterness may be redeemed by healing and love, and inner despair transformed by the joy of knowing you and serving others; through Jesus Christ our Lord.

Susan Williams

See also:
Birth, Adoption and Fostering, 967–77
Trouble and Conflict, 223–57

part six

INTERCESSION

LEADING INTERCESSIONS IN CHURCH SERVICES

Part 6 begins with some orders of intercession for use in worship, which can be taken as they stand or abbreviated. Later sections contain shorter prayers about a variety of situations. One way of using those is to weave a few of them into a full act of intercession, with a single sentence of introduction to each prayer (e.g., 'We ask for God's blessing on the church:'), then use a prayer from Nos. 525 to 554.

To avoid the intercessions becoming too long, it is best not to use more than three or four prayers in this way. It doesn't always work to include a set prayer within a pre-designed order of intercession because it can interrupt the flow of the prayer.

RESPONSES

Intercessions can be spoiled when worshippers are asked to repeat at regular intervals a fairly long sentence which they have never heard before! Some people tell me that they are so worried about remembering the given phrase that they cannot concentrate on the rest of the prayer. Or else they receive a jolt every time the 'lead-in phrase' comes up (because you have to remember that too), and stumble with embarrassment, and none too accurately, through the response.

Short responses are safer, e.g.:

'Lord in your mercy: Hear our prayer',
or: 'Lord hear us: Lord, graciously hear us',
or: 'Let us pray to the Lord: Lord have mercy.'

So, if these are not regularly used in your church, it is best to tell people what the response will be before you start. Anything more complicated than that needs to be printed out on a service sheet, even when the response seems relatively short – e.g., 'Jesus, Lord of life: In your mercy, hear us' – as in No. 389 below.

SILENCE

It is good to include moments of quietness, to give people a chance to enter more deeply into the prayers (though you need to watch that the prayers don't become too long). If worshippers are warned about this, they won't think you have lost your place, and the pauses can become a natural part of the rhythm of the prayers.

MUSIC

Spoken prayers can be interspersed with a simple sung chorus such as one from Taizé. This needs careful preparation and practice, with a group of singers who can lead others confidently. Instrumental or taped music can also be played as a background to prayer (see No. 390 below). This again needs careful preparation, to make sure that the balance, volume and timing are right for the particular building you are in.

SOME FURTHER POINTS

- Make sure you can be heard; speak slowly and clearly.
- Avoid preaching a mini-sermon through the medium of your intercessions.
- Don't be too long, and don't try to cover every problem in the world; time your prayers at home first: between three and five minutes is usually best.
- Be careful about mentioning people in the congregation by name; this is usually all right if they are ill, but if in doubt, check with them or their families first; avoid references to anybody's personal problems if there is any danger of embarrassment.
- It is good to pick up, briefly, a key point from the sermon; you can jot down a sentence during the service and incorporate it into the beginning of your prayers.
- Pegs on which to hang intercessions may include creation and the environment, the church, the nations of the world, the local community, the sick and those in trouble, people who are bereaved, and, if this is part of your tradition, those who have died.

Some Orders of Intercession for Worship

⁓ ⊙ ⊙⌣

389   Jesus, light of the world,
bring the light and peace of your Gospel to the nations
(and especially . . .)
Jesus, Lord of life
in your mercy, hear us.

Jesus, bread of life,
give food to the hungry (and especially . . .)
and nourish us all with your word.
Jesus, Lord of life
in your mercy, hear us.

Jesus, our way, our truth, our life,
be with us and all who follow you in the way,
(and especially . . .)
deepen our appreciation of your truth,
and fill us with your life.
Jesus, Lord of life
in your mercy, hear us.

Jesus, good shepherd who gave your life for the sheep,
surround with your care
those in particular need (and especially . . .)
Jesus, Lord of life
in your mercy, hear us.

Jesus, the resurrection and the life,
we give you thanks
for all who have lived and believed in you

(and especially . . .)
raise us with them to eternal life.
Jesus, Lord of life
in your mercy, hear us.
accept our prayers, and be with us always. Amen.

Patterns for Worship

390   INTERCESSION WITH BACKGROUND MUSIC
Taped music, e.g., from Taizé, in the background, such as 'O Lord hear my Prayer' (on the tape 'Laudate')

Suggested pattern:
Play the chorus once through before you start to speak:
  'O Lord hear my prayer, O Lord hear my prayer, When I call, answer me,
  'O Lord hear my prayer, O Lord hear my prayer, Come, and listen to me.'
  (Then turn the volume down to low.)

In our prayers today, we remember that we are part of the world-wide body of Christ, and we give thanks in particular for places where Christians from many nations come together, especially Taizé, whose music we are listening to today.

When I say the words, 'Let us pray to the Lord,' the response will be, 'Lord have mercy.'

For men, women and children without homes:
For men, women and children without food:
For men, women and children without love:
Let us pray to the Lord.
Lord, have mercy.

For the bewildered and the worried:
For those who feel they can no longer cope:
For the sick, the dying and the despairing:
Let us pray to the Lord.
Lord, have mercy.

For our families and friends:
For our congregation and neighbours,

and all those whose paths cross ours:
Let us pray to the Lord.
Lord, have mercy.

For our bishops and clergy:
For the brothers of Taizé, and all who go to their meetings:
For Christians working in television and radio,
and for ourselves, that we may spread God's love
by prayer, by word and deed:
Let us pray to the Lord.
Lord, have mercy.

We offer these prayers in the strength and the love of Jesus, our
Lord and Saviour.
Amen.

*(Turn the volume up again for another verse or verse-and-a-bit
of 'O Lord hear my Prayer'. Then fade out slowly.)*

391   O Lord our God,
You are Love, living and dancing through creation;
You are Light, challenging and purifying our hearts;
You are Peace, deep and unfathomable, working through and
beyond all pain and conflict;

We praise you for the gift of life itself;
we praise you for our fragile and beautiful planet;
we praise you for the richness and variety of different races and
cultures;
we praise you for human love and laughter;
we praise you for the sheer fun of celebration.

Use us now as channels of blessing for those in need:
for victims of famine, especially in . . . ,
for victims of war, especially in . . . ,
for victims of hatred, prejudice and injustice;
for those who are ill or depressed,
the lonely, and those longing to be alone;
and for those who have lost all hope of finding a home,
or finding work.

Lord, in your mercy,
hear our prayer.

Risen Christ,
breaking the bonds of evil and death,
shine on us, and on those for whom we pray,
with your eyes of compassion and glory.
Let your light flood the darkness in us and in our world,
and make us bearers of
    your healing for people,
    your delight in this planet,
    and your outrageously generous forgiveness,
on which we all depend,
through Christ, our Lord, our Lover and our Saviour, Amen.

A.A.

392   Let us pray for those who are going through dark times – a time
    of trouble,
    a time when it is not clear what to do, especially . . .
    God in your mercy
    Hear our prayer.

Let us thank God for those people whose courage and hope
have lit up the dark places of this world, especially . . .
God, in your mercy
Hear our prayer.

We pray for ourselves, that God will give us the courage
to see things clearly and tell the truth . . .
God, in your mercy
Hear our prayer.

The light of God to make us unafraid
The power of God to protect us
The joy of God to heal us
The grace of God to bless us and keep us truthful
now and for evermore.
Amen.

Ruth Burgess

393   Lord God,
       In Jesus, you came in the body:
       Flesh of our flesh, and bone of our bone;
       One with us in searing pain and delirious laughter.

       We thank you that you did not remain an idea,
               even a religious idea,
       But walked, wept, and washed feet among us.

       By your love,
       Change our ideas, especially our religious ideas,
       Into living signs of your work and will.

       Through our lives and by our prayers, your kingdom come.

       Lord God,
       In Jesus, you touched the scabby (suffering),
           listened to the ignored,
           gave the depressed something to hope for.
       You bandaged the broken with love
       And you healed them.

       We believe that your power to heal is still present,
       So on your help we call.
       We remember those whose minds are menaced by thoughts
           which worry or wound them, *(pause)*
       We remember those whose hearts are broken because love
           has gone,
           or because the light they lived by has turned to darkness,
       (pause)
       We remember those whose feet walk in circles,
           stopping only when they are tired,
           resting only to walk in circles again, *(pause)*
       We remember those whose flesh and bone or mind and spirit
           are filled with pain, *(pause)*
       We remember those who feel discarded or disposable. *(pause)*

       O Christ, put your hands where our prayers beckon.

       Through our lives and by our prayers, your kingdom come.

       Lord God,
       In Jesus your body was broken

By the cowardly and the powerful.
The judgement hall of Pilate
Knew your silence as surely as your critics knew your voice.

In word and silence,
Take on the powerful of the world today:
those whose word sentences some to cruelty or unmerited dismissal;
those whose word transfers wealth or weapons for the sake of profit or prejudice;
those whose silence condones the injustice they have the power to change.

O Saviour of the Poor, liberate your people.

Through our lives and by our prayers, your kingdom come.

Lord God,
By the authority of the Scripture,
We learn that we are the body of Christ . . .
Yes, even we who worship in different ways,
    even we whose understanding of you is so changeable,
        even we, who in our low moments, make an idol of our insignificance.

We are your body, we are told.

Then, Lord,
Make us like you,
That our souls may be the stained glass
Through which your light and purpose
Bring beauty and meaning into the world.

Through our lives and by our prayers, your kingdom come.

Your kingdom come
In joy and generosity,
In the small and the large,
    the ordinary and the special,
And to you be the glory
Now and always.
Amen.

John L. Bell

394   *(Explain to the congregation: After the words, 'Let us pray to the Lord,' the response is, 'Lord, have mercy.')*

For the peace of the world, that a spirit of respect and forbearance may grow among nations and peoples, let us pray to the Lord.
Lord, have mercy.

For the holy Church of God, that it may be filled with truth and love and be found without fault at the day of your coming, let us pray to the Lord.
Lord, have mercy.

For those in positions of public trust, (especially . . .), that they may serve justice and promote the dignity and freedom of all people, let us pray to the Lord.
Lord, have mercy.

For a blessing upon the labours of all, and for the right use of the riches of creation, let us pray to the Lord.
Lord, have mercy.

For the poor, the persecuted, the sick, and all who suffer; for refugees, prisoners, and all who are in danger, that they may be relieved and protected, let us pray to the Lord.
Lord, have mercy.

For this community; for those who are present, and for those who are absent, that we may be delivered from hardness of heart and show forth your glory in all that we do, let us pray to the Lord.
Lord, have mercy.

For our enemies and those who wish us harm; and for all whom we have injured or offended, let us pray to the Lord.
Lord, have mercy.

For all who have died in the faith of Christ, that, with all the saints, they may have rest in that place where there is no pain or grief, but life eternal, let us pray to the Lord.
Lord, have mercy.

                    Ancient Byzantine Litany

395 Let us say a prayer for those who need to be remembered tonight
(today):

Those who have made the news headlines today
because of what they have done or said . . .
(A name or a short prayer may be offered, each being fol-
lowed by a said or sung response, e.g., 'Lord, draw near'.)

Those who have been brought to our attention
through a meeting or conversation . . .

Those who are in hospital, in care,
or in a place which is strange to them . . .

Those in whose family, marriage or close relationship,
there is stress or a break-up . . .

Those who are waiting for a birth,
or a word which someone else must say . . .

Those who need to forget the God they do not believe in
and meet the God who believes in them . . .

Those whose love or need we should not forget to
share with God tonight . . .

Lord, we believe that you hear our prayer
And will be faithful to your promise to answer us.

When our eyes open again,
May they do so,
Not to end our devotions,
But to expect your kingdom,
For Jesus' sake.

John L. Bell

396 *(You can have two voices reading alternative sentences in this*
prayer, with a pause between each one.)

For all Christians throughout the world, that each person may
be a servant of Christ, truly and faithfully following his teach-
ings, Lord we pray.

Renew your peace in our hearts, and give us the courage of faith in our daily life, Lord we pray.

Free us from all prejudice and fear, deepen our understanding and our love, Lord we pray.

May those in authority work to establish justice and freedom in their countries and throughout the world, and especially in . . . , Lord we pray.

Show us the way to bring your compassion to the poor, the sick, the lonely and the unloved, Lord we pray, especially remembering . . .

For those who seek to be bearers of friendship to young and old, across all age-barriers, Lord we pray.

For all who are in prison, condemned, or exiled from their home, Lord we pray.

For parents and teachers and all those entrusted with the care of children and young people, Lord we pray.

Forgive those who hurt us or distort our best intentions; forgive us also and remedy our acts of injustice, Lord we pray.

Console those who are bereaved or in sorrow Lord we pray.

God our Father, you care for us and know all our needs; may we find rest in your love.

Taizé Community

397   Most loving Lord, holy and immortal, by your cross and resurrection you have overcome the world. We pray tonight for all who lie in the shadow of the cross.
Holy and immortal, have mercy upon us.

Give healing to every broken life.
Holy and immortal, have mercy upon us.

Give release to those consumed by bitterness.
Holy and immortal, have mercy upon us.

Give light to those who sit in darkness.
Holy and immortal, have mercy upon us.

Give peace to the tormented.
Holy and immortal, have mercy upon us.

Give joy to those in despair.
Holy and immortal, have mercy upon us.

Give relief to all in pain.
Holy and immortal, have mercy upon us.

Give hope to the dying.
Holy and immortal, have mercy upon us.

Give faith to the searching.
Holy and immortal, have mercy upon us.

John Michael Mountney

The righteous will ask, Lord, when did we see you hungry or
thirsty, or a stranger or needing clothes, or sick or in prison?
And the King will say, 'As you did it for one of the least of
these, you did it for me.

MATTHEW 25:37, 40

398   Abba, Father,
       with you, in my sinfulness,
            offering the world;
        with you in my weariness,
            offering the world;
       with you in my need of you,
            offering the world;
      with you in unbounded trust,
            offering the world.

A.A.

399   Lord, may this room become a castle of prayer, a place of com-
      munion with you, from which my prayer may flow out in love
      to the world.

after St. Teresa of Avila (1515–1582)

400   Make me
         a still place of light
         a still place of love
         of you
         your light radiating
         your love vibrating

your touch and your healing
far flung and near
to the myriads caught
in darkness, in sickness
in lostness, in fear

make a heart-centre here,
Light of the world.

Malling Abbey

401   Spirit of Christ, sanctify me.
            Accept and transform
            my small energy of desire,
            that it may become
         part of your great energy of desire
            for the redemption of the world.
               Your will be done!

Evelyn Underhill (1875–1941)

402 Lord, let me be a channel of your blessing to others. I do not
know how you will use my prayers, but I trust you absolutely,
that I may play my part in your healing and redeeming work in
the world.

A.A.

403 O God, enlarge my heart
        that it may be big enough to receive the greatness of your love.
     Stretch my heart
        that it may take into it all those who with me around the
        world
        believe in Jesus Christ.
     Stretch it
        that it may take into it all those who do not know him,
        but who are my responsibility because I know him.
     And stretch it
        that it may take in all those who are not lovely in my eyes,
        and whose hands I do not want to touch;
     through Jesus Christ, my Saviour.

Prayer of an African Christian

404 Let the healing grace of your love, O Lord, so transform me,
that I may play my part in the transfiguration of the world,
from a place of suffering, death and corruption
to a realm of infinite light, joy and love.
Make me so obedient to your Spirit
that my life may become a living prayer,
and a witness to your unfailing presence.

Martin Israel

405 Lord, make us quiet, as we place in your hands those for whom
we want to pray. We know that you love them with a love
greater than we could ever imagine. In the stillness we are here,
with you, for them. Use us, Lord.

A.A.

406 O Lord, save us from self-centredness in our prayers,
and help us to remember to pray for others.
May we be so lovingly absorbed with those for whom we pray
that we may feel their needs as keenly as our own,
and intercede for them sensitively,
with understanding and imagination.
We ask this in Christ's name. Amen.

after John Calvin (1509–1564)

407 We cannot measure how you heal
Or answer every sufferer's prayer,
Yet we believe your grace responds
Where faith and doubt unite to care.
Your hands, though bloodied on the cross
Survive to hold and heal and warn,
To carry all through death to life
And cradle children yet unborn.

John L. Bell and Graham Maule (verse 1 from a song)

FOR CHILDREN AND YOUNG PEOPLE

*Jesus said, See that you do not despise one of these little ones;
for I tell you that in heaven their angels always behold the face
of my Father.*

MATTHEW 18:10

(Note: prayers for use by children and teenagers are in Parts 15 and 16.)

෬ ෬

408 A PARENT'S PRAYER
Lord, I offer my daily life with my children
as a prayer
for all children of the world,
especially those who are
unloved,
abused,
starving,
bullied,
orphaned,
or afraid.

I offer my struggle with the demands of parenthood
as a prayer
for other parents,
those who face similar difficulties,
and those whose problems are different.

I offer my delight in my children
as a prayer
for childless couples,
bereaved parents,
single parents who ache for someone to share the load,
adopted children who have been told the truth too late,

women who have had abortions,
aborted babies,
and for all the secure and contented children too.

A.A.

409   Lord Christ,
      we bring before you the world of children.
      We bring their openness and friendliness,
      their sense of enquiry and creativity.
      Forgive our readiness to classify and divide,
      to label and separate.
      Forgive our voices of experience,
      and our demand for their conformity.
      Help us to understand and encourage them,
      that their spirits may be lifted,
      their imaginations quickened,
      and their vision broadened,
      for your world's sake.

J. Dickson Pope (adapted)

410   God our Father, be near to our children growing up in the peril
      and confusion of these times. Guard them from the forces of evil
      at work in our society, and lead them in the paths of goodness
      and truth; and enable us as parents to give them at all times the
      security of our love, and the help of our example and prayers;
      through Jesus Christ our Lord.

Frank Colquhoun

411   CHILDREN AT RISK
      Heavenly Father, we pray for children in all kinds of danger: on
      the roads; from the stranger offering sweets; from the unseen and
      often unknown cruelty of men and women. Give us the courage
      to speak out against all that may corrupt them. Show us, with
      your wisdom, how to warn them without frightening them, and
      help us assure them of your presence with them everywhere.

The Mothers' Union Prayer Book

412   Lord, help us to be patient
      With our children,
      To give them time
      When they need it,
      To listen to their views
      However much they may differ from ours.
      Help us in our conversations together
      That we may always trust each other.
      As our children search for knowledge
      Help us to learn with them.
                              Frank Topping

413   O God, we place our children in your hands.
      We ask
      not that you will shield them from difficulty,
          but that you will give them the strength to face it;
      not that you will protect them from making mistakes,
          but that they may be able to learn from them;
      not that their lives will be easy,
          but that they will deal with its challenges courageously.
      Be with them when they are vulnerable,
      protect them from lasting harm,
      and keep them always in your love.
                              A.A.

414   Lord God,
      help us to learn from our teenagers
      how best to accompany them
      through these turbulent years.
      Make us sensitive and patient,
      and give us the wisdom to support them
      in our challenging and confusing world.
      May they grow in understanding
      of what matters most in life,
      so that they become generous, strong and thoughtful adults;
      through Christ our Lord.
                              A.A.

415 God,
     we pray for our young people,
     growing up in an unsteady and confusing world.

     Show them that your ways give more life
         than the ways of the world,
     and that following you is better
         than chasing after selfish goals.

     Help them to take failure,
     not as a measure of their worth,
     but as a chance for a new start.

     Give them strength to hold their faith in you,
     and to keep alive their joy in your creation.

     We ask this through Christ our Lord.
     The Book of Common Prayer of the Episcopal Church, USA

416 Lord, when our children have different tastes and ideas from our
     own,
         show us when not to speak.
     When they disagree with us over what we allow them to do,
         give us the wisdom to be neither over-protective nor irre-
         sponsible.
     And when they move away from us,
         help us to welcome their freedom,
         and to be always there for them when they need us.
                              A.A.

417 We pray for young people growing up in today's world:
         – for the bewildered and seeking, that they may find faith in
         you,
         – for the unemployed and frustrated, that they may find
         spheres of usefulness and satisfaction,
         – for those who have been led into paths of anarchy and
         violence, that they may find a way of escape.
     May our discipline be wise and just; and may our love make it
     easier for them to understand the love of God.
                      Women of Ireland (adapted)

LEAVING HOME FOR THE FIRST TIME

418   Lord, we pray for our young people as they leave home for the first time. Help them to settle into their new surroundings, and be with them as they make friends and adjust to different patterns of living. Watch over them, Lord, and guard them.

A.A.

419   Heavenly Father, we ask you to bless ... who, for the first time, is leaving home and family and friends. Help him to know your love and constant presence wherever he is, and protect him in mind and body. Fill him with the power and joy of your Holy Spirit and keep him faithful to your Son, Jesus Christ.

The Mothers' Union Prayer Book

FOR THE ELDERLY

The glory of young men is their strength, but the beauty of the aged is their grey hair.

PROVERBS 20:29

420 We thank you, Lord, for the privilege of knowing elderly people:
thank you for their experience and wisdom,
and the stories they can tell us;
be with them when they feel lonely or unwanted,
help them if frustration makes them difficult,
and surround them with your peace,
that they may be aware how very close you are.

A.A.

421 We pray today for all elderly people; some are ill; some have had
to give up their own homes; some have no one to care for them.
Be especially near to those approaching death. Make them certain of your constant presence with them that they may have no
fear. This we ask in Jesus' name.

Kathleen A. Goodacre

422 Lord Jesus Christ, you are the same yesterday, today and for ever,
and you have promised to be with us all our days. We pray for
all elderly people, especially those who are ill or house-bound.
In their weakness may they find your strength and in their loneliness know the joy of your presence. Be to them a sure and certain hope of the life that you have prepared for them in heaven.

The Mothers' Union Prayer Book

FOR THE SICK AND THOSE WHO CARE FOR THEM

Bless the Lord, O my soul, let all that is within me, bless his holy name; for he forgives all your sin and heals all your diseases.

PSALM 103:1, 3

⁂

423 Jesus our Healer,
    we place in your gentle hands those who are sick.
    Ease their pain,
    and heal the damage done to them
    in body, mind or spirit.
    Be present to them through the support of friends
    and in the care of doctors and nurses,
    and fill them with the warmth of your love
    now and always.

A.A.

424 Living God, source of light and life,
    we come to you as broken members of your body;
    your strength is our strength,
    your health is our health,
    and your being is our being.
    Grant us your wisdom in our work,
    your love in our pain
    and your peace in our hearts.
    Send your blessing on all those who care for the sick,
    and those whom they serve,
    and give us the joy of everlasting love.
    In the name of Jesus your Son.

CARA (adapted)

425   Lord God, whose son, Jesus Christ, understood people's fear and
      pain before they spoke of them, we pray for those in hospital;
      surround the frightened with your tenderness; give strength to
      those in pain; hold the weak in your arms of love, and give hope
      and patience to those who are recovering; we ask this through
      the same Jesus Christ, our Lord.
                                        Christine McMullen

AIDS

426   Lord, help us to accept the challenge of AIDS:
          To protect the healthy, calm the fearful;
          to offer courage to those in pain;
          to embrace the dying;
          to console the bereaved;
      and to support all those who attempt to care
          for the sick and dying.

      Enable us to offer our energies,
      our imaginations,
      and our trusting in the mysteries of love,
      to be united with and through one another
      in liberating each other
      from fear of this disease.

      We offer these thoughts and prayers
      in the mystery of the loving
      that can and does bear all our woundings,
      whatever their source,
      through the spirit of love's concern
      for every single person.
          based on a prayer from the Terrence Higgins Trust

427   Lord, you came into the world so that we would know that you
      love and care for us. By your grace let me share your loving and
      caring with those whose lives are being changed by the AIDS
      virus, and help me to bring them help and comfort.
                                        CARA

428   Lord Jesus, you reached out to touch the leper and the outcast: reach out in love to those with HIV and AIDS, and those who love them. Give courage to their doctors, nurses and friends, so that their touch may be a channel for your healing and strengthening grace.

Lord Jesus, you were brought to the cross by hostility and prejudice: open our eyes to the challenge of HIV and AIDS. Make us ready to learn before we speak; may our words dispel hatred and build up compassion; and may we serve your spirit of truth and your kingdom of goodness.

Newcastle Churches' AIDS Awareness

429   Heavenly Father, Lord of the living and the dead: hold in your arms of love those who are dying with AIDS. Give them the knowledge of your closeness and the conviction that nothing can separate them from the love you showed us in Jesus Christ.

Newcastle Churches' AIDS Awareness

MENTAL ILLNESS

430   Lord, we are concerned for the mentally ill, for those who do not have the ability to learn and think clearly, or who have deep personal problems.

They are part of our community; they are one with us . . .

Help us to care for them, to help them find a place in society and to know that they are loved and wanted.

written by young people in Kenya

431   Father, we pray for the mentally ill, for all who are of a disturbed and troubled mind. Be to them light in their darkness, their refuge and strength in time of fear. Give special skills and tender hearts to all who care for them, and show them how best to assist in your work of healing; through Jesus Christ our Lord.

Timothy Dudley-Smith

Nursing

432 Dearest Lord, may I see you today and every day in the person
of your sick, and, while nursing them, minister to you.

Even when you hide yourself behind the unattractive disguise
of the irritable, the exacting, the unreasonable, may I still recognize you and gladly serve you.

O Jesus, bear with my faults, and look only at my intention,
which is to love and serve you in the person of each of your sick.

Lord, increase my faith, and bless my efforts and work, now and
for evermore.

Mother Teresa of Calcutta (adapted)

FOR THE UNHAPPY
AND THE LONELY

In you, O Lord, have I put my hope; in you have I trusted,
let me not be ashamed, nor let my enemies triumph over me.

PSALM 25:1–2

433   Lord,
      show us where there is loneliness,
         that we may take friendship.
      Show us where individuals are not seen as persons,
         that we may acknowledge their identity.
      Show us where there is alienation,
         that we may take reconciliation.

Women of Jamaica (adapted)

434   Lord Jesus, when you walked among hurt and lonely people,
      you looked at them with understanding
      and approached them with arms outstretched,
      showing them that they were truly loved.
      Come, now, we pray,
      and touch all who are in pain and distress;
      heal those who have stopped believing in themselves,
      comfort those who are at the end of their tether,
      and pour into their hearts the gentle balm of your Spirit.

A.A.

435   Lord Jesus, by the loneliness of your suffering on the cross, be
      near to all who are desolate, and in pain and sorrow; let your
      presence transform their sorrow into comfort, and their loneli-
      ness into fellowship with you; for the sake of your tender mercy.

George Appleton

436   Lord, we pray for all who are lonely:
      children who are being bullied and dare not tell anyone;
      shy people who find it hard to make friends;
      those who feel rejected and isolated;
      those whose partner has died or left them;
      and elderly people who miss their families and old friends.
      Lord, be with them all, in your infinite love.

                          A.A.

FOR THE POOR, THE HUNGRY AND THE DESPERATE

Is not this the fast that I choose, to share your bread with the hungry, and bring the homeless poor into your house? says the Lord.

ISAIAH 58:6–7

437   Christ, let me see You in others.
      Christ, let others see You in me.
      Christ, let me see:

      You are the caller
      You are the poor
      You are the stranger at my door.

      You are the wanderer
      The unfed
      You are the homeless
      With no bed.

      You are the man
      Driven insane
      You are the child
      Crying in pain.

      You are the other who comes to me
      Open my eyes that I may see.
                              David Adam

438   Make us worthy, Lord, to serve our fellow human beings
      throughout the world who live and die in poverty and hunger.
      Give them through our hands this day their daily bread, and, by
      our understanding love, give peace and joy.
                    Mother Teresa of Calcutta (adapted)

439 O God, who created us out of love, we pray for all who are destitute and without hope. Help us to understand what it is like to be poor or marginalized, to have no clean water, or to be exhausted by the sheer struggle to survive. Fire our imaginations, and empower us to work for the relief of their suffering; through Jesus Christ our Lord.

A.A.

440 Lord, when we say 'Give us today our daily bread,' may we remember our brothers and sisters who live below the poverty-line and pray, 'Give them today their daily bread'. Give us the wisdom and courage to challenge the policies and structures which make the poor ever poorer, while we have more than enough. Grant us such deep compassion that we will not rest while surplus food rots in one part of the world, and families starve in another; for your love's sake.

based on the words of Sister Margaret Magdalen CSMV

441 We pray for people
so poor
that they cannot help themselves;
whose subsistence crops
have been destroyed by climatic disasters;
for people who live in areas
where rainfall is unreliable
and varies from year to year.
We pray for small children
who die of malnutrition,
and others who suffer from disease
because their mothers do not understand the values of different kinds of foods.

We pray for little children,
too young
to pray for themselves.

written by young people in Kenya

442   We pray, mighty God, for those who struggle
that their life's flickering flame may not be snuffed out.
We pray for the poor and deprived,
for those exploited by the powerful and greedy,
and for a more human sharing of the plenty
you have given your world.

Worship in an Indian Context (abridged)

443   Lord Jesus Christ, who will, in the end, acknowledge all acts of
mercy as done to you;
grant that we may never pass by the poor, but may respond
with generous hearts to the voice of the helpless, whose cry is
your own.

Source unknown

444   We pray for those who live
crowded in shanty towns
with paper-thin walls,
inadequate sanitation,
and little, if any, clean water;
for those families who
squeeze into one squalid room;
for those who sleep rough
in the freezing cold.
There are so many people
with no place to call home.
O Lord, help us to help them.

Michael Hollings and Etta Gullick (abridged)

445   O God, graciously comfort and tend all who are imprisoned,
hungry, thirsty, naked and miserable; also all widows, orphans,
sick and sorrowing. In brief, give us our daily bread, so that
Christ may abide in us and we in him for ever, and that with him
we may worthily bear the name of 'Christian'.

Martin Luther (1483–1546)

446   We bring before you, O Lord,
     the troubles and perils of peoples and nations,
     the frustration of prisoners and captives,
     the anguish of the bereaved,
     the needs of refugees,
     the helplessness of the weak,
     the despondency of the weary,
     the failing powers of the aged
     and the hopelessness of the starving.
     O Lord, draw near to each,
     for the sake of Jesus Christ our Lord.

after St Anselm (1033–1109)

447   A LITANY OF PENITENCE
In sorrow, Lord, we pray for our sisters and brothers whose lives
are crippled by the greed and injustice of the world:
We remember women in factories in Brazil, working long hours
for little money, making shoes for us in the West.
Lord, have mercy.
We remember workers on tea-plantations in Sri Lanka, who
never know if the price of tea will enable them to survive.
Lord, have mercy.
We remember small children who work adult hours inhaling
dangerous fibres in rug-making factories in India.
Lord, have mercy.
We remember farmers in Uganda, already in debt, whose fami-
lies are hungry because world coffee prices have slumped.
Lord, have mercy.
Lord, we offer our anger and frustration for all people in con-
ditions like these, and we confess our apathy concerning their
misery. Strengthen all who work to alleviate their hardship, and
let loose your spirit of fairness and generosity among us. For
your love's sake.

A.A.

INNER CITIES

448   From the theatres, galleries and shops
       We cross the road and descend the steps
       To the pedestrian underpass
       Where they live
       In cardboard shacks.
       The homeless.
       The under-class.

       You seem to be everywhere here, Lord.
       You are the prophet screaming at political leaders
       That homelessness strips a society of dignity and value.

       You are the priest declaring to pious congregations
       That your mansion in heaven has many rooms.

       But above all
       You are the saviour
       Who gave up your home in heaven
       To be born into a feeding trough
       And who in the faces around me here
       Is very present.
                                        Martin Wallace

449   Our Father, we pray for the homes and families and for the chil-
       dren of the inner cities; for those whose families are broken, for
       the badly housed, the lonely and the handicapped, and for all
       whose lives seem purposeless or who cannot find work.

           We remember especially young people growing up amid
       urban deprivation and decay.

       Give to us all the will to seek for them a better quality of life,
       true opportunity, a future and a hope.

       In the name of him who loved Jerusalem, and wept for it, even
       Jesus Christ our Lord.
                                        Timothy Dudley-Smith

FOR VICTIMS OF WAR, OPPRESSION AND DISASTER, AND FOR REFUGEES

Give justice to the weak and the orphan: vindicate the lowly and the oppressed. Rescue the poor and the needy: deliver them from the hands of the wicked.

PSALM 82:3–4

450   O God, you bring hope out of emptiness
energy out of fear
new life out of grief and loss;
comfort all who have lost their homes
through persecution, war, exile,
or deliberate destruction.
Give them security, a place to live,
and neighbours they trust
to be, with them,
a new sign of peace to the world.

Janet Morley (abridged)

451   We pray
for all who have been maimed or murdered,
and those who were traumatized through watching the brutality
of others.
We pray
for people buried under bombed-out buildings,
and the victims of earthquakes, fires and mining accidents.
We pray
for those with smoke in their nostrils and dust in their mouths,
lost and perhaps unremembered.
Lord, in your tenderness, hold them.

A.A.

452   O Brother Jesus, who as a child was carried into exile,
       Remember all those who are deprived of their home or country,
       Who groan under the burden of anguish and sorrow,
       Enduring the burning heat of the sun,
       The freezing cold of the sea, or the humid heat of the forest,
       Searching for a place of refuge.
       Cause these storms to cease, O Christ.
       Move the hearts of those in power
       That they may respect the men and women
       Whom you have created in your own image;
       That the grief of refugees may be turned into joy.
                            African Prayer for Refugees

453   This prayer could be used for the children of any conflict area:
       Almighty God, Father of all,
       you have concern for all peoples,
       and you call us to live with compassion for others,
       as well as responsibility for ourselves.
       We commend to you the children of Rwanda (or . . .),
       and all who have suffered so terribly there.

       We remember especially
       the children who have lost their parents,
       and those who are struggling to keep alive.

       We ask that you will bless the work of UNICEF (or . . .) and all
       who are bringing comfort and hope to the children. May they be
       strengthened as they help those in such great need.

       We offer these prayers through Jesus Christ our Lord.
                UNICEF 1994 prayer for the children of Rwanda

454   Give comfort, O Lord, to all who are torn away from their
       homes and their loved ones by war, famine or the cruelty of their
       fellows; grant that we who dwell secure in this insecure world
       may be generous in caring for our displaced sisters and brothers.
                    Quarterly Intercession Paper, No 322.

455   O Lord our God, whose compassion fails not: support, we
      entreat you, the peoples on whom the terrors of invasion have
      fallen; and if their liberty be lost to the oppressor, let not their
      spirit and hope be broken, but stayed upon your strength till the
      day of deliverance; through Jesus Christ our Lord.

Eric Milner-White (1884–1963) and G. W. Briggs (1875–1959)

FOR PRISONERS OF CONSCIENCE

Let justice roll down like waters, and righteousness like an everflowing stream.

Amos 5:24

456 It must be the hardest thing, not to know what has happened,
or what wounds have been inflicted,
or what cell or grave marks the spot,
or whether there will ever be a home-coming.

Heavenly Father, the whole family of humanity is yours
and in your care.
So we remember in your presence
those who have been torn from their families,
those who have taken them away,
and those who are left . . .
Help us today to be signs of your care for them.

Bernard Thorogood

457 Lord, I pray for my brothers and sisters
who are in prison because of their stand against injustice,
and for all the other people who have 'disappeared'.
I pray for those undergoing torture;
Lord, give them strength, and the sense that they are not alone.
In particular I hold before you
those who believe that the world has forgotten them.
May they know that there are people who care,
and who are praying for them.
Jesus, arrested and tortured yourself,
be with them now,
and hold them in your wounded hands.

A.A.

458   May the fitful tremblings of our prayer move through the world
       with compassion to give to someone in prison, neglected and for-
       gotten, at least a moment's respite from despair.

Jim Cotter

459   O Jesus, King of the poor,
       shield today
       those who are imprisoned without charge,
       those who have 'disappeared'.
       Cast a halo of your presence around those who groan in sorrow
       or in pain.

       Encircle us with your power,
       compass us with your grace,
       embrace your dying ones,
       support your weary ones,
       calm your frightened ones –

       and as the sun scatters the mist on the hills,
       bring us to a new dawn,
       when all shall freely
       sit at table in your kingdom,
       rejoicing in a God who saves them.

Kate McIlhagga (adapted)

460   Use us now, Lord, as channels of your blessing for those in
       detention, especially any who are in particular distress at this
       moment.
       We thank you for the courage of those who suffer for truth
       and freedom; and we ask not only that they may be strengthened
       by our prayers but also that we will be inspired by their exam-
       ple; in the love of Jesus Christ our Lord.

A.A.

461   Uphold, O God, all those who are
       persecuted or imprisoned for their beliefs.
       Be to them a light showing the way ahead;
       a rock giving them strength to stand;
       a song singing of all things overcome.

Richard Harries

The Book *of a* Thousand Prayers

462 God of love and strength, your Son forgave his enemies even while he was suffering shame and death. Strengthen those who suffer for the sake of conscience. When they are accused, save them from speaking in hate; when they are rejected, save them from bitterness; when they are imprisoned, save them from despair. Give us grace to discern the truth, that our society may be cleansed and strengthened. This we ask for the sake of our merciful and righteous judge, Jesus Christ our Lord.

The Book of Common Prayer of the Episcopal Church, USA

463 FOR THOSE WHO DIED AS PRISONERS
Grant peace and eternal rest to all the departed, but especially to the millions known and unknown who died as prisoners in many lands, victims of the hatred and cruelty of others. May the example of their suffering and courage draw us closer to thee through thine own agony and passion and thus strengthen us in our desire to serve thee in the sick, the unwanted and the dying wherever we may find them. Give us the grace so to spend ourselves for those who are still alive, that we may prove most truly that we have not forgotten those who died.

Sue Ryder and Leonard Cheshire

PRAYERS FOR PEACE AND JUSTICE

The Lord shall judge between many peoples; they shall beat their swords into ploughshares, and their spears into pruning hooks; nation shall not lift up sword against nation, neither shall they learn war any more.

MICAH 4:3

464   Lord, I am part of the tension and injustice of the world.
     Forgive our human selfishness, to which I contribute;
     heal the resentment between people, of which I am a part;
     and come into the world's conflicts, in which I share by being human.
Take my unworthiness and sorrow,
and use them in your great work
of healing and redeeming humanity.

A.A.

465   In this land
bricks and mortar have become
not keystones of community
but weapons of occupation;
ploughing an act of resistance
not care for the open soil;
the growth of trees
no sign of shared blessing,
but proof of legal rights.
May all who love this land so fiercely
now build together for peace
with stones that no longer wound,
and work with friendly ploughshares
not forced to act like swords.

Janet Morley

466   Lord Jesus Christ, you are the way of peace.
       Come into the brokenness of our lives and our land with your
       healing love.
       Help us to be willing to bow before you in true repentance, and
       to bow to one another in real forgiveness.
       By the fire of your Holy Spirit, melt our hard hearts and con-
       sume the pride and prejudice which separate us.
       Fill us, O Lord, with your perfect love which casts out fear and
       bind us together in that unity which you share with the Father
       and the Holy Spirit.

                              Cecil Kerr
             This could be used as a prayer for any country torn by conflict.
         In line 2 the name of a place or places could replace the words 'our land'.

467   Bless our beautiful land, O Lord,
       with its wonderful variety of people,
       of races, cultures and languages.
       May we be a nation
       of laughter and joy,
       of justice and reconciliation,
       of peace and unity,
       of compassion, caring and sharing.
       We pray this prayer for a true patriotism,
       in the powerful name of Jesus our Lord.

                       Archbishop Desmond Tutu

468   O Lord Jesus,
       stretch forth your wounded hands in blessing over your people,
       to heal and restore,
       and to draw them to yourself and to one another in love.

                       Prayer from the Middle East

469   Lord, Christ, you see us
       sometimes like strangers on the earth,
       taken aback by the violence,
       by the harshness of oppositions.

And you come to send out a gentle breeze
on the dry ground of our doubts,
and so prepare us to be bearers
of peace and of reconciliation.

Brother Roger of Taizé

470   O God, teach us to distinguish
      negotiation and betrayal:
      when to defend our truth until the end;
      and when to climb down
      from our embattled certainties
      in search of real peace.

Janet Morley

471   O God,
      it is your will to hold both heaven and earth
      in a single peace.
      Let the design of your great love
      shine on the waste of our wraths and sorrows,
      and give peace to your Church,
      peace among nations,
      peace in our homes,
      and peace in our hearts.

A New Zealand Prayer Book

472   O God, make us children of quietness,
      and heirs of peace.

St Clement of Alexandria (c.150–215)

473   God of revelation,
      whose mercy embraces all peoples and nations:
      tear down the walls which divide us,
      break open the prisons which hold us captive
      and so free us to celebrate your beauty
      in all the earth;
      through Jesus, our Brother and Redeemer.

Celebrating Common Prayer

474 You have shown us, Lord, what is good.
   Enable us, we pray,
    to act justly,
    to love mercy,
    and to walk humbly with you, our God.

based on Micah 6:8

475 Grant, O Lord, that your Holy and life-giving Spirit may so
   move every human heart, that barriers which divide us may
   crumble, suspicions disappear and hatred cease; that our divisions being healed, we may live in justice and peace, through
   Jesus Christ our Lord.

The National Council of Churches of the Philippines

476 Show us, good Lord,
   the peace we should seek,
   the peace we must give,
   the peace we can keep,
   the peace we must forgo,
   and the peace you have given
   in Jesus Christ our Lord.

Caryl Micklem, used by the Corrymeela Community, N. Ireland

477 Tongue of God, keep on speaking,
   so that the peoples of earth
   may speak your language to each other
   and all may hear you in their own.

   Speak peace where nations meet,
   justice where ideas clash,
   mercy where power reigns,
   healing where minds and bodies hurt,
   and love where churches seek your unity,
   and wherever else Babel drowns out the sound of Pentecost.

Graham Cook

478   Lord, we pray for peace,
       not peace at any price
       but peace at your price.
       Make us and all your children so rich with your love,
       your generosity, your justice,
       that we can afford
       to pay the cost of your peace.
              The Mothers' Union Anthology of Public Prayers

479   Almighty God, ever-loving Father,
       your care extends beyond the boundaries of race and nation
       to the hearts of all who live.
       May the walls, which prejudice raises between us,
       crumble beneath the shadow of your outstretched arm.
       We ask this through Christ our Lord.
                            The Liturgy of the Hours

480   We pray for world peace,
       that ways of aggression and violence against fellow-humans
       and against God's creation may be renounced,
       and that world leaders may lessen the threat of nuclear
       destruction;
       we pray especially for our leaders
       and all others who strive to bring peace.
       Let there now be light for all, Light of all creation.
                    Worship in an Indian Context *(abridged)*

481   O God of earth and altar,
           Bow down and hear our cry;
       Our earthly rulers falter,
           Our people drift and die;
       The walls of gold entomb us,
           The swords of scorn divide;
       Take not thy thunder from us,
           But take away our pride.

       From all that terror teaches,
           From lies of tongue and pen,

From all the easy speeches
  That comfort cruel men,
From sale and profanation
  Of honour and the sword,
From sleep and from damnation,
  Deliver us, good Lord!

        G.K. Chesterton (1874–1936)

482   God of hope, you have given the rainbow as a symbol of your
faithfulness;
in its colours, you have shown us the variety of human life and
your call to unity;
its span between heaven and earth reminds us that our hopes for
the future are founded on your grace;
you have turned your face from judgement to redemption and
have called us to be peacemakers;

We pray for people whose humanity is denied by others;
for those persecuted or imprisoned because of their religion or
their politics;
for those who try to oppress and manipulate others and in so
doing lose sight of their own humanity;
for those who work for peace and justice, whatever the cost.

Lord God, make us your rainbow people, glorying in our God-
given variety, passionate for peace, trusting in your grace; in the
name of Jesus Christ, the hope of the world.

        Patterns and Prayers for Christian Worship

483   Giver of Life,
we wait with you to bear
your hope to earth's darkest places:
we wait at the places where darkness is
deeper than the deepest pain:
where love is denied:
let love break through.
Where justice is destroyed:
let righteousness rule.

Where hope is crucified:
let faith persist.
Where peace is no more:
let passion live on.
Where truth is denied:
let the struggle continue.
Where laughter has dried up:
let music play on.
Where fear paralyses:
let forgiveness break through.

Robin Green

FOR THE LEADERS
OF THE NATIONS

*Let all people know that God is ruler, even to the ends of
the earth.*

BASED ON PSALM 59:13

ᴄᴏ Gᴏ

484   Eternal God, Fount of wisdom;
       we ask you to bless the national leaders we have elected;
       grant that through their discussions and decisions
       we may solve our problems effectively,
       enhance the well-being of our nation,
       and achieve together a fairer and more united society.

       A New Zealand Prayer Book (adapted)

485   Almighty Father,
       whose will is to restore all things
           in your beloved Son, the king of all:
       govern the hearts and minds of those in authority,
       and bring the families of the nations,
       divided and torn apart by the ravages of sin,
       to be subject to his just and gentle rule;
       who is alive and reigns with you and the Holy Spirit,
       one God, now and for ever.

       The Alternative Service Book, *1980*

486   Destroy, O Lord, the spirit of self-seeking, in us as individuals
       and in our nations. Give to the peoples and their leaders a vision
       of peace and reconciliation. For you, O Lord, can find a way
       where human beings do not know what to do.

       Prayer from Sweden (adapted)

487   Lord God, all wise, all merciful, hear us as we pray for those
       who bear the responsibility of leadership among the nations of
       the world.
       Give them in all their deliberations wisdom to know your will,
       regard for your laws, and respect for human rights; that they
       may seek to lead all people in the paths of truth, freedom and
       peace, for the glory of your name, through Jesus Christ our Lord.

Frank Colquhoun (adapted)

488   Almighty God, from whom all thoughts of truth and peace pro-
       ceed:
          Kindle, we pray you, in the hearts of all people the true love
       of peace; and guide with your pure and peaceable wisdom those
       who take counsel for the nations of the earth; that in tranquil-
       lity your kingdom may go forward, till the earth be filled with
       the knowledge of your love: through Jesus Christ our Lord.

Francis Paget (1851–1911)

489   FOR GOOD GOVERNMENT
       Spirit of justice, creator Spirit;
       help us to make and keep this country
       a home for all its different peoples,
       and grant to our government and all its representatives
       imagination, skill and energy
       that there may grow amongst us good neighbourliness and
       peace.

A New Zealand Prayer Book

FOR OUR COMMUNITIES

Love one another with mutual affection. Rejoice with those
who rejoice; weep with those who weep.

ROMANS 12:10, 15

490   Grant us a vision, Lord
       To see what we can achieve
       To reach out beyond ourselves
       To share our lives with others
       To stretch our capabilities
       To increase our sense of purpose
       To be aware of where we can help
       To be sensitive to your Presence
       To give heed to your constant call.

David Adam

491   Guide us that we may be more sensitive to our neighbour's needs.
       We pray for awareness of those needs:
           the need of the old to know they are wanted,
           the need of the young to know they are listened to,
           the need of all people to know they are of value.
       Lord, keep us aware.

Women of New Zealand (adapted)

492   We thank you, our Father, for those whose work sustains our
       nation, and this community in which we live; for all who create
       the wealth by which we trade, for those who grow and provide
       our food, or who in industry, commerce and transport bring it
       to our homes.
           We thank you for those who, day and night, maintain the pub-
       lic services; for the police, for those who respond to emergencies,
       and for all whose work is in health or healing or social care.

Teach us to remember that all our lives depend upon the work
of many minds and hands; and we pray that we may live thank-
fully and in unity as members of one human family; through
Jesus Christ our Lord.

Timothy Dudley-Smith

493 God of our daily lives,
we pray for the people of the cities of this world
working and without work;
homeless or well housed;
fulfilled or frustrated;
confused and cluttered with material goods
or scraping a living from others' leavings;
angrily scrawling on walls, or reading the writing on the wall;
lonely or living in community;
finding their own space and respecting the space of others.
We pray for our sisters and brothers,
mourning and celebrating–
may we share in their sufferings and hope.

Jan Pickard

494 Lord God, you have taught us
that we are members one of another
and that we can never live to ourselves alone:
we thank you for the community of which we are part;
for those who share with us in its activities,
and for all who serve its varied interests.
Help us, as we have opportunity,
to make our own contribution to the community
and to learn to be good neighbours,
that by love we may serve one another,
for the sake of Jesus Christ our Lord.

Frank Colquhoun (adapted)

495   O God, the source of our common life,
       when we are dry and scattered,
       when we are divided and alone,
       we long for connection, we long for community.
       Breath of God, breathe on us.

       With those we live beside,
       who are often strange to us,
       whom we may be afraid to approach,
       yet who have riches of friendship to share,
       we long for connection, we long for community.
       Breath of God, breathe on us.

       With those we have only heard of,
       who see with different eyes,
       whose struggles we try to imagine,
       whose fierce joy we wish we could grasp,
       we long for connection, we long for community.
       Breath of God, breathe on us.

       With those we shall never know,
       but whose lives are linked with ours,
       whose shared ground we stand on,
       and whose common air we breathe,
       we long for connection, we long for community.
       Breath of God, breathe on us.

       When we are dry and scattered,
       when we are divided and alone,
       when we are cut off from the source of our life,
       open our graves, O God,
       that all your people
       may be free to breathe, strong to move,
       and joyful to stand together
       to celebrate your name.

                                        Janet Morley

FOR RACIAL HARMONY

496 God of peace,
     we pray for a spirit of mutual interest and concern
     between men and women of different colours, cultures and
     creeds.
     Touch the wounds that racism has inflicted,
     heal those who have suffered verbal or physical abuse,
     and make whole the people who inflicted those hurts.
     Teach us to enjoy our diversity
     and help us to move, always in hope,
     towards a truly peaceful community of peoples.

                              A.A.

497 Almighty God,
     as your Son our Saviour
     was born of a Hebrew mother,
     but rejoiced in the faith of a Syrian woman
     and of a Roman soldier,
     welcomed the Greeks who sought him,
     and needed a man from Africa to carry his cross;
     so teach us to regard the members of all races
     as fellow heirs of the kingdom of Jesus Christ our Lord.

                          Toc H

498 We pray for our brothers and sisters of other faiths,
     that dark walls of separation may be broken down.
     Open all our hearts, great Saviour,
     and attune us to each other's hopes,
     that we may learn to know and respect each other.

                  Worship in an Indian Context

WORK

499 INDUSTRIAL RELATIONS
     Almighty God, we pray for all who work in industry. Bless
     all meetings between employers and employees. Remove all

bitterness, distrust and prejudice from their deliberations. Give to all a spirit of tolerance and an earnest desire to seek for justice and for truth; that all may work together for the common good, through Jesus Christ our Lord.

William A. Hampson

500 Lord, you toiled at the carpenter's trade: we pray for all who work in industry and commerce, in agriculture and at sea.

Lord, you offered to the heavily laden your easy yoke: we pray for all whose labour is hard, monotonous or exposes them to danger.

Lord, your ministry took you far from home: we pray for all who serve their country abroad, and those whose work parts them from their families.

Lord, you constantly met the demands of the needy: we pray for all whose work is deeply demanding or causes them stress.

John Michael Mountney (abridged)

501 FOR A SHOP, OFFICE, FACTORY OR OTHER PLACE OF WORK
God of creation,
bless all who work in this building,
and those who come to use it [*or* buy in it].
May it be a place
of care and honesty,
justice and kindness,
so that all who enter it
may glimpse something of your kingdom.

A.A.

Unemployment

502 Thank you for our country, Lord. Thank you for the talents of each person living here. Forgive us when we allow people to count for nothing, when we cannot share our resources fairly, and when we want more for ourselves, although our neighbour has less.

Be with those who, at the height of their powers, have been deprived of their jobs, and give hope to those who have never known the prospect of employment; through Jesus Christ, our Lord.

Church Action with the Unemployed (adapted)

503   We pray, O Lord, for all those people for whom life has no obvious pattern, no routine, no challenge. We think particularly of the unemployed, and of any known to us personally. Give wisdom and imagination to all who plan new patterns of work and leisure for our society, that no one may feel useless, unproductive, or unfulfilled.

Kathleen A. Goodacre (adapted)

SEAFARERS

504   O Lord, we commend to your keeping all who sail the seas: enrich them with your presence, guard them in danger, protect them in temptation, sustain them in loneliness, and support them in sickness and anxiety. Bless those who minister to them, and guide us all to the haven of eternal life; through Jesus Christ our Lord.

Missions to Seamen (adapted)

505   Eternal Father, strong to save,
Whose arm hath bound the restless wave,
Who bidd'st the mighty ocean deep
Its own appointed limits keep:
   O hear us when we cry to thee
   For those in peril on the sea.

William Whiting (1825–1878)

THE JUDICIAL SYSTEM

506   THE JUDICIARY AND THE POLICE
God of truth and justice;
we ask you to help the men and women

who administer and police our laws;
grant them insight, courage and compassion,
protect them from corruption and arrogance
and grant that we, whom they seek to serve,
may give them the support and affection they need;
so may our people be strengthened more and more in respect and
concern for one another.

A New Zealand Prayer Book

507 PRISONERS

We pray, our Father, for those whose freedom has been taken
from them: for all who suffer imprisonment, whether for crime
or for conscience' sake; for all whose vision of your world is seen
through bars, and in whose heart the lamp of hope burns low.
God of mercy, give them help, according to their need, and hear
our prayer for Jesus Christ's sake.

Timothy Dudley-Smith

ARTS AND THE MEDIA

508 THE MEDIA

We pray, O God, for those who as writers, speakers and enter-
tainers influence the thought of our people through the press,
radio and television. Help them to exercise their gifts with
responsibility and understanding, that they may enrich the common life of the nation and strengthen the forces of truth and
goodness; through Jesus Christ our Lord.

The Mothers' Union Prayer Book

509 TELEVISION

Lord God, you have placed in human hands great power for
good or evil through television.
We pray for those whose faces and voices are thus known in millions of homes; for those who decide the policies and plan sched-
ules; and those who direct and produce programmes.

We pray that their skills and gifts may be devoted to what is true and good, so that those who watch and listen may be informed and entertained without being debased or corrupted; through Jesus Christ our Lord.

Christopher Idle

510   THE ARTS
Spirit of God, creative inspiration of all that we do which is beautiful and of good report, we thank you for painting, sculpture, music, drama and literature, and all the endeavours which point us beyond ourselves. We thank you for every enrichment of our humanity and for the rededication which so naturally follows.

Colin Semper

FOR PLACES
OF EDUCATION

Happy are those whom you discipline, O Lord, and whom you teach out of your law. For the Lord will not forsake his people.

PSALM 94:12, 14

ംൟ ൕ

511   Good Jesus, you have deigned to refresh our souls with the sweet stream of knowledge; grant that one day we may come to you, its source and spring.

Alcuin of York (735–804)

512   May we explore together the territory of knowledge;
May we learn together the mysteries of truth;
May we share together the experience of beauty;
May we release in each other the spark of creativity;
May we always remember that you, the author of all knowledge, yourself Goodness, Truth and Beauty, delight to share all experience with us.

Kathleen A. Goodacre

513   Father, we thank you for the gift of language, and for the written word.
We thank you for writers, publishers and printers, for books and libraries, and for the spread of knowledge and the sharing of experience which comes to us through the printed page.
We thank you for the books which have helped to shape our lives and to mould our tastes and values; they have furnished our minds, spoken to our hearts, enriched or entertained us, both in health and sickness.
Teach us to value literacy and to use it rightly; through him whose words are words of life, our Saviour Jesus Christ.

Timothy Dudley-Smith

514   O God, we pray for our schools and universities, (especially . . .).
Help us to value the experience of studying for its own sake.
Bless our life together as a learning and teaching community,
and make us wise but not cunning,
    perceptive but not cynical,
    and generous in a world where greed and ruthlessness often
prevail;
in the name of Jesus Christ our Lord.

                                  A.A.

515   Grant, Lord, to all who study and those who teach them,
the grace to love that which is worth loving,
to know that which is worth knowing,
to value what is most precious to you,
and to reject whatever is evil in your eyes.
Give them a true sense of judgement,
and the wisdom
to see beneath the surface of things.
Above all, may they search out and do
what is pleasing to you;
through Jesus Christ our Lord.

                after Thomas à Kempis (1380–1471)

516   STUDENTS FROM OVERSEAS
O God, the Father of all, we remember before you those who
come from many lands to study in our schools and universities.
Guide and protect them in the difficulties which beset them in
their new surroundings. Keep alive in their hearts the love of all
that is good in their life at home, and give them insight to appre-
ciate and share that which is good in ours. Pardon the faults of
temper and manners by which we so often offend them; and
grant unto us true humility, love, and patience, that we may welcome them in the spirit of the master whom we desire to serve,
Jesus Christ our Lord.

        The Mothers' Union Prayer Book *(abridged)*

Science and Technology

The earth is the Lord's, and all that is in it.
PSALM 24:1

517 Praise to you, God, for all your work among us.
Yours is the vigour in creation,
yours is the impulse in our new discoveries.
Make us adventurous, yet reverent and hopeful
in all we do.

A New Zealand Prayer Book

518 God of energy and power,
in the risk of creation
you have entrusted to us
a vast and dangerous knowledge of your world.
Give us wisdom
and generosity of spirit,
to use the skills of science
and the resources of technology
for the needs of the poor and forgotten,
and for the enriching and healing of us all.

A.A.

519 God of action, you gave us fingers to dance amidst clay and
chemicals, to build and to burn. You invested us with energies
to transform our planet. Today our commission is to share in the
divine work. Help us in all we do to learn to trace the design of
heaven upon the material of our world, and to speak, act and
think with gentle reverence.

Jonathan Blake (abridged)

520   Grant us prudence in proportion to our power,
      wisdom in proportion to our science,
      and humaneness in proportion to our wealth and might.
      For in your will, O God, is our peace.

                  Conference of European Churches (CEC)

521   Lord, we have found out so much knowledge and yet possess
      so little wisdom. We pray that in your mercy you will save us
      from ourselves. Help us to learn the right use of nature no less
      quickly than we unlock her new treasures; and give us hearts and
      wills made new in Christ to dedicate your gifts of knowledge to
      the service of others and to the praise of your name.

                  Timothy Dudley-Smith

522   O God whose wisdom has set within our hearts
      the quest for knowledge and dominion in the natural world,
      teach us to use all science, invention and technology
          not to hurt but to heal,
          not to destroy but to build,
          not to divide but to unite your human family in prosperity
              and dignity together.
      And let not our knowledge outstrip our wisdom;
      through Jesus Christ our Lord.

                  Timothy Dudley-Smith

523   Awesome God, your Love embraces all the powers of creation,
      and in the presence of Love we need never be afraid. Give us
      steadiness and courage and skill to strive with the energies you
      have placed in our hands, that the wise use of heat and light, of
      atom and laser, may enable the earth and its peoples to flourish
      and prosper, according to your will shown to us in Jesus Christ,
      true image of you, our Creator.

                  Jim Cotter

524   Yours, O Lord, is the power of the computer,
      Yours, O Lord, is all power;

Yours, O Lord, is the power of the aeroplane,
Yours, O Lord, is all power;
Yours, O Lord, is the power of television,
Yours, O Lord, is all power;
Yours, O Lord is the power of electricity,
Yours, O Lord, is all power;

Yours, O Lord, is all power,
As stewards we act,
The power is not ours.
Let us use it aright
To disclose your might.
Yours, O Lord, is all power.

Brian Bell

FOR THE CHURCH: ITS UNITY AND INTEGRITY

Jesus prayed, Father, the glory which you have given to me, I have given to them, that they may be one, even as we are one, so that the world may know that you have sent me.

JOHN 17:22–3

525 Lord, look in your mercy on your Church,
     lest we, your people who know you well,
     should shut the doors against the others
     whom you love to draw to yourself;
     because they are too different,
     too difficult,
     or too demanding.

                                        Betty Scopes

526 We pray, O Lord, for the Church which is one in the greatness
     of your love, but divided by the littleness of our own. May we
     be less occupied with the things that divide us, and more with
     those we hold in common, and the love that enfolds us all.

                        USPG 'Network' Winter 1978

527 Lord, we pray for the unity of your Church.
     Help us to see ourselves as rays from the one sun,
     branches of a single tree,
     and streams flowing from one river.
     May we remain united to you and to each other,
     because you are our common source of life;
     and may we send out your light
     and pour forth your flowing streams over all the earth,
     drawing our inspiration and joy from you.

                    after St Cyprian of Carthage (c.200–258)

528   Lord, heal your Church:
heal the wounds of the past,
and those we inflict on each other now.
Free us from party-spirit,
and forgive us when we fail to listen to each other.
Lift up our hearts to you,
so that we may be filled
with resurrection joy beyond all division,
and with your spirit of love
which nothing can destroy.

A.A.

529   Lord God, we thank you
For calling us into the company
Of those who trust in Christ
And seek to obey his will.
May your Spirit guide and strengthen us
In mission and service to your world;
For we are strangers no longer
But pilgrims together on the way to your Kingdom.

Prayer of the Inter-Church Process (The Swanwick Declaration)

530   O God of peace, good beyond all that is good, in whom is calmness and concord: Heal the dissensions which divide us from one another, and bring us into unity of love in you; through Jesus Christ our Lord.

St Dionysius of Alexandria (c.190–265)

531   Gracious Father, we pray for your Church.
Fill it with your truth, and keep it in your peace.
Where it is corrupt, purge it;
where it is in error, direct it;
where it is right, strengthen and confirm it;
where it needs help, provide for it;
where it is divided, heal it,
and unite it in your love,
through Jesus Christ our Saviour.

after William Laud (1573–1645)

532   Lord Jesus Christ, who prayed for your disciples that they might
       be one, even as you are one with the Father; draw us to yourself,
       that in common love and obedience to you we may be united to
       one another, that the world may believe that you are Lord, to the
       glory of God the Father.

                        William Temple (1881–1944)

533   Father, we pray for your Church throughout the world,
       that it may share to the full in the work of your Son,
       revealing you to men and women
       and reconciling them to you and to one another;
       that Christians may learn
       to love one another and their neighbours,
       as you have loved us;
       that your Church may more and more reflect
       the unity which is your will and your gift;
       we pray through Jesus Christ our Lord.

              Prayer from the Chapel of Unity, Coventry Cathedral

534   Gracious God, you have called us to be a new community in
       Christ, and yet we remain divided. Forgive us our fear, anxiety,
       prejudice and misunderstandings. Strengthen our common bonds
       and deepen our resolve to promote the unity of your Church.

                        Celebrating Community

535   O God, give to us who are still divided the thirst and hunger for
       communion in faith, life and witness. Keep us restless until we
       grow together in accord with Christ's prayer that we who believe
       in him may be one.

                        Celebrating Community

I heard the voice of the Lord saying, Whom shall I send, and who will go for us? Then I said, Here am I! Send me.

ISAIAH 6:8

⊷⊙ ⊙⊶

536   Draw your Church together, O God,
into one great company of disciples,
together following our Lord Jesus Christ
into every walk of life,
together serving him in his mission to the world,
and together witnessing to his love
on every continent and island.

A New Zealand Prayer Book

537   God our healer,
whose mercy is like a refining fire:
touch us with your judgement,
and confront us with your tenderness;
that, being comforted by you,
we may reach out to a troubled world,
through Jesus Christ.

Janet Morley

538   We praise and thank you, Holy Spirit of God,
for the men and women you have called to be saints;
from your first fallible, frightened friends
who followed you to Jerusalem,
through the centuries of discovery and growth,
people of every class and temperament
down to the present day.

We praise you, Holy Spirit, for calling us
to serve you now,
for baptizing us to represent you
in this broken world.
Help us to be Christ's united body to heal and reconcile;
help us to share Christ's life with everyone.

A New Zealand Prayer Book

539   Gather us, Lord, or scatter us;
      do as Thou deemest right,
      building us all into one Church:
      a Church with open doors and large windows,
      a Church that takes the world seriously,
      ready to work and to suffer,
      and even to bleed for it.

Béla Vassady

540   Set our hearts on fire with love for you, O Christ,
      that in its flame we may love you
      with all our heart,
      with all our mind,
      with all our soul,
      and with all our strength,
      and our neighbours as ourselves,
      so that, keeping your commandments,
      we may glorify you,
      the giver of all good gifts.

Kontakion for Love, Eastern Orthodox Church

541   Lord, make us, your Church, into the people you want us to be,
      and forgive us where we fall short.
      Teach us to be generous in judgement,
      bold in commitment,
      and sensitive in listening.
      Where we find no love, let us bring love,
      and make us more like you.

A.A.

542   O God, forgive our attempts at piety, that prevent us from being part of your world; and forgive our worldliness, that prevents us from being part of your kingdom.

Bring us closer to you, that we may be more actively involved in your work of reconciliation and healing.

Mark Wakelin (adapted)

543   Save us, Jesus, from hurrying away,
because we do not wish to help,
because we know not how to help,
because we dare not.
Inspire us to use our lives serving one another.

A New Zealand Prayer Book

544   O God, our Creator,
who gave us all that we are and have;
release us from self-love
to be able to share
     what we are
     what we know
     what we have
with one another
and in the world which you love.
In the name of Christ, who makes this a possibility.

Christian Conference of Asia

545   Holy God, whose name is not honoured
where the needy are not served,
and the powerless are treated with contempt:
may we embrace our neighbour
with the same tenderness
that we ourselves require;
so your justice may be fulfilled in love,
through Jesus Christ.

Janet Morley

546 O Lord, you have told us
that you will ask much of those to whom much is given;
may we, who enjoy so rich an inheritance of faith,
work together the more fruitfully,
by our prayers and labours,
to share with those who do not know you
the gifts we so plentifully enjoy;
and, as we have entered into the labours of others,
so may others enter into ours,
through Christ our Lord.

Anonymous (fifth century)

547 Forgive us, Lord, when we build worlds which are dependent on
us and not on you ...
Forgive us when we cannot see you in the midst of suffering and
darkness. Help us, however feebly, to realize that the coming of
the kingdom is your work, and not ours.

Subir Biswas (died c.1980)

548 Father in heaven,
form in us the likeness of your Son
and deepen his life within us.
Send us as witnesses of gospel joy
into a world of fragile peace and broken promises;
and touch the hearts of all with your love
that they in turn may love one another.

The Roman Missal (adapted)

549 Lord, you have consecrated your world
by sending your Son into the midst of it
and by making all things new in him.
We ask you to give us and all your people
the courage and power we need
to share fully in his mission to the world
and to further his kingdom.

Paul Iles

550   Lord Jesus, killed by hate and raised by love,
        help us to be Your witnesses in a hostile world,
        to show most love where there is most hate,
        and to live united with one another until You come again.

Susan Williams

551   All-loving Christ,
        we pray for those who have lost their faith,
        and all who are questioning and searching.
        Make us sensitive in listening to them,
        and keep us from being judgemental or inward-looking.
        We also pray for those who have recently found new faith;
        help us to accompany them with warmth and wisdom,
        so that, together, we may grow into a deeper knowledge of you,
        for your love's sake.

A.A.

552   Almighty God, you called us to labour in your vineyard: Keep
        us faithful in your service, whether the harvest be plentiful, or
        the soil seem barren and our labour unprofitable; knowing that
        the harvest is yours, and you will reap in your own appointed
        time; to the glory of your holy Name.

Eric Milner-White (1884–1963) and G.W. Briggs (1875–1959)

553   Heavenly Father,
        we pray for those who have gone to other countries
        with the good news of Jesus:
        when their work is difficult and tiring,
        make them strong;
        when they are lonely and homesick,
        remind them that you are with them;
        when they are uncertain what to do,
        guide them.
        Keep them at all times loving you;
        for Jesus' sake.

Michael Botting

554   Father, by your Spirit
bring in your kingdom.

You came in Jesus to bring good news to the poor,
sight to the blind, freedom to the captives,
and salvation to your people:
anoint us with your Spirit;
rouse us to work in his name:
Father, by your Spirit
bring in your kingdom.

Send us to bring help to the poor
and freedom to the oppressed:
Father, by your Spirit
bring in your kingdom.

Send us to tell the world
the good news of your healing love:
Father, by your Spirit
bring in your kingdom.

Send us to those who mourn,
to bring joy and gladness instead of grief:
Father, by your Spirit
bring in your kingdom.

Send us to proclaim that the time is here
for you to save your people:
Father, by your Spirit
bring in your kingdom.

Lord of the Church,
hear our prayer,
and make us one in heart and mind
to serve you in Christ our Lord. Amen.
Patterns for Worship

See also:

Intercession for Christmas, 720, 722 and 734; Easter, 827;
and Harvest, 884–86

Prayers in a Healing Ministry, 555–63

Prayers for Peace and Justice, 464–83

Prayers for Harvest, 876–87

Prayers for Remembrance Day, 888–92

Prayers for the Hungry, Poor and Oppressed, 437–55

Prayers for the Leaders of the Nations, 484–89

Prayers for Peace and Justice, 464–83

Prayers under Saints and Angels, 893–927

Also:

No. 201: A prayer of thanksgiving for the variety of our human races.

part seven

Prayers in a Healing Ministry

*Are any among you sick? They should call for the elders of the
church and have them pray over them, anointing them with
oil in the name of the Lord.*

JAMES 5:14

⤫◎ ◎⤫

555   Christ, You are behind me to protect me from evil, defending me
       from all that would creep up on me. You stand between me and
       all that seeks to defile me.
       Christ, You enter through the door of the past with Your love
       and forgiveness. You can come where doors are closed and bring
       light and peace.
       Christ, I put my hand in Yours, for I am afraid; I bring memo-
       ries that hurt and a past that pains, for Your healing and renewal.
       Christ, come enter through the door of the past;
              into the remembered and the forgotten,
              into the joys and sorrows,
              into the recording room of memories,
              into the secret room of sin,
              into the hidden room of shame,
              into the mourning room of sorrow,
              into the bright room of love,
              into the joyful room of achievement.
       Come, Christ.

David Adam

PRAYERS TO ACCOMPANY THE LAYING ON OF HANDS

556   PRAYER FOR USE BY THOSE WHO WILL BE LAYING HANDS ON OTHERS
       And now, O God, I give myself to you.
       Empty me of all that is not of you,
       Cleanse me from all unrighteousness,
       And, according to your will,
       Take my hands and use them for your glory.

Dorothy Kerin (1889–1963) (adapted)

557   May the healing power of our risen Lord, Jesus Christ, fill your
whole being, body, mind and spirit. May he take away all that
hurts or harms you, and give you his peace.

Source unknown

558   In the name of God Most High, and through his infinite love and
power, may release from all sickness and infirmity to be given to
you [*and those for whom you pray*].

Dorothy Kerin (1889–1963)

*The words in italics may be used if a person receives
the laying-on of hands on behalf of someone else.*

559   In the name of Jesus Christ, may the healing power of the Holy
Spirit make you whole, and keep you entire, working in you
according to his most loving will.

Dorothy Kerin (1889–1963) (adapted)

560   May the wonderful energy of God's healing power flow into you,
fill you with new life, and give you peace and calm.

Source unknown

561   May the light of God surround you,
the presence of God enfold you,
and the power of God heal you,
today and always.

A.A.

ANOINTING

562   I lay my hands upon you in the Name of our Lord and Saviour
Jesus Christ, beseeching him to uphold you and fill you with his
grace, that you may know the healing power of his love.

The Book of Common Prayer of the Episcopal Church, USA

563 I anoint you with this holy oil.
Receive Christ's forgiveness and healing.
The power of the Saviour who suffered for you
flow through your mind and body,
lifting you to peace and inward strength.

A New Zealand Prayer Book

See also:
Intercessions for the Sick, 423–32
Intercessions for the Unhappy, 433–36

part eight

DEATH AND DYING

OUR OWN DYING

Into your hands, O Lord, I commend my spirit.
PSALM 31:5

564   Lord Jesus, receive my spirit.
St Stephen in Acts 7:59

565   One day, Lord, I will be with you.
I will stand in your presence,
tired of wandering,
weary of the inconsequential.
Then I want to bathe in innocence
and experience the freedom of the children of God.
I will lay aside my failures
like old clothing.
Then I will know what holiness is:
to be chosen,
to be near you,
and to survive the fire of your purity.
Ulrich Schaffer

566   Gentle and mysterious God,
you gave me the gift of life,
and will be with me at my death;
I am afraid of dying suddenly, violently or painfully,
and I dread leaving behind those I love.
I give you my fears, as a gift of trust in you.
Help me to face the truth that we are all dying,
and let me remember
that if I can face up to my mortality with honesty,
I can live more fully now.
A.A.

567   In the evening of this life, I shall appear before you with empty hands, for I do not ask you, Lord, to count my works. All our goodness is stained and imperfect. I wish, then, to be clothed with your own goodness, and to receive you yourself eternally, out of your love. I want no other place or crown but you, my beloved.

Lord, even if my conscience were burdened with every sin it is possible to commit, I would still throw myself into your arms, my heart broken with contrition. And I know how tenderly you welcome any prodigal child of yours who comes back to you.

St Thérèse of Lisieux (1873–1897)

568   Jesus, remember me,
as you remembered the man who was dying next to you;
Jesus, remember me,
as you remember all who are lonely and frightened;
and, when I die, take me into your loving arms,
and show me that your kingdom has never been far away.

A.A.

569   FACING A TERMINAL ILLNESS
As a boat is tossed by the storm,
so my trust in you, God, is wavering.
I have prayed for healing,
cried to you for a miracle,
but am still left suffering.
My confidence in you is shaken.
Can it be that in my vulnerability
you will come to be with me?
Living Jesus, transform by brokenness
so death may be the gateway to new life.
Your faithful love is sufficient,
so I rest in you.

Ann Shepherdson

570   Lord,
      may I ever speak
      as though it were the last word that I can speak.
      May I ever act
      as though it were the last action that I can perform.
      May I ever suffer
      as though it were the last pain that I can offer.
      May I ever pray
      as though it were for me on earth
      the last chance to speak to you.
                                    Chiara Lubich

571   Swift to its close ebbs out life's little day;
      Earth's joys grow dim, its glories pass away;
          Change and decay in all around I see;
          O thou who changest not, abide with me.
                        Henry Francis Lyte (1793–1847)

572   O God, in your love you have kept me vigorously and joyfully
      at work in the days gone by, and now you send me, joyful and
      contented, into silence and inactivity. Grant me to find happi-
      ness in you in all my solitary and quiet hours. In your strength,
      O God, I bid farewell to all. The past you know; I leave it at your
      feet. Grant me grace to respond to your divine call; to leave all
      that is dear on earth, and to go on alone to you. Behold, I come
      quickly, says the Lord. Come, Lord Jesus.
                        Prayer by an Indian priest in old age.

573   IN EXTREME AGE
      Accept me,
      maimed, deformed and stunted,
      take me from myself unto thy own great uses.
      Lo, I outgrow this body;
      painfully my life ebbs yet
      and flows again within it.
      These hands and feet, these eyes and brain,
      these senses, faculties, have served their turn.

The dinted tools I render back to thee.
So little– one life–
so brief, slight a thing,
till now, at length,
feeling thee gathering around me close,
close, closer, closer yet,
at last the bounds dissolve which keep us twain,
and I and thou are one,
and I alone am not.

Edward Carpenter (1844–1929) (Part of a longer poem)

574   I beseech you, good Jesus, that as you have graciously given to me here on earth the sweet delight of partaking of your wisdom and knowledge, so you will grant that I may at some time come to you, the fountain of all wisdom, and may always appear before your face; for you live and reign, world without end.

The Venerable Bede (671–735)

575   O God, each day and every moment comes from you as gift;
    –enable us to live fully in the present, cherishing the moment that is now ours.
Your son, Jesus, told us not to be anxious about the needs of each day, for your loving care is with us;
    –calm our fears about the future and give us the gift of inner peace.
Peter was told he would be led by a path not of his own choosing;
    –help us to surrender to the way you are leading us and give us the gift of trust.

The Woman's Prayer Companion

576   Lord of eternity,
whose power is infinite,
whose days are without number
and whose mercy is beyond our fathoming:
keep our faces turned always towards you,
so that, each day, we remember
that life is your gift,
and the hour of death unknown.

And when finally we meet you face to face,
transform us in the fire of your love,
and receive us into your eternal kingdom.

A.A.

577   Bring us, O Lord, at our last awakening
into the house and gate of heaven,
to enter into that gate and dwell in that house
where shall be no darkness nor dazzling,
        but one equal light;
no noise nor silence, but one equal music;
no fears nor hopes, but one equal possession;
no ends nor beginnings, but one equal eternity
in the habitations of your glory and dominion,
world without end.

John Donne (1573–1631)

See also:
        Prayers in Old Age, 983–87
Also:
        No. 244: 'O Love that wilt not let me go'

WITH THE DYING

Lord, now let your servant depart in peace.
LUKE 2:29

ᐦᐦ

578   Go forth, O Christian soul,
      upon your journey from this world;
      go in the name of God the Father
      who created you;
      go in the mercy of Jesus, the Redeemer,
      who suffered for you;
      go in the power of the Holy Spirit
      who was poured out for you.
      In communion with the angels and saints,
      may you be given eternal peace
      and rest for ever in the presence of God.
         Commendation of a soul, Western Rite (adapted)

579   I commend you, dear brother, to almighty God,
      and entrust you to your Creator's love.
      May Christ who was crucified for you
      give you freedom and peace.
      May Christ who died for you
      forgive all your sins.
      And may you see your Redeemer face to face,
      and enjoy the vision of God for ever.
         The Roman Missal (adapted)

580   Lord, we pray for those
      whose life on earth is almost at an end,
      especially for this your beloved child . . . ,
      may she be filled with your peace,

and surrender herself totally into your hands,
knowing that you have loved her
with an everlasting love.

A.A.

581 God of the dark night,
     you were with Jesus praying in the garden,
     you were with Jesus all the way to the cross
     and through to the resurrection.
     Help us to recognize you now, as we watch with . . .
     and wait for what must happen;
     help us through any bitterness and despair,
     help us accept our distress,
     help us to remember that you care for us
     and that in your will is our peace.

A New Zealand Prayer Book

FOR THOSE WHO HAVE DIED

God will wipe away every tear from their eyes, and death shall be no more, neither shall there be mourning nor crying nor pain any more, for the former things have passed away.

REVELATION 21:4

౼ఴ ౬ఴ

582   Welcome, Lord, into your calm and peaceful kingdom those who, out of this present life, have departed to be with you; grant them rest and a place with the spirits of the just; and give them the life that knows not age, the reward that passes not away; through Jesus Christ our Lord.

St Ignatius Loyola (1491–1556)

583   We commend into your hands, O Lord,
those whom we have loved ...
You gave them breath,
and loved them through their lives.
Receive them now in your infinite tenderness,
and give them peace.

A.A.

584   Give rest, O Christ, to your servants, with your saints, where sorrow and pain are no more, neither sighing, but life everlasting.

You only are immortal, our Creator and Maker; and we are mortal, formed of the earth, and to earth we shall return. All of us go down to the dust; yet even at the grave we make our song: Alleluia, alleluia, alleluia.

Give rest, O Christ, to your servants, with your saints, where sorrow and pain are no more, neither sighing, but life everlasting.

Russian Orthodox Kontakion of the Departed

585 Father of all, we pray to you for those we love, but see no longer.
     Grant them your peace; let light perpetual shine upon them; and
     in your loving wisdom and almighty power, work in them the
     good purpose of your perfect will; through Jesus Christ our Lord.
     The Book of Common Prayer of the Episcopal Church, USA

586 Into the darkness and warmth of the earth
     We lay you down
     Into the sadness and smiles of our memories
     We lay you down
     Into the cycle of living and dying and rising again
     We lay you down
     May you rest in peace, in fulfilment, in loving
     May you run straight home into God's embrace.

     Into the freedom of wind and sunshine
     We let you go
     Into the dance of the stars and the planets
     We let you go
     Into the wind's breath and the hands of the star maker
     We let you go
     We love you, we miss you, we want you to be happy
     Go safely, go dancing, go running home.
                                          Ruth Burgess

See also:
     Bereavement, 587–99

BEREAVEMENT

*O my son Absalom, my son, my son, my son! Would to God
I had died for you, my son.*

KING DAVID, 2 SAMUEL 18:33

587   My God,
       why have you let this happen?
       why did you forsake us?
       Creator – why uncreate?
       Redeemer – why destroy wholeness?
       Source of love – why rip away
       the one I loved so utterly?
       Why? Why, O God?

       In this pit of darkness,
       hollowed out by grief and screaming,
       I reach out to the one I loved
       and cannot touch.

       Where are you, God?
       Where are you,
       except here
       in my wounds
       which are also yours?

       God,
       as I hurl at you
       my aching rage and bitterness,
       hold me,

       and stay here
       until this hacked-off stump of my life
       discovers greenness again.

                 A.A.

588   I pray you
      take this weeping heart
      and all the broken thing
      that lies within Your hand
      Distil the agony
      until
      from all its hurt
      a single drop of sweetness
      may remain
      changing the substance
      of this death in earth
      to make all new –
      a rising sap
      to bring the transformation
      of the spring

                              Margaret Torrie

589   O God who brought us to birth,
      and in whose arms we die:
      in our grief and shock
      contain and comfort us;
      embrace us with your love,
      give us hope in our confusion,
      and grace to let go into new life,
      through Jesus Christ.

                              Janet Morley

590   We remember, Lord, the slenderness of the thread which separates
      life from death, and the suddenness with which it can be broken.
      Help us also to remember that on both sides of that division we
      are surrounded by your love. Persuade our hearts that when our
      dear ones die neither we nor they are parted from you. In you
      may we find our peace and in you be united with them in the glo-
      rious body of Christ, who has burst the bonds of death and is
      alive for evermore, our Saviour and theirs for ever and ever.

                              Dick Williams

591   We give back to you, O God, those whom you gave to us. You
did not lose them when you gave them to us, and we do not lose
them by their return to you. Your Son has taught us that life is
eternal and love cannot die. So death is only a horizon, and a
horizon is only the limit of our sight. Open our eyes to see more
clearly, and draw us closer to you, so that we may know we are
nearer to our loved ones, who are with you. You have told us
that you are preparing a place for us: prepare us, that where you
are we may be always, O dear Lord of life and death.
William Penn (1644–1718)

592   God of life and love, we come to you in our need. Be with us as
we experience the abyss of death and grief. Be there in our sorrow and pain; be with us in our fear, that we may find light in
darkness, comfort in your Word; in the name of Jesus, who by
death has conquered death.
The Service Book of The United Reformed Church

593   O Lord our God, from whom neither life nor death can separate
those who trust in your love, and whose love holds in its embrace
your children in this world and the next; so unite us to yourself
that in fellowship with you we may always be united to our
loved ones whether here or there; give us courage, constancy and
hope; through him who died and was buried and rose again for
us, Jesus Christ our Lord.
William Temple (1881–1944) (adapted)

594   Father of mercies and God of all consolation,
you pursue us with untiring love
and dispel the shadow of death
with the bright dawn of life.

Comfort your family in their loss and sorrow.
Be our refuge and our strength, O Lord,
and lift us from the depths of grief
into the peace and light of your presence.

Your son, our Lord Jesus Christ,
by dying has destroyed our death,
and by rising, restored our life.
Enable us therefore to press on toward him,
so that, after our earthly course is run,
he may reunite us with those we love,
when every tear will be wiped away.

We ask this through Christ our Lord.

The Order of Christian Funerals

595 Lord Jesus,
you wept at the death of Lazarus whom you loved.
We pray for our friends in their loss;
give courage and companionship as they adjust to their new
 situation,
and be with them as they grieve.

A.A.

596 Most merciful God, whose wisdom is beyond our understanding: Deal graciously with ... in their grief. Surround them with your love, that they may not be overwhelmed by their loss, but have confidence in your goodness, and strength to meet the days to come; through Jesus Christ our Lord.

The Book of Common Prayer of the Episcopal Church, USA

597 AFTER A VIOLENT DEATH
Eternal God, the savagery that has taken ... has wounded us as well. We are reeling under the blow, unable to think clearly and aware of the cruel ways life can end. In all the anger and perplexity of this time, help us to cling to you as the calm at the centre of the storm; through Jesus Christ our Lord.

Patterns and Prayers for Christian Worship

BLESSING FOR A FUNERAL

598   May the love of God
and the peace of the Lord Jesus Christ
bless and console us,
and gently wipe every tear from our eyes:
in the name of the Father,
and of the Son,
and of the Holy Spirit.

The Order of Christian Funerals

599   LITURGY AMONG FAMILY OR FRIENDS AFTER SOME-ONE HAS DIED

The setting for this liturgy can be any kind of shared gathering, e.g., a family meal, a picnic, a meeting of friends. The physical setting should be relaxed. The liturgy is participative, and leadership should be shared. Take responsibility for each others' feelings. Laughter and tears are appropriate in this setting.

OPENING RESPONSES
Come among us, God.
You who cast the planets into space
and cradle the sparrow in her nest.
Come God and meet us here.

Come among us, God.
You who bless the poor and the broken
and stand by the sad and the strong.
Come God and meet us here.

Come among us, God.
You who dance in the silence
and shine in the darkness.
Come God and meet us here.

READINGS
Psalm 139:7–10
Revelation 21:3–4
John 14:1–3

SPACE TO REMEMBER

A space to remember those who have died–to retell stories, to sing songs, to share common memories, to bring into the present the things that we want to recall, to share silence. Use a ritual action that is meaningful to those present, e.g. light a candle, place a stone or flower on a grave, float petals in water, place centrally something that recalls those who have died.

All our laughter, all our sadness,
Safe now in God's hands.

All our anger, all our gladness,
Safe now in God's hands.

All our stories, all our memories,
Safe now in God's hands.

Those we remember, those we love,
Safe now in God's hands.

Sing a song together or listen to some favourite music; have a coffee.

CLOSING RESPONSES
We ask for the love of God
and the messages of angels.

The laughter of Jesus
and the stories of the saints.

The power of the spirit
and the strong hands of friends.

To bless us on life's journey
and lead us safely home, Amen.

Ruth Burgess

See also:
Prayers for Those Who Have Died, 582–86

A MISCARRIAGE, A STILL-BORN CHILD, OR THE DEATH OF A NEW-BORN BABY

I am convinced that neither death, nor height, nor life, nor depth, nor anything else in all creation, will be able to separate us from the love of God in Jesus Christ our Lord.

ROMANS 8:38–9

ᑫᕟᕟᕟᕟᕟᕟ

600   Lord, you love us from all eternity and from the moment when you shaped and formed us in our mother's womb. We give thanks for ..., for the wonder of his being, so closely knit with ours. Lord, you know ... through and through and you love him, for you created his innermost self. Help us now as we entrust ... to you knowing that he is safe in your care.

Be close to these parents in their grief. May ... bring them new understanding and a deepening love for one another. May we know ourselves to be enfolded in your love until with ... and all your children we are gathered into one through Jesus Christ our Lord.

The Service Book of The United Reformed Church

601   O God, in whose hands are both life and death,
be with us as we struggle to understand
the dying of this tiny child.
We entrust that life into your care.
Comfort ... on this day of grief,
and in the weeks that lie ahead;
in the love of Jesus Christ our Lord.

A.A.

602   O God, whose beloved Son took children into his arms and blessed them: Give us grace to entrust ... to your never-failing care and love, and bring us all to your heavenly kingdom; through Jesus Christ our Lord.

The Book of Common Prayer of the Episcopal Church, USA

603   Lord, we lose sight of you sometimes, though you are always with us in our need.
Lord have mercy.
Christ, you forgive us when we blame ourselves, others, or even you.
Christ have mercy.
Lord you help our little faith.
Lord have mercy.

We pray for ..., the departed child of ... and ...

[or, if this is an act of remembrance for a group of bereaved people:
    We pray for the departed children of all here present, and we give them into God's loving arms.]

    We pray for all those who wrongly blame themselves for the loss of a child, that they may forgive themselves and be healed.
    We pray for all aborted children, that they may know the eternal love of their creator.
    We pray for the parents of aborted children that they may know and accept the loving forgiveness of God.
    And we pray for all those who have hurt or angered us in our loss by not comprehending our grief.

Devised by a group of women from Newcastle upon Tyne

part nine

PRAYERS IN
QUIETNESS

My soul waits in silence for God; from him comes my salvation.

PSALM 62:1

604   In the depths of my being
      I become quiet and still;
  I wait for you, my God,
      source of my salvation.

Jim Cotter

605   To the place of your choosing
      I come
emptied of all but desire to know
even as I am known

without words
in the silence of love
my unlikeness yields to your like
your quickening touch penetrating
every fibre vibrating its
     'yes'
to the making
    one

Malling Abbey

606   Abba, Father,
           I am here,
            for you,
          for myself,
        for the world,
      for this moment,
        I am here ...

A.A.

607   Lord God
      I meet you in the mystery of life
      the sudden silences
      intensity of presence that makes me stop
      catch my breath
      lift up head high to catch the glory of your moment

      and then bow low
      lost in the misery of my meagre self

      so small
      so weak
      so far from you

      God
      you are of a grandeur and glory I long after and shrink from.
      Have mercy! In your glory let your pity touch me.

                              Nicola Slee

608   Prompt me, God,
      But not yet. When I speak
      Though it be you who speak
      Through me, something is lost.
      The meaning is in the waiting.

                              R. S. Thomas

609   Calm steadfast love
                          still deep
                      within your peace
                          and keep
                    our fluctuating hearts

                      our inability
                          anchor
                      in your stability
                    your changeless energy
                        of burning love
                          Malling Abbey

610   O Christ,
      Serene and tranquil light,
      Shine into the depth of my being,
      Come, and draw me to yourself.

      Free me from the chatter of my mind,
      And draw me through and beyond
      All words and symbols,
      Into the silence,

      That I may discover You,
      The unspoken Word,
      The pure Light,
      Piercing and transforming the darkness
      That veils the ground of my being.
                          based on words by F. C. Happold

611   In the silence
      I receive once more
      this gift of my life
      from you.
            Hold me in your stillness,
            simplify me,
            and take possession of me,
            my God.
                          A.A.

612   Jesu I love,
      Jesu I adore,
            hide me in thyself,
            wrap me in the stillness of thy peace,
                  that no voice may be heard,
                  no thought conceived,
                  but only of thee.
                          Gilbert Shaw (1886–1967)

613   To be there before you, Lord, that's all.
       To shut the eyes of my body,
       To shut the eyes of my soul,
       And be still and silent,
       To expose myself to you who are there,
       exposed to me.
       To be there before you, the Eternal Presence.
       I am willing to feel nothing, Lord,
          to see nothing,
          to hear nothing.
       Empty of all ideas,
          of all images.
       In the darkness.
       Here I am, simply,
       To meet you without obstacles,
       In the silence of faith,
       Before you, Lord.

Michel Quoist

614   I weave a silence on to my lips
       I weave a silence into my mind
       I weave a silence within my heart
       I close my ears to distractions
       I close my eyes to attractions
       I close my heart to temptations

       Calm me, O Lord, as you stilled the storm
       Still me, O Lord, keep me from harm
       Let all the tumult within me cease
       Enfold me Lord in your peace.

David Adam

615   Teach me the power and the strength of silence,
       that I may go into the world
       as still as a mouse
       in the depths of my heart.

after Mechtild of Madgeburg (1207–1294)

616 You, Lord, are in this place,
     Your presence fills it.
     Your presence is peace.

     You, Lord, are in my heart,
     Your presence fills it.
     Your presence is peace.

     You, Lord, are in my life,
     Your presence fills it.
     Your presence is peace.

                          David Adam

617 Drop thy still dews of quietness,
     Till all our strivings cease;
     Take from our souls the strain and stress,
     And let our ordered lives confess
     The beauty of thy peace.

              John Greenleaf Whittier (1807–1892)

618 O my divine Master, teach me to hold myself in silence before
     you, to adore you in the depths of my being, to wait upon you
     always and never to ask anything of you but the fulfilment of
     your will. Teach me to let you act in my soul, and form in it the
     simple prayer that says little but includes everything. Grant me
     this favour for the glory of your name.

                          Père Grou (1731–1803)

619 Like weary waves,
     thought flows upon thought,
     but the still depth beneath
     is all thine own.

                George Macdonald (1824–1905)

620 I sit in church, Lord,
     Very aware of your presence,
     Glad I can draw aside
     From the hustle and bustle of the street.

Yet even in here
I can hear
The regular beeping of the pedestrian crossing monitor,
The distinctive rattle of the diesel taxi engine,
The screech of brakes at the traffic lights.

Somehow I hear you telling me
Never to sever the relationship
Between the silence of mystery in worship
And the noise of everyday life,
For in the junction of the two
Is you
The Lord of Heaven and Earth.

Martin Wallace

621   Lord, in your presence
I do not concern myself with great matters,
or with things that are too hard for me.

But I become still and calm,
like a child on its mother's breast;
my God, you hold me close to you,
like a mother,
so that my soul is quieted within me.

based on Psalm 131:1–2

622   Lord, teach me the silence of love, the silence of wisdom, the silence of humility, the silence of faith, the silence that speaks without words.

O Saviour, teach me to silence my heart that I may listen to the gentle movement of the Holy Spirit within me, and sense the depths which are God, today and always.

Frankfurt, sixteenth century

623   I ask for that quietness of mind and spirit
which reflects the stillness in the heart of God,
as a calm sea reflects the shining stars.

Enable me, Lord, to hear the still, small voice of eternity
speaking through the sounds of time,
that I may dwell in your peace
and be one with your love,
through Jesus Christ our Lord.

based on words by Raymond Hockley in
'The Order for Evening Prayer', York Minster

624 God help us to live slowly:
To move simply:
To look softly:
To allow emptiness:
To let the heart create for us.
Amen

Michael Leunig

625 O Risen Christ,
you breathe your Holy Spirit upon us
like a gentle breeze
and tell us: 'Peace be yours.'
Opening ourselves to your peace,
letting it penetrate the harsh and rocky ground
of our hearts,
means preparing ourselves to be bearers of
reconciliation wherever you may place us.
But you know that at times we are at a loss.
So come and lead us to wait in silence,
to let a ray of hope shine through in our world.

Brother Roger of Taizé

626 Lift up our souls, O Lord,
above the weary round of harassing thoughts,
to your eternal presence.
Lift up our minds
to the pure, bright, serene
atmosphere of your presence,

that we may breathe freely,
and rest there in your love.
From there, surrounded by your peace,
may we return to do or to bear
whatever shall best please you,
O blessed Lord.

Edward Pusey (1800–1882)

627   Lord, make us people of stillness.
Help us to be empty before you,
that we may be filled with your peace;
teach us to be quiet in your presence,
that we may listen to your words;
and give us confidence to expose our whole being to you,
and meet you in the silence.

A.A.

part ten

MORNING PRAYERS

O Lord, in the morning you hear my voice; in the morning I make my offering and keep watch.

PSALM 5:3

ᘓᘐ

628   This day, Lord, may I dream your dreams;
this day, Lord, may I reflect your love;
this day, Lord, may I do your work;
this day, Lord, may I taste your peace.

A.A.

629   In this morning light
Some of the things I have to do
Seem to loom large before me,
And I carry the prospect of work
Like a heavy burden weighing me down
Even before I begin.
Yet by this evening many of today's
Difficulties will have passed.
Maybe they will prove to have been
Far less arduous than I imagined.
The thought of a problem
So often turns out to be worse
Than the problem itself.
Lord, lift my spirit,
Give me energy and a sense of humour
Throughout the hours of this day.
Lord of the morning, help me.

Frank Topping

630   Come into my soul, Lord,
as the dawn breaks into the sky;
let your sun rise in my heart
at the coming of the day.

Traditional

631   Thank you, God, for opportunity.
      Here is a new day, untouched by my hand, but held in yours.
      I need you, and you have chosen to need me.
      Together, we can bring to fruition
      some of life's endless possibilities.
      Thank you, God.

                              Michael Forster

632   Lord, I do not know what this day may bring, but each moment
      is in your hands and I offer it to you in advance. Nothing that
      will happen or be said today can separate me from you. Let me
      rest assured in that peace.

                              Subir Biswas (died c. 1980)

633   Each morning, Lord, I hold out my life to you,
      an empty vessel for you to fill.
      I give back to you this gift of a new day.
      In your mercy
      redeem today's mistakes
      and rescue its good intentions,
      so that what I am
      may reflect your life in me.

                              A.A.

634   Let this day, O Lord, add some knowledge or good deed to
      yesterday.

                              Lancelot Andrewes (1555–1626)

635   All I speak, be blessed to me, O God;
      All I hear, be blessed to me, O God;
      All I see, be blessed to me, O God;
      All I sense, be blessed to me, O God;
      All I taste, be blessed to me, O God;
      Each step I take, be blessed to me, O God.

      And may I serve you all my life,
      For the love of the Father who created me,
      The Son who redeemed me,
      And the Holy Spirit who strengthens and guides me.

                              W. Mary Calvert

636   O secret Christ,
      Lord of the rose of dawn,
      hide me
      within thy silent peace,
      that throughout the turmoil of the day,
      I may abide within the quiet of the daybreak.

      Source unknown (used in the chapel at Launde Abbey)

637   Lord, grant me strength to do what has to be done today,
      and wisdom calmly to leave on one side what cannot be done.
      Fill me with prayer,
      draw together my scattered preoccupations,
      and help me to respond to every moment with my full attention;
      for your love's sake.

                           A.A.

638   I go out
      Into the grace of this day's light;
      In the power of our great God;
      With the blessing of Jesus;
      And the radiance of the Holy Spirit.

          May the joy and the peace
          and the strength of the Creator
          be with us always.

                           W. Mary Calvert

639   Lord, I my vows to thee renew,
      Scatter my sins as morning dew;
      Guard my first springs of thought and will,
      And with thyself my spirit fill.

      Direct, control, suggest this day,
      All I design or do or say;
      That all my powers, with all their might,
      In thy sole glory may unite.

                  Thomas Ken (1637–1711) (adapted)

640 I arise today
     through God's mighty strength,
     his power to uphold me,
     his wisdom to guide me,
     and his hand to guard me.
     I arise today,
     through Christ's mighty strength,
     through his death and resurrection,
     through the Spirit's empowering,
     through the presence of angels
     and the love of the saints,
     through the threefold Trinity
     to protect me from evil.
                    St. Patrick (c.389–c.461)

641 My soul hath desired thee all night, O eternal wisdom! and in
     the early morning I turn to thee from the depths of my heart.
     May the holy presence remove all dangers from my soul and
     body. May thy many graces fill my heart, and inflame it with thy
     divine love. O most sweet Jesus! turn thy face towards me, for
     this morning with all the powers of my soul I fly to thee.
                    Henry Suso (c.1295–1366)

642 God protect me this day,
     May the God of life surround me;
     Christ, protect me this day,
     May the love of Christ surround me;
     Spirit, protect me this day,
     May the Spirit of power surround me;
     Circle me, with me, before me;
     Life, love, power;
     Life, love, power.
                    W. Mary Calvert

643 Lord, help me today to realize that you will be speaking to me
     through the events of the day, through people, through things,
     and through all creation.

Give me ears, eyes and heart to perceive you, however veiled
your presence may be.
Give me insight to see through the exterior of things to the
interior truth.
Give me your Spirit of discernment.
O Lord, you know how busy I must be this day.
If I forget you, do not forget me.

Jacob Astley (1579–1652)

This was written before the battle of Edgehill in 1642.

644   Let me now go forth, O Lord my God, to the work of another
      day, still surrounded by thy wonderful lovingkindnesses, still
      pledged to thy loyal service, still standing in thy strength and not
      my own.

John Baillie (1886–1960)

645   Eternal God,
      grant to us this day and every day
      such readiness and delight in following Christ,
      that whether our lives are short or long
      we shall have lived abundantly.

A New Zealand Prayer Book

646   The night has passed and the day lies open before us;
      as we rejoice in the gift of this new day,
      so may the light of your presence, O God,
      set our hearts on fire with love for you;
      now and for ever. Amen.

Celebrating Common Prayer

647   Eternal God,
      early in the morning, before we begin our work,
      we praise your glory.
      Renew our bodies as fresh as the morning flowers.
      Open our inner eyes, as the sun casts new light upon the darkness
      which prevailed over the night.
      Deliver us from captivity.

Give us wings of freedom like the birds in the sky,
to begin a new journey.
Restore justice and freedom, as a mighty stream
running continuously as day follows day.
We thank you for the gift of this morning,
and a new day to work with you.

Masao Takenaka

648   O God who loves us,
we offer this day into your keeping:
our plans into your providence,
our concerns into your love,
our words into your silence,
our activity into your stillness.

Look upon us in your steadfast love
and grant us your saving health,
so that we may be instruments
of your healing for others,
and all may grow into wholeness
in your praise.

Julie M. Hulme

649   Lord, set your blessing on us
As we begin this day together.
Confirm in us the truth by which we rightly live;
Confront us with the truth from which we wrongly turn,
As we offer this day and ourselves for you and to you.

John L. Bell

650   Holy and ever-living God,
by your power we are created
and by your love we are redeemed;
guide and strengthen us by your Spirit,
that we may give ourselves to your service
and live this day in love to one another and to you;
through Jesus Christ our Saviour.

A New Zealand Prayer Book

651 Father,
    may everything we do
    begin with your inspiration
    and continue with your saving help.
    Let our work always find its origin in you
    and through you reach completion.
    We ask this through our Lord Jesus Christ.
                    The Liturgy of the Hours

652   O God of love,
            true light and radiance of our world,
        shine into our hearts like the rising sun,
    and banish the darkness of sin and the mists of error.
        May we, this day and all our life,
            walk without stumbling
        along the way which you have set before us;
        through your Son Jesus Christ our Lord.
                    Erasmus (1466–1536)

653 O Lord, the day is yours, and the night is yours;
    you have prepared the light and the sun;
    they continue this day according to your ordinance,
    for all things serve you.
    Blessed are you, O Lord,
    for you turn the shadow of death into the morning,
    and renew the face of the earth.
                    Lancelot Andrewes (1555–1626)

654 Blessèd are you, Sovereign God of all,
    to you be glory and praise for ever!
    In your tender compassion,
    the dawn from on high is breaking upon us
    to dispel the lingering shadows of night.
    As we look for your coming among us this day,
    open our eyes to behold your presence
    and strengthen our hands to do your will,

that the world may rejoice and give you praise,
Father, Son and Holy Spirit:
Blessèd be God for ever.

Celebrating Common Prayer

655   SUNDAY MORNING
This is the day that the Lord has made:
    let us rejoice and be glad in it!
This is the day of the Lord;
    our Saviour, Christ, is risen!
He has conquered sin and death,
the power of love has overcome,
and God has given us the victory!
        Alleluia!
        based on Psalm 118:24 and 1 Corinthians 15:55–7

part eleven

EVENING AND NIGHT
PRAYERS

Behold now, praise the Lord, you who by night stand in the house of the Lord.

PSALM 134:1

ⱸⱺ ꙅⱺ

656   I will lie down in peace and take my rest;
for you alone, Lord, make me dwell in safety.
Into your hands I commend my spirit,
for you have redeemed me, O Lord, God of truth.

Psalm 4:8, 31:5

657 You are the healer of my soul,
Shield me from shame and sin.
Keep me at noon,
Keep me at nightfall.
Keep me at nightfall.

You are my hope and shield,
In my tiredness,
In my stumbling.
Be you my rest tonight.
Be you my rest tonight.

W. Mary Calvert

658 While I sleep, O Lord,
let my heart not cease to worship you;
fill my sleep with your presence,
while creation itself keeps watch,
singing psalms with the angels,
and taking up my soul into its paean of praise.

St Gregory of Nazianzus (c.330–389)

659 INSOMNIA
Jesus,
you sometimes spent whole nights alone in prayer:
be with me tonight if I cannot sleep.

Calm me in the dark silence,
and fill me with the peace of your presence
in the depth of the night-time quietness.

A.A.

660   God with me lying down,
God with me rising up,
God with me in each ray of light,
Nor I a ray of joy without Him,
Nor one ray without Him.

Christ with me sleeping,
Christ with me waking,
Christ with me watching,
Every day and night,
Each day and night.

God with me protecting,
The Lord with me directing,
The Spirit with me strengthening,
For ever and for evermore,
Ever and evermore, Amen.
Chiefs of chiefs, Amen.

Carmina Gadelica, *Vol. 1, p. 5*

661   Glory to thee, my God, this night
For all the blessings of the light;
Keep me, O keep me, King of kings,
Beneath thine own almighty wings.

Forgive me, Lord, for thy dear Son,
The ill that I this day have done,
That with the world, myself, and thee,
I, ere I sleep, at peace may be.

Thomas Ken (1637–1711)

662   The Lord has granted his loving-kindness in the daytime;
          and now in the night season will I sing of him.
                Let my prayer be set forth
                in your sight, O Lord, as incense;
                and let the lifting up of my hands
                    be an evening sacrifice,
                    now and always.
                Lancelot Andrewes (1555–1626)
                    Psalm 141:2

663   The day ends, darkness descends,
        Now Lord let troubles cease,
        Let your servant depart in peace.
        Labours are over, my task here done,
        Now Lord your victory be won.

        Lord when everything trembles
        Give me a firm foundation;
        Faith founded on facts
        Prayers founded on your Presence
        Life founded on your love
        Peace founded on your power.
                        David Adam

664   May the song of your Spirit soothe us,
                    your gentle arms cradle us,
                    your tenderness ease our tiredness
              and your welcome enfold our weariness,
                        this night
                    and all our nights.
                        A.A.

665   Light of the world,
        Enter into the depths
            of our lives.
        Come into the dark
            and hidden places.

> Walk in the storehouse
>   of our memories.
> Hear the hidden secrets
>   of the past.
> Plumb the very depth
>   of our being.
> Be present through
>   the silent hours,
> And bring us safely
>   to your glorious light.
>   *David Adam*

666   O God, our Father, we thank You for this day.

We thank You for those who have given us guidance, counsel, advice and good example.

We thank You for those in whose company the sun shone even in the rain, and who brought a smile to our faces even when things were grim.

We thank You for those in whose company the frightening things were not so alarming, and the hard things not so difficult.

We thank You for those whose presence saved us from falling to temptation,and enabled us to do the right.

We thank You for those whom it is joy to be with, and in whose company the hours pass all too quickly.

We thank You for happy times to be to us for ever happy memories.

We thank You for times of failure to keep us humble, and to make us remember how much we need You.

Most of all we thank You for Jesus Christ, who in the daytime is our friend and our companion and who in the night is our pillow and our peace.

Hear this our evening thanksgiving for Your love's sake.
                    William Barclay (1907–1978)

667   As our evening prayer rises before you, O God,
      so may your mercy come down upon us
            to cleanse our hearts
      and set us free to sing your praise,
      now and for ever.

                    Celebrating Common Prayer

668   Watch, dear Lord, with those who wake or weep tonight, and
      let your angels protect those who sleep. Tend the sick. Refresh
      the weary. Sustain the dying. Calm the suffering. Pity the dis-
      tressed. We ask this for your love's sake.

                    St Augustine of Hippo (354–430)

669   Lord, you have brought us through this day
      to a time of reflection and rest.
      Calm us,
      and give us your peace to refresh us.
      Keep us close to you
      that we may be closer to one another
      because of your perfect love.
      In Christ's name we pray.

                    Daily Prayer: The Worship of God *(adapted)*

670   Be present, merciful God, and protect us through the silent hours
      of this night, so that we who are wearied by the changes and
      chances of this fleeting world, may rest upon your eternal
      changelessness; through Jesus Christ our Lord.

                    Leonine Sacramentary

671   Lighten our darkness,
      Lord, we pray;
      and in your mercy defend us
      from all perils and dangers of this night;
      for the love of your only Son,
      our Saviour Jesus Christ.

                    The Alternative Service Book 1980

672   O God our Creator, by whose mercy and might the world turns safely into darkness and returns again to light: we give into your hands our unfinished tasks, our unsolved problems and our unfulfilled hopes, knowing that only those things which you bless will prosper. To your great love and protection we commit each other, and all for whom we have prayed, knowing that you alone are our sure defender; through Jesus Christ our Lord.

The Book of Common Worship, Church of South India (adapted)

673   Lord God, send peaceful sleep
to refresh our tired bodies.
May your help always renew us
and keep us strong in your service.
We ask this through Christ our Lord.

The Liturgy of the Hours

674   O Lord, support us all the day long of this troublous life, until the shadows lengthen, and the evening comes, and the busy world is hushed, and the fever of life is over, and our work is done.

    Then, in your mercy, give us safe lodging, a holy rest, and peace at the last, through Jesus Christ our Lord.

John Henry Newman (1801–1890)

675   Visit, Lord, we pray, this place,
and drive far from it all the snares of the enemy.
Let your holy angels dwell here to keep us in peace,
and may your blessing be upon us evermore;
through Jesus Christ our Lord.

The Office of Compline

676   Look down, O Lord, from your heavenly throne;
lighten the darkness of the night
with your celestial brightness;
and from the children of light
banish the deeds of darkness;
through Jesus Christ our Lord.

The Office of Compline

677   Now as the sun sets in the west,
        the lamps glow with their soft light and evening comes;
        thus, light from light, God's blessed Son comes forth from
            the immortal Father's heart.
        We therefore sing our joyful songs to Father, Son and Holy
            Spirit,
        to whom in every age be universal praise.
        Lord Jesus, Son of God, from you all life and joy come forth
            this night;
        the world and the gentle light of evening lamps reflect your
            glory.
        Praise to you!
   Orthodox hymn (third century) at the lighting of candles at Vespers

678   God, that madest earth and heaven,
            Darkness and light;
        Who the day for toil hast given,
            For rest the night;
        May thine angel-guards defend us,
        Slumber sweet thy mercy send us,
        Holy dreams and hopes attend us,
            This livelong night.
                    Reginald Heber (1783–1826)

679   THE EVENING BEFORE A COMMUNION SERVICE
        As the night-watch looks for the morning,
            so do our eyes wait for you, O Christ.
        Come with the dawning of the day,
            and make yourself known in the breaking of bread,
            for you are the risen Lord for ever and ever.
                        Traditional

part twelve

GRACE AT MEALS

The eyes of all look to you, O Lord, and you give them their food in due season.

PSALM 145:15

⌒⊙ ⊙⌒

680 Risen Lord,
we thank you for love, laughter, bread, wine and dreams;
fill us with green-growing hope,
and make us a people whose name is love.

Adapted from words found by a Welsh craftsman

681 Sun, earth and air
Have wrought by God's care,
That the plants live and bear.

Praise God for this food
In truth would we live,
Bearing beauty and good.

Diana Carey and Judy Large

682   God of all bounty and goodness,
as we break bread together
strengthen the bonds between us;
help us to grow closer to you
and give us thankful hearts.

A.A.

683 Bless to us, God, the fruits of your earth
Bread to keep us healthy, wine to bring us joy.
Bless to us, God, our loving and our laughter
Today and every day that we sit and eat together.

Ruth Burgess

684   Blessèd are you, Lord God of all creation.
You hold in your care all that you have made.
Bless us as we share this meal,
and touch our hearts to serve all whom we meet;
through Christ our Lord.

Traditional, based on the Hebrew blessing, 'Berakah Attah Adonai'

685   Blessèd are you, Lord God of all creation.
Generously you give us the fruits of the earth
to delight and nourish us.
Bless this meal
and strengthen us in your service;
through Christ our Lord.

Traditional

686   Bless these thy gifts, most gracious God,
From whom all goodness springs;
Make clean our hearts and feed our souls
With good and joyful things.

Source unknown

687   Bless, O Lord, this food to our use
and ourselves to your service,
and make us mindful of the needs of others;
for your love's sake.

Traditional

part thirteen

BLESSINGS

Now may the Lord of peace himself give you peace, at all times and in all ways; the Lord be with you all.

Some blessings have the word 'me', some have 'us', and some have 'you'. These words are interchangeable.

688   Be thou a bright flame before me,
Be thou a guiding star above me,
Be thou a smooth path below me,
Be thou a kindly shepherd behind me,
Today – tonight – and for ever.

                              St Columba (c. 521–597)

689   On our heads and our houses
the blessing of God;
on our coming and going,
the peace of God;
in our life and believing,
the love of God;
at our end and new beginning,
the arms of God to welcome us
and bring us home.

                              John L. Bell

690   Blessing and laughter and loving be yours.
The love of a Great God
    who names you
    and holds you while the earth turns and the flowers grow,
    this day
    this night
    this moment
    and forever.

                              Ruth Burgess

691   The blessing of God, the eternal goodwill of God, the shalom of God, the wildness and the warmth of God, be among us and between us, now and always.

                              Jim Cotter

692   The peace of God
      which passes all understanding,
      keep our hearts and minds
      in the knowledge and love of Jesus Christ our Lord;
      and the blessing of God Almighty,
      the Father, the Son and the Holy Spirit,
      be upon us and remain with us always.
                              based on Philippians 4:7

693   Bless to us, O God, the road that is before us,
      Bless to us, O God, the friends who are around us,
      Bless to us, O God, your love which is within us.
      Bless to us, O God, the light that leads us home.
                                     Ruth Burgess

694   Peace of the running waves to you,
      Deep peace of the flowing air to you,
      Deep peace of the quiet earth to you,
      Deep peace of the shining stars to you,
      Deep peace of the shades of night to you,
      Moon and stars always giving light to you,
      Deep peace of Christ, the Son of Peace, to you.
                          Traditional Gaelic blessing

695   The love of the Lord Jesus
      draw you to himself,
      the power of the Lord Jesus
      strengthen you in his service,
      the joy of the Lord Jesus fill your hearts;
      and the blessing of God almighty,
      the Father, the Son, and the Holy Spirit,
      be among you and remain with you always.
                        The Alternative Service Book *1980*
          Based on an original prayer by William Temple (1881–1944)

696   May the road rise up to meet you,
               may the wind be always at your back,
               may the sun shine upon your face,

the rains fall soft upon your fields
and, until we meet again,
may God hold you in the palm of His hand.
Ancient Irish Blessing

697 May Christ dwell in your hearts through faith;
and may you be rooted and grounded in love,
and comprehend, with the saints,
what is the breadth and length and height and depth
of the love of Christ,
so that you may be filled
with all the fullness of God.
based on Ephesians 3:17–19

698 May the warmth of Christ heal you,
the eyes of Christ gaze on you,
and the peace of Christ shine through you,
today and evermore.
A.A.

699 The Lord bless you and keep you,
The Lord make his face to shine upon you and be gracious
unto you;
The Lord lift up the light of his countenance upon you and
give you peace,
now and always.
Numbers 6:24–6

700 May the everlasting Father Himself take you
In His own generous clasp,
In his own generous arm.
May the everlasting Father shield you
East and west wherever you go.
Carmina Gadelica, *Vol. 3, pp. 201–2*

701 May the blessing of the Lord rest and remain upon all his people,
of every race and language;
may the Lord meet in mercy all who seek him;

may the Lord comfort with tenderness all who suffer and mourn;
and may the Lord hasten his coming,
and give us the blessing of peace.

Source unknown

702   The blessing of the God of Sarah and of Abraham,
the blessing of the Son born of Mary,
the blessing of the Holy Spirit
who broods over us as a mother over her children,
be with us all.

Worship in an Indian Context

703   BLESSING FOR A PERSON GOING ON A JOURNEY
Gracious Father,
maker of all the world,
bless this our friend as *she* prepares for *her* journey.

Be with *her* on every road,
on every hill, meadow and stream,
under cloud, under stars,
through storm and in sunshine.

Guard *her*, O Father,
protect *her*, O Christ,
guide *her*, O Holy Spirit,
now, and in weariness,
now, and in happiness,
now, and in danger,
now, and in journey's ending.

Enfold *her* in your love,
and surround *her* with your care,
that *she* may sing your song
every step of the way.

A.A.

Inspired by ancient Celtic 'journey prayers'

See also:
Blessing for Christmas, 736
Blessing for Good Friday, 811
Blessings for Easter, 828–31
Blessings for Pentecost, 858–59

∽part fourteen∾

THE CHRISTIAN YEAR

THE ANNUNCIATION –
MARY'S 'YES'

Behold the servant of the Lord. Let it be it unto me according to your word.

LUKE 1:38

৵৹ ৹৲

704 Loving God,
    calling your friends in new and unexpected ways,
    choosing Mary from the powerless and unnoticed in the world,
    yet greatly loved and cherished in your sight,
    that she should be the mother of our Saviour,
    so fill us with your grace
    that we too may accept the promptings of your Spirit,
    and welcome your angel with glad and open arms,
    ready to be pierced with pain and filled with joy,
    rejoicing in the cost of your salvation,
    in and through the same Jesus our Messiah.

                    Jim Cotter

705 Father of love,
    through your most Holy Spirit,
    Mary the Jewish girl conceived your Son;
    may his beauty, his humanity,
    his all-transforming grace be born in us,
    and may we never despise the strange and stirring gentleness
    of your almighty power.

                    A New Zealand Prayer Book

706 God we thank you
    that you made yourself known
    to someone without power, wealth or status;

and we praise you
for the courage of Mary,
this young woman from Galilee,
whose Yes to the shame and shock
of bearing your Son
let loose the unstoppable power of love
which changed the world.

A.A.

707   We praise you, our Father, for the marvellous news announced
      to Mary;
      for the grace of life that prepared her for her call;
      for her obedience to your will and her humility in accepting it;
      for her loving care and patience in fulfilling it.
      Give us such grace and obedience that we may be accounted
worthy to bear the good news to our world; through Jesus Christ
our Lord.

Basil Naylor

ADVENT

708   Your coming is like freedom to the prisoner,
      like the return of those long captive.
      You are the movements of the dance I had forgotten,
      you are the face of satisfied desire.

      My soul is stirred for you, my beloved,
      I cannot contain my heart;
      for you have seen my longing,
      and your eyes are dark with love.
      Your love is stronger than death,
      your passion more relentless than the grave.
      You will but speak the word,
      and I shall be healed;
      though your touch is the touch of a stranger,
      yet is your voice my home.

                          Janet Morley (abridged)

709   A MORNING IN ADVENT
      As the new day dawns,
      we rejoice in the first glimmers of light
      which remind us of your coming, O Christ.
      We give thanks
      that your light has overcome all our darkness;
      may we share in the mystery of your presence in the world,
      and be always ready to live each day for you.

                          A.A.

710   Christ our Advent hope,
      bare brown trees,
      etched dark across a winter sky,
      leaves fallen, rustling,
      ground hard and cold,
      remind us to prepare for your coming;

remind us to prepare for the time
when the soles of your feet will touch the ground,
when you will become one of us
to be at one with us.

Kate McIlhagga

711   God of all hope and joy,
open our hearts in welcome,
that your Son Jesus Christ at his coming
may find in us a dwelling prepared for himself;
who lives and reigns with you and the Holy Spirit,
one God now and for ever.

A New Zealand Prayer Book

712   Father in heaven,
the day draws near when the glory of your Son
will make radiant the night of the waiting world.

May the lure of greed not impede us from the joy
which moves the hearts of those who seek him.
May the darkness not blind us
to the vision of wisdom
which fills the minds of those who find him.

The Roman Missal

713   Come, Lord Jesus,
Come as King.

Rule in our hearts,
Come as love.

Rule in our minds,
Come as peace.

Rule in our actions,
Come as power.

Rule in our days,
Come as joy.

Rule in our darkness,
Come as light.

Rule in our bodies,
Come as health.

Rule in our labours,
Come as hope.

Thy Kingdom come
Among us.

David Adam

714   Father in heaven,
our hearts desire the warmth of your love
and our minds are searching for the light of your Word.

Increase our longing for Christ our Saviour
and give us the strength to grow in love,
that the dawn of his coming
may find us rejoicing in his presence
and welcoming the light of his truth.

The Roman Missal

715   Stir up your power, Lord, and with great might come among us;
and, because we are sorely hindered by our sins, let your boun-
tiful grace and mercy speedily help and deliver us; through Jesus
Christ our Lord.

Gelasian Sacramentary (eighth century)

716   Our heavenly Father, as once again we prepare for Christmas, help
us to find time in our busy lives for quiet and thought and prayer;
that we may reflect upon the wonder of your love and allow the
story of the Saviour's birth to penetrate our hearts and minds. So
may our joy be deeper, our worship more real, and our lives wor-
thier of all that you have done for us through the coming of your
Son, Jesus Christ our Lord.

Frank Colquhoun

THE SEVEN GREAT O'S OF ADVENT

717　*The following seven prayers originate in the Advent antiphons, an ancient part of the Church's liturgy, sung at Evensong from December 17 to 23 as part of the preparation for Christmas. They can be used separately or as a sequence.*

O WISDOM, mysterious Word of God,
　　　coming forth from the Father
　　　and filling all creation with your life-giving power:
Come and show us the way of truth.

O LORD OF ISRAEL, ruler of your ancient people,
　　　you appeared to Moses in the burning bush
　　　and gave the law on Mount Sinai:
Come, and reach out your hand to save us.

O FLOWER OF JESSE'S LINE, Son of David,
　　　you have been lifted up as a sign of peace,
　　　drawing all kings and peoples to stand silent in your presence:
Come quickly and help us, we beseech you.

O KEY OF DAVID, and sceptre of the house of Israel,
　　　you have opened to us the way of hope,
　　　and shut the door on the powers of evil:
Come and free us from our prisons of darkness.

O MORNING STAR, radiance of the Father's love,
　　　you are the brightness that disperses the shadows of our
　　　　　hearts:
Come, cleanse and renew us in your glory.

O KING OF THE NATIONS, you alone bring joy when you
reign in our hearts,
　　　and you are the cornerstone of our lives:
Come and strengthen us, who were formed by you.

O EMMANUEL, God with us,
　　　hope of the world, and Saviour of all,
　　　come and live in us, now and for ever.
　　　　　　　　Western Rite (adapted by A.A.)

718   *Taking their pattern and inspiration from the traditional Advent
       antiphons, these prayers remind us of our experience of what
       God is like and call upon God to come to our aid.*

O God, you speak through your prophets,
        your words hold us and challenge us
            and keep us right:
Come and tell us the truths that we need to know
        and write them into our hearts and lives.

O Lover of the little ones,
        their Guardian and Defender:
Come with your angels and cradle your children
        and guide their stumbling feet
        along the homeward roads.

O Maker of Laughter,
        who plays with Leviathan in the deep waters:
Come, stretch out your hands
        to cuddle and tickle your children
        through the moments of their days.

O Pilgrim God, abandoning that which
        is no longer needed:
Come with us on our journey,
    show us how to travel lightly
    keeping only what we need to grow.

O God, you love me:
        Come, come quickly,
            I need your help.

O Wind of God, you blow through
        the holes in our defences,
        and lay bare our fear:
Come, breathe on us gently,
        as at the beginning,
        and give us life.

                                        Ruth Burgess

Christmas, Epiphany and the Presentation of Jesus

Christmas Eve

719   When all things in silence lay,
        and the night was in the midst of her course,
your Word leaped down from your royal throne, O God.
            So we rejoice and give you praise,
              that your Word may live in us,
         and that we may glorify you for ever.
based on Wisdom of Solomon 18:14, Orthodox liturgy

720   INTERCESSION FOR CHRISTMAS EVE
Father, in this holy night your Son our Saviour was born as a human child. Help the Church also to be the Body of Christ.
Lord in your mercy
hear our prayer.

In this holy night Christians the world over are celebrating his birth. Open our hearts that he may be born in us today.
Lord in your mercy
hear our prayer.

In this holy night there was no room for your Son in the inn. Protect with your love those who have no home and all who live in poverty.
Lord in your mercy
hear our prayer.

In this holy night Mary in the pain of labour brought your Son to birth. Hold in your hand . . . and all who are in any kind of pain or distress today.
Lord in your mercy
hear our prayer.

In this holy night your Christ came as a light shining in the darkness. Bring comfort to ... and all who suffer in the sadness of our world.
Lord in your mercy
hear our prayer.

In this holy night shepherds in the fields heard good tidings of joy. Give us grace to preach the gospel of Christ's redemption.
Lord in your mercy
hear our prayer.

In this holy night the angels sang 'Peace to God's people on earth'. Strengthen those who work for your peace and justice in ... and in all the world.
Lord in your mercy
hear our prayer.

In this holy night strangers saw Mary and Joseph, and the baby lying in the manger.
Bless our homes and all whom we love.
Lord in your mercy
hear our prayer.

In this holy night heaven is come down to earth, and earth is raised to heaven. Keep in safety ... and all those who have gone through death in the hope of heaven.
Lord in your mercy
hear our prayer.

In this holy night angels and shepherds worshipped at the manger throne. Receive the worship we offer in fellowship with blessed Mary and all the saints.
Merciful Father,
accept these prayers
for the sake of your Son
our Saviour Jesus Christ.

Patterns for Worship

721 O God, who made this most hallowed night resplendent with the glory of the true Light; grant that we who have known the mysteries of that Light on earth may enter into the fullness of his joys in heaven.

Ancient Western Rite, Christmas Midnight

CHRISTMAS MORNING

722   INTERCESSION FOR CHRISTMAS MORNING
We gather this morning
to celebrate the feast of God's incarnation,
in which the creative power
to which the universe owes its being
is discovered in the powerless,
and the means of God's action
is found, not in the wielders of power,
but in a village girl
and a working man,
in foreigners
and in the unrespectable.

We ask for the insight
to find the work of God
not where it fits
but where it is;
not in comfort
but in justice;
not in cosy security
but in our risks.
Lord in your mercy
hear our prayer.

Christ, you came to us
from the womb of Mary.
There was pain at your bearing,
confusion in your rearing
and astonishment at the man you came to be:
we bring to mind now
all who are in pain
of the body, mind or soul;
(we particularly bring to God . . . .).
We pray too
for all who are facing change,
and all who struggle
to understand where they are being led.
We remember all involved in conflict,
and we pray for the peace of the world (especially in . . .).

Lord in your mercy
hear our prayer.

God, in this day we find you at the edge of things:
an unremarkable town
in an unremarkable province
of an immense empire:
since then your Church has gained much,
but at your birth, you lacked much.
Teach us this day's simplicity.
Lord in your mercy
hear our prayer.

God, in this day we find you at the heart of things:
in birth
in journey
in the work of people
and amid the lives of animals.
Teach us this day's centre.
Lord in your mercy
hear our prayer.

At this season of beginnings
we remember also with thanksgiving
those we knew and loved who have died.
Help us, Lord, to live close to you
and to find a place in your presence in heaven.
Merciful Father,
accept these prayers
for the sake of your Son
our Saviour, Jesus Christ.

Peter Armstrong

723   Jesus, Son of God,
       now that we have heard the angels sing,
       may we not lose our sense of the joy of heaven;
       now that we have been with the shepherds to Bethlehem,
       make us witnesses
       of the wonder of the love we have seen.
       Fill us with the quiet joy of Mary,
       so that we, too,

may keep all these things
and ponder them in our hearts.
                              A.A.

CHRISTMASTIDE

724 O consuming Fire, Spirit of Love,
     descend within me
     and reproduce in me, as it were,
     an incarnation of the Word,
     that I may be to Him
     another humanity
     wherein He renews His mystery.
                    Elizabeth of the Trinity (d.1184)

725 Moonless darkness stands between
     Past, O Past, no more be seen!
     But the Bethlehem star may lead me
     To the sight of him who freed me
     From the self that I have been.
     Make me pure, Lord: Thou art holy;
     Make me meek, Lord: Thou wert lowly;
     Now beginning, and alway:
     Now begin, on Christmas Day.
                    Gerard Manley Hopkins (1844–89)

726 Mary could not have known
     what she was saying 'Yes' to:
     we pray for her trust.

     Joseph could not have known
     where his trust was leading him:
     we pray for his patience.

     The travellers could not have known
     the end of their journey:
     we pray for their boldness and adventure.

     The shepherds could not have known
     the meaning of their vision:
     we pray for their open minds.

The Christ-child could not have known
what was happening to him:
we join with him
in his fragile humanity
in bringing before
the unknown of divinity
our prayer, praise and wonder this Christmas Day.
Peter Armstrong

727 God, who became as we are,
     may we become as you are.
                    after William Blake (1757–1827)

728 For the huge risk you took
     in becoming human
     in order to bring out the best in us,
     we praise you.

     For the huge risk you took
     in entrusting yourself to us
     and sharing our vulnerability,
     we praise you.

     For the incalculable risk you took
     in emptying yourself
     and allowing yourself to be abused and killed
     to free us from the power of evil,
     we praise you.

     God in Jesus,
     God with us,
     Emmanuel.
          A.A. (Inspired by words of the late Sister Jane SLG)

729 What shall we offer you, O Christ,
     Who for our sakes appeared on earth as man?
     Every creature made by you offers you thanks.
     The angels offer you a hymn;
     The heavens, a star;
     The Magi, gifts;
     The shepherds, their wonder;

The earth, a cave;
And from our human race we offered you a Virgin Mother.
God before all ages, have mercy upon us.
from The Festal Menaion of the Russian Orthodox Church

730   O God of Peace, you fill our hearts with hope at every
Christmastide, for we remember again that this is the world
that you have loved. May that hope, peace and joy fill our
hearts this night.

Wesley Ariarajah

731   O holy Child of Bethlehem,
    Descend to us, we pray;
Cast out our sin, and enter in:
    Be born in us today.
We hear the Christmas angels
    The great glad tidings tell:
O come to us, abide with us,
      Our Lord Emmanuel.

Phillips Brooks (1835–93)

732   O God, we thank you for the message of peace that Christmas
brings to our distracted world. Give peace among nations, peace
in our land, peace in our homes, and peace in our hearts, as we
remember the birth at Bethlehem of the Prince of peace, Jesus
Christ our Lord.

Worship Now

733   We pray you, Lord, to purify our hearts
that they may be worthy to become your dwelling-place.
Let us never fail to find room for you,
but come and abide in us,
that we also may abide in you,
for at this time you were born into the world for us,
and live and reign, King of kings and Lord of lords,
now and for ever.

William Temple (1881–1944)

734   INTERCESSION FOR CHRISTMASTIDE
Holy Child of Bethlehem,
    whose parents found no room in the inn;
    we pray for all who are homeless.

Holy Child of Bethlehem,
    born in a stable;
    we pray for all who are living in poverty.

Holy Child of Bethlehem,
    rejected stranger;
    we pray for all who are lost, alone,
        all who cry for loved ones.

Holy Child of Bethlehem,
    whom Herod sought to kill;
    we pray for all in danger,
        all who are persecuted.

Holy Child of Bethlehem,
    a refugee in Egypt;
    we pray for all who are far from home.

Holy Child of Bethlehem,
    in you the Eternal was pleased to dwell;
    help us, we pray, to see the divine image
        in people everywhere.

In your name we offer this prayer.
                 David Blanchflower

735   CONFESSION AT CHRISTMASTIDE
Lord of grace and truth,
we confess our unworthiness
to stand in your presence as your children.
We have sinned:
forgive – and heal us.

The Virgin Mary accepted your call
to be the mother of Jesus.
Forgive our disobedience to your will.

We have sinned:
forgive – and heal us.

Your Son our saviour
was born in poverty in a manger.
Forgive our greed and rejection of your ways.
We have sinned:
forgive – and heal us.

The shepherds left their flocks
to go to Bethlehem.
Forgive our self-interest and lack of vision.
We have sinned:
forgive – and heal us.

The wise men followed the star
to find Jesus the King.
Forgive our reluctance to seek you.
We have sinned:
forgive – and heal us.

May the God of all healing and forgiveness
draw us to himself,
that we may behold the glory of his Son,
the Word made flesh,
and be cleansed from all our sins
through Jesus Christ our Lord.

Patterns for Worship

BLESSING FOR CHRISTMAS

736   May the humility of the shepherds,
the perseverance of the wise men,
the joy of the angels,
and the peace of the Christ-child
be God's gifts to us and to people everywhere
this Christmas time.
And may the blessing of the Christ-child
be upon us always.

The Promise of His Glory

HOLY INNOCENTS (DECEMBER 28TH)

737   O God, how can this be endured?
Babies slaughtered then,
      children bombed now?
The innocent massacred then,
      villagers mutilated now?
Mothers inconsolable,
systematic torture,
apathy,
mindlessness . . .
O God, how can this be borne,

except by you
and with you

as it always has been?

A.A.

738   We remember today, O God, the slaughter of the holy innocents
of Bethlehem by King Herod. Receive, we pray, into the arms
of your mercy all innocent victims; and by your great might frus-
trate all evil designs, and establish your rule of justice, love and
peace; through Jesus Christ our Lord.
The Book of Common Prayer of the Episcopal Church, USA *(abridged)*

EPIPHANY (JANUARY 6TH)

739   God of gold, we seek your glory:
      the richness that transforms our drabness into colour,
      and brightens our dullness with vibrant light;
your wonder and joy at the heart of all life.

God of incense, we offer you our prayer:
      our spoken and unspeakable longings, our questioning of truth,
      our search for your mystery deep within.

God of myrrh, we cry out to you in our suffering:
      the pain of all our rejections and bereavements,
      our baffled despair at undeserved suffering,
      our rage at continuing injustice;

and we embrace you, God-with-us,
in our wealth, in our yearning, in our anger and loss.
Jan Berry

740   Jesus,
       we offer you the gold of our desire to love,
           even though our hearts are often cold;
       we offer you the incense of our longing to pray,
           although our spirits can be luke-warm;
       we offer you the myrrh of our frustrations and troubles,
           even when self-pity and bitterness creep in.
       Receive and make good our gifts
       out of your great love for us,
       and grant that we, like the wise men,
       may find some kneeling-space at Bethlehem.
                        A.A.

741   O God, who guided by a star the Wise Men to the worship of
       your Son: lead to yourself, we pray, the wise and the great in every
       land, that unto you every knee may bow, and every thought be
       brought into allegiance; through Jesus Christ our Lord.
       The Book of Common Worship, *Church of South India (adapted)*

742   Almighty God, you have revealed the incarnation of your Son by
       the bright shining of a star, which the wise men saw and offered
       costly gifts in adoration; let the star of your justice always shine
       in our hearts, that we may give as our treasure all that we are and
       all that we possess to your service, through Jesus Christ our Lord.
                Gelasian Sacramentary (eighth century)

743   A LITANY FOR EPIPHANY
       The Magi journeyed far to find you, Redeemer and Saviour; we
       too must search for you all our lives.
           Help us to find you, Lord.

       The Magi brought precious gifts to you. Our treasure must be
       the gift of building up your kingdom here and now.
           Help us to find you, Lord.

The coming of the strangers from the East marked the showing forth of Christ to the whole world. As Christians we are called to show forth Christ's love in our everyday lives.
Help us to find you, Lord.

You were in the world but they did not know you. You came to your own and they did not receive you. There was no room for you at the inn. Is there any room for you in our hearts?
Help us to respond to you.

The Magi were prepared to leave their homes to search for the new king whose sign was a star in the east. We too must be prepared to search and become a pilgrim people.
Give us the strength to put false security behind us and live as if we were on a journey.

God has called us out of darkness into the light. May we experience his kindness and blessing and be strong in faith, hope and love.
Because we are followers of Christ, who came as a light shining in the darkness, may we show the light of God to the people we find around us.

Ianthe and Oliver Pratt

THE PRESENTATION OF JESUS IN THE TEMPLE (FEBRUARY 2ND)

744   Lord we praise you for the quiet strength of Joseph,
            the prophetic insight of Simeon,
            the self-dedication of Anna,
            and the courage of Mary
            as she faced the truth
            that a sword would pierce her heart.
        Make us bearers of your light which lightens the world,
        and help us, like Simeon, to live for you and to depart in peace.
            A.A.

745   Come, and with divine songs let us also go to meet Christ, and let us receive him whose salvation Simeon saw. This is he whom David announced: this is he whose words the prophets uttered, who for our sakes has taken flesh and speaks to us in his new law. Let us worship him.

Ancient Orthodox Liturgy

NEW YEAR

Behold I am doing a new thing; now it springs forth, do you not perceive it? says the Lord.

ISAIAH 43:19

746   Almighty God,
by whose mercy my life has continued for another year,
I pray that, as my years increase, my sins may not increase.
As age advances,
let me become more open, more faithful and more trusting in you.
Let me not be distracted by lesser things
from what is truly important.
And if I become infirm as I grow old,
may I not be overwhelmed by self-pity or bitterness.
Continue and increase your loving kindness towards me,
so that, when you finally call me to yourself,
I may enter into eternal happiness with you,
through Jesus Christ my Lord.

Dr Samuel Johnson (1709–84)

It was Dr Johnson's custom to write a prayer in the early hours
of New Year's Day; he did this every year from 1745 onwards.

747   We thank you, Father, Lord of all time,
for the gifts of food, warmth and company,
for your love and the protection of our homes,
and, in all that this year may hold,
for the friendship of Jesus Christ, our Lord.

The Promise of His Glory *(adapted)*

748   God of day and night,
of frost and sunshine,
of rest and growth,
we praise you for the rhythms and patterns of life:

for the gentle dying of each season
and the coming of the next;
for the wonder of new life, in all its forms,
and the quiet flowing of youth into age.
Give us eyes and hearts to perceive you
in the unfolding of our years,
and help us in this new-born year
to make more space for you,
the Giver of it all.

A.A.

749   O Lord, as the years change, may we find rest in your eternal
      changelessness. Help us to meet this new year bravely, in the
      faith that, while life changes all around us, you are always the
      same, guiding us with your wisdom and protecting us with your
      love; through our Saviour Jesus Christ.

William Temple (1881–1944)

750   For all the possibilities ahead in this new year,
      make us thankful, O Lord.
      Give us wisdom, courage and discernment
      in the face of so much chaos, despair and fear.
      Help us to see how, in our circumstances,
      we can contribute towards peace, faith and love;
      and give us the will to translate our desires into actions.

Brother John Charles SSF

751   God and Father of our Lord Jesus Christ,
      whose years never fail
      and whose mercies are new each returning day:
      let the radiance of your Spirit renew our lives,
      warming our hearts and giving light to our minds;
      that we may pass the coming year
      in joyful obedience and firm faith;
      through him who is the beginning and the end,
      your Son Christ our Lord.

David Silk

752   God, bless our year
      giving us
      time for the task
      peace for the pathway
      wisdom for the work
      friends for the fireside
      love to the last.
           The Mothers' Union Anthology of Public Prayers

JESUS' LIFE – THE CHALLENGE OF THE INCARNATION

When many followers drew back and no longer went about
with him, Jesus said to the twelve, 'Do you also wish to go?'
Peter said, 'Lord, to whom shall we go? You have the words
of eternal life.'

JOHN 6:66–68

753   Thank you, God, for incarnation:
      For taking the risk of being human,
         of making friends,
         of offering love,
         of living in hope.
      Thank you for being here, for calling me to do that, too.
      Thank you, God, for incarnation.

Michael Forster

754   Father you never forget us or turn away from us
      even when we fail you.
      You sent your Son Jesus, who gave his life for us,
      cured those who were sick,
      cared for those who were poor
      and cried with those who were sad.
      He forgave sinners and taught us to forgive each other.

      For all your love we give you thanks.
      We open our hearts to him;
      we remember how he died and rose again
      to live now in us.

Scottish Liturgy

755 Lord Jesus Christ,
    you were born in poverty,
    when we might have anticipated riches;
    you are King of all the earth,
    yet you were content to visit one nation.
    From beginning to end
    you upturned our human values
    and held us in suspense.
    Come to us, Lord Jesus.
    Do not let us take you for granted
    or pretend that we ever fully understand you.
    Continue to surprise us
    so that, kept alert,
    we may always be ready
    to receive you as Lord
    and to do your will.

Donald Hilton (adapted)

JESUS' BAPTISM — *See under Baptism, 928–34*

JESUS IN THE WILDERNESS — *See under Lent, 768–77*

JESUS' TEACHING

756 Who are you, Jesus, that you speak with such authority?
    Not like scholars and teachers, simply repeating each other,
    you speak the Word of God to us and all who will listen.
        The power of God living within you shines through
            everything you say.

    Lord Jesus, help us
        to hear what you are saying,
        to understand what you are teaching,
        to know God's power in our lives
        and in the words we speak of you.

Kay Bullock

JESUS' MIRACLES

757   JESUS WALKING ON THE WATER
       Jesus, Saviour in storm,
       when the waters of the deep are broken up,
       when the landmarks are washed away or drowned,
       come to us across the water.

                              A New Zealand Prayer Book

JESUS' HEALING

758   Lord Jesus, touch our eyes,
       as you did those of the blind;
       then we shall see
       in things that are visible
       those things which are invisible.
       Lord Jesus, open our ears,
       heal our wounds and purify our lives,
       as you did those who came to you;
       then we shall hear and perceive what is true
       amidst the sounds of the world,
       and find wholeness in ourselves.

                              after Origen (185–254)

759   THE WOMAN WITH A HAEMORRHAGE (Luke 8:43–8)
       Lord,
       I want to reach you
       and I try to touch you,
       but many forces jostle me,
       and my own fears thrust me aside.

       I want to reach you
       and I try to touch even your garment,
       but they say I am a fool
       and I am filled with doubt.

       I want to reach you
       and I try to touch even the hem of your garment,

and my fingers brush the homespun cloth
and I am flooded with healing
and you turn and ask who touched you
and I fall on my face
and you bend down, lifting me gently, and telling me
that my own faith, that fragment of hope,
has healed me.

And you love me,
and my life is changed.

A.A.

760   THE PARALYSED MAN (Mark 2:1–12)
They broke through the roof,
and lowered him down,
paralysed.
We too are stiffened by fear and need you to release us;
overloaded with guilt and need you to lift it from us;
powerless to change and need you to take charge of us.
Help us to realize there are no limits to your love and power,
nothing which you cannot heal and forgive.

Duncan Wilson

761   BARTIMAEUS (Mark 10:46–52)
Lord Jesus Christ, who stopped to listen
to blind Bartimaeus in his frustration,
look also on us
with your still gaze of love.
Restore our inward sight,
renew our sense of self-worth,
and take hold of our hands
as we join you on the way.

A.A.

762   THE FEEDING OF THE FIVE THOUSAND (Mark 6:35–44)
Lord, we give you our love;
accept it, as you accepted loaves and fishes from a young lad.

Use our small offering to bless many,
and make good the poverty of our efforts
by the richness of your bounty.

A.A.

Also on the Feeding of the Five Thousand, see No. 261

THE TRANSFIGURATION

763   When I look into Your holiness,
when I gaze into Your loveliness,
when all things that surround become shadows in the light of You;
when I've found the joy of reaching Your heart,
when my will becomes enthrall'd in Your love,
when all things that surround become shadows in the light of You:
I worship You,
I worship You,
the reason I live, is to worship You.

Cathy and Wayne Perrin

764   Christ our only true light,
before whose bright cloud
your friends fell to the ground:
we bow before your cross
that we may remember in our bodies
the dead who fell like shadows;
and that we may refuse to be prostrated
before the false brightness of any other light,
looking to your power alone
for hope of resurrection from the dead.

Janet Morley

The church remembers the Transfiguration of Jesus on 6 August,
which is also the day the nuclear bomb was dropped on Hiroshima.

765   May the light and love of God shine in our hearts and through
the universe that the whole creation may be transfigured to
glory, in and through Jesus Christ, radiant in the splendour of
the wounds of love.

Jim Cotter

See also No. 853

JESUS ENCOUNTERING PEOPLE

766   THE RICH YOUNG MAN (Mark 10:17–22)
        Lord, what are my riches?
        What stops me giving everything to you?
        What weighs me down and ties my hands?
        What denies me true freedom?
        Show me, and give me grace to abandon my idols,
        so that, when you look at me with love,
        I shall not walk away
        still cluttered.

                        A.A.

767   JESUS AND THE MONEY-LENDERS (Mark 11:15–19)
        Forgive us, Lord Jesus, when we let fund-raising get in the way
            of faith;
        when we become so concerned with the amount in the collection
        that we fail to see you at the centre of our worship and
            our world.

        Give us the determination to tear down the tables of greed–
        not only in our churches but in our hearts as well;
        help us to overturn our materialistic attitudes
        and offer ourselves, wholly, in your service.

                        Carol Dixon

See also:
        No. 393: 'Lord God, in Jesus you came in the body, flesh of
        our flesh . . .'

LENT

Lord, hear my prayer; do not hide your face from me in the day of my trouble; my heart is scorched and withered like grass; I have become like an owl in the wilderness; I have eaten ashes for bread, and mingled my drink with my tears.

PSALM 102:1, 2, 4, 6.

JESUS IN THE WILDERNESS

768   Jesus, my true King,
       when you were tempted in the wilderness,
       you rejected the way of easy popularity
       and chose instead a path of humiliation
       at the hands of those you had come to love.
       Give me the wisdom to see
       when it is necessary
       to be, like you,
       a fool in the eyes of the world,
       and keep me always true to you.

A.A.

769   Lord Jesus Christ,
       who for our sake drew to yourself the world's hate,
       grant us the courage to be vulnerable,
       grace to expose ourselves to the furies without and the furies
         within;
       and in our frailty send your holy angels to minister to us.

Richard Harries

770   God of the desert,
       as we follow Jesus into the unknown,
       may we recognize the tempter when he comes;

let it be your bread we eat,
your world we serve
and you alone we worship.
                    A New Zealand Prayer Book

771   Servant-Christ,
      help us all to follow you into the desert,
      with you to fast, denying false luxury,
      refusing the tempting ways of self-indulgence,
      the way of success at all costs,
      the way of coercive persuasion.
      Servant-Christ, help us all to follow you.
                    Worship in an Indian Context

ASH WEDNESDAY

772   Dust and ashes touch our face,
      mark our failure and our falling.
          Holy Spirit, come,
          walk with us tomorrow,
          take us as disciples,
      washed and wakened by your calling.
          Take us by the hand and lead us,
          lead us through the desert sands,
          bring us living water,
          Holy Spirit, come.
                        Brian A. Wren

773   Life-giving God,
      we thank you for creating us out of the dust of the earth,
      and breathing your life into us;
      may these ashes be to us a sign
      that life is more than our physical bodies,
      and that our hope of eternal life
      depends, not on our merits, but on your mercy alone,
      to which we now turn
      in sorrow for our sins,
      and with the trust of children.
                        A.A.

774   Lord,
        take my small offering of self-denial this Lent,
            as a sign of my great longing for you.
              I hunger for your presence in my life,
                  and I thirst for your love.
    I hunger for justice for those who are wronged and oppressed,
                 and I thirst for your peace.
              I hunger for a glimpse of your glory,
            and I thirst for your stillness in my heart.
          God of giving, God of longing, God of pain,
                  I hunger for you.
                          A.A.

775   Lord, in these days of mercy, make us quiet and prayerful;
      in these days of challenge, make us stronger in you;
      in these days of emptiness, take possession of us;
      in these days of waiting, open our hearts to the mystery of your
         cross.
                          A.A.

776   God our Father,
      in your love and goodness
      you have taught us
      to overcome our sins with prayer, fasting and generosity;
      accept our Lenten disciplines,
      and when we fall by our weakness,
      raise us up by your unfailing mercy;
      through Jesus Christ our Lord.
                          David Silk

777   Blessed are you, O Lord our God,
      the shepherd of Israel,
      their pillar of cloud by day,
      their pillar of fire by night.
      In these forty days you lead us
      into the desert of repentance
      that in this pilgrimage of prayer

we might learn to be your people once more.
In fasting and service
you bring us back to your heart.
You open our eyes to your presence in the world
and you free our hands to lead others
to the radiant splendour of your mercy.
Be with us in these journey days
for without you we are lost and will perish.
To you alone be dominion and glory,
for ever and ever.

Praise God in Song

Mothering Sunday / Mother's Day

(This falls during Lent in the UK)

As one whom his mother comforts, so will I comfort you.
ISAIAH 66:13

778 Thank you, God,
  that you are tender as a mother,
  as well as strong as a father.
  You give us life,
  and care for us
  like a mother who will not forsake her children.
  We pray for our mothers today,
  putting them into your hands
  for time and for eternity;
  and we ask your blessing on all our relationships
  in the families of our homes,
  our churches,
  and our communities.

A.A.
Isaiah 49:15

779 Jesus, as a mother you gather your people to you: you are
  gentle with us like a mother with her children.
  In your love and tenderness, remake us.

  Often you weep over our sins and our pride: tenderly you draw
  us from hatred and judgment.
  In your love and tenderness, remake us.

  You comfort us in sorrow and bind up our wounds: in sickness
  you nurse us and with pure milk you feed us.
  In your love and tenderness, remake us.

Jesus, by your dying we are born to new life: by your anguish and labour we come forth in joy.
In your love and tenderness, remake us.

Despair turns to hope through your sweet goodness: through your gentleness we find comfort in fear.
In your love and tenderness, remake us.

Your warmth gives life to the dead: your touch makes sinners righteous.
In your love and tenderness, remake us.

In your compassion bring grace and forgiveness: for the beauty of heaven may your love prepare us.
In your love and tenderness, remake us.

St Anselm (1033–1109)

HOLY WEEK

My God, my God, why have you forsaken me?
PSALM 22:1 AND MATTHEW 27:46

PALM SUNDAY

780   Lord, you rode straight into the power of the enemy to suffer
and die; give us the strength to follow you to the centres of oppo-
sition in this world, and the confidence which confronts power
with love.

Susan Williams

781   Jesus, Lord of the Journey,
   we thank you
   that you set your face firmly towards Jerusalem,
   with a single eye and pure intention,
   knowing what lay ahead but never turning aside.

Jesus, Lord of the Palms,
   we thank you
   that you enjoyed the Hallelujahs of ordinary people,
   living fully in that moment of delight
   and accepting their praise.

Jesus, Lord of the Cross,
   we thank you
   that you went into the heart of our evil and pain,
   along a way that was both terrible and wonderful,
      as your kingship became your brokenness
   and your dying became love's triumph.

A.A.

782   Jesus, when you rode into Jerusalem
       the people waved palms
       with shouts of acclamation.
       Grant that when the shouting dies
       we may still walk beside you even to a cross.

A New Zealand Prayer Book

783   Lord, on this Palm Sunday you were given a hero's welcome
       as one who was going the way of the crowd; but you had cho-
       sen the way of the cross, and the applause was short lived.
          Keep bright and clear before us the vision of our calling, that
       we may never be diverted from the way you have chosen for us,
       but may follow in the steps of you, our crucified and risen Lord,
       to whom be all glory, laud and honour, this day and for evermore.

Basil Naylor

784   King of the universe, whose son entered Jerusalem riding on a
       donkey to the praise of the crowds, help us to recognize in him
       the one who comes in the name of the Lord, and to acclaim him,
       crying, 'Hosanna in the highest!' May we make sacrifices for the
       coming of your kingdom, giving not only our hallelujahs, but
       also our hearts.

Alan Sayers

785   Lord Jesus, we greet your coming,
       pilgrim messiah, servant king, rejected saviour.

       You rode into Jerusalem on a donkey, symbol of
       humility and lowliness, mocking our dream of pomp
       and glory, demonstrating the foolishness of God before
       the eyes of the world.
          You have shown us the way of humble service, the
       way of true greatness.
          Lord Jesus, help us to follow.

Patterns and Prayers for Christian Worship

MAUNDY THURSDAY

786   Infinite, intimate God;
this night you kneel before your friends
and wash our feet.
Bound together in your love,
trembling, we drink your cup
and watch.

A New Zealand Prayer Book

787   Great God, in Christ you call our name
and then receive us as your own,
not through some merit, right or claim
but by your gracious love alone.
We strain to glimpse your mercy-seat
and find you kneeling at our feet.

Then take the towel, and break the bread,
and humble us, and call us friends.
Suffer and serve till all are fed,
and show how grandly love intends
to work till all creation sings,
to fill all worlds, to crown all things.

Brian A. Wren

788   O Christ,
pouring yourself out,
love drained to the last drop,
we adore you.

O Christ,
kneeling as a servant,
washing the disciples' feet,
shocking in your humility,
we adore you.

O Christ,
taking bread and wine,
crystal-clear in your awareness
of the work you must complete,
we adore you.

O Christ,
entering Gethsemane,
falling on your face to pray,
uncontainable in your broken heart,
we adore you.

A.A.

789   GETHSEMANE
Servant-Christ, we follow you into the garden,
to watch with you.
Help us to be ever vigilant
for signs of the dawning of your day;
to struggle unsparingly to understand,
and to be obedient to your perfect will.

Worship in an Indian Context *(adapted)*

GOOD FRIDAY AND THE PASSION OF CHRIST

790   Lord, I realize that what I see of your love
is only the beginning.
One drop from the whole ocean.
And, like the sea, moving, surging.
All-embracing.
Seeking to surround me,
not to overwhelm, to drown,
but to hold me, buoy me up.
A love with room to spare.
No rejections.
No high-tide mark of rubbish,
pushed up and thrown aside.

I wish Judas could have known that.
I wish that somehow
in his own agony in the garden,
so different, Lord, from yours,
so like to mine,
he could have reached out

from the depths of his despair
and felt your hand.
There's nothing I can do about that.
I leave it with you, Lord,
as I leave so much.
You've got strong hands.

Eddie Askew

791   When I survey the wondrous cross,
      On which the Prince of Glory died,
      My richest gain I count but loss,
      And pour contempt on all my pride.

      Were the whole realm of nature mine,
      That were an offering far too small;
      Love so amazing, so divine,
      Demands my soul, my life, my all.

Isaac Watts (1674–1748)

792   Jesus, what have you not suffered,
          what have you not given for me?
      I can never comprehend you,
          but I can love you
          and wonder
          at the depth of the darkness
          that you entered on the cross,
          and the depth of the love
          that held you there.

A.A.

793   Fashion in me, Lord,
          eyes within my eyes,
          so that, with new eyes,
          I may contemplate your divine sacrifice.

      Create in me a pure heart,
          so that, through the power of your Spirit,
          I may inhale your salvation.

Joseph the Visionary (a Syrian Father of eighth-century Iraq)

794   Ah, holy Jesus, how hast thou offended,
        That man to judge thee hath in hate pretended?
        By foes derided, by thine own rejected,
            O most afflicted.

        Who was guilty? Who brought this upon thee?
        Alas, my treason, Jesus, hath undone thee.
        'Twas I, Lord Jesus, I it was denied thee:
            I crucified thee.

        Therefore, kind Jesus, since I cannot pay thee,
        I do adore thee, and will ever pray thee,
        Think on thy pity and thy love unswerving,
            Not my deserving.
                              Robert Bridges (1844–1930)

795   O Jesus, blessed Jesus, I gaze on thy Cross,
        O Saviour suffering to draw my love:
            was ever love like thine, or thanks so poor as mine?
        Thy hands are outstretched for love of me and all mankind,
            and with my sin I have pierced thee and keep on wounding
                thee;
        Bitterly I sorrow, deepen my penitence.
        Give me tears that I may weep.
        Give me strength that I may amend.
        Take me to thyself,
            keep me in thy wounds,
            ever mindful of thy presence,
            ever to love thee,
            in pain and in bliss,
            on earth and in heaven,
            with thee for ever.
                              Gilbert Shaw (1886–1967)

796   Oh King of grief! (a title strange, yet true,
            To thee of all kings only due)
        Oh King of wounds! how shall I grieve for thee,
            Who in all grief preventest* me?
                    * 'Pre-ventest' in the sense of 'goes before'

Shall I weep blood? Why thou hast wept such store
   That all thy body was one door.
Shall I be scourged, flouted, boxed, sold?
   'Tis but to tell the tale is told.
Then for thy passion – I will do for that –
   Alas, my God, I know not what.

George Herbert (1593–1633)

797   Soul of Christ, sanctify me;
Body of Christ, save me;
Blood of Christ, inebriate me;
Water from the side of Christ, wash me;
Passion of Christ, comfort me;

Good Jesu, hear me;
Within your wounds, hide me;
Never let me be separated from you;
From the deadly enemy, defend me;
In the hour of my death, call me,
And ask me to come to you,
That with the saints I may sing your praise
For ever and ever.

The 'Anima Christi' (fourteenth century)

798   O my sweet Saviour, who in your undeserved love towards us so kindly suffered the painful death of the cross, suffer me not to be cold or lukewarm in love towards you.

St Thomas More (1478–1535)

799   In this thy bitter Passion,
   Good Shepherd, think of me
With thy most sweet compassion,
   Unworthy though I be:
Beneath thy Cross abiding
   For ever would I rest,
In thy dear love confiding,
   And with thy presence blest.

Translated by Sir Henry W. Baker (1821–1877) (adapted)

800   Lord Jesus,
      forgive us for failing you,
      as even the disciples did.
      Through thoughtlessness
      we betray you;
      through fear
      we run away from you;
      through cowardice
      we deny you,
      not wanting people to know that we are your followers.
      Have mercy on us,
      as you had mercy on Peter and the others,
      and when the cock crows in our hearts
      and we realize what we have done,
      help us to bear your gaze of love.
                              A.A.

801   Christ our victim,
      whose beauty was disfigured
      and whose body torn upon the cross;
      open wide your arms
      to embrace our tortured world,
      that we may not turn away our eyes,
      but abandon ourselves to your mercy.
                              Janet Morley

802   Jesus our Saviour, we thank you that you endured a criminal's
      death for us. When we are carried away with pride, remind us
      that you were betrayed, whipped, and publicly humiliated. When
      we are full of resentment, may we remember that you prayed,
      'Father, forgive.' Show us your way of overcoming hatred with
      love, and keep our eyes fixed on you, now and always.
                              A.A.

803   Blessed be the name of Jesus,
      who died to save us.
      Blessed be Jesus,
      who had compassion on us.

Blessed be Jesus,
who suffered loneliness, rejection and pain,
for our sakes.
Blessed be Jesus,
through whose cross I am forgiven.
Lord Jesus, deepen my understanding
of your suffering and death.

Written by young people in Kenya

804   Almighty God,
as we stand at the foot of the cross of your Son,
help us to see and know your love for us,
so that in humility, love and joy
we may place at his feet
all that we have and all that we are;
through Jesus Christ our Saviour.

Celebrating Common Prayer

805   Crucified Christ,
we draw near with awe
to this holy place of Calvary;
here you transformed evil into the victory of love,
and violence into the victory of peace.
On this painful and mysterious day
accept our thanksgiving
for the cost of what you endured,
and give us the courage to stay with you
until it is finished.

A.A.

806   O Saviour of the world,
who redeemed us by your Cross and precious Blood,
save us, and help us, we humbly beseech you.

Western Rite, Good Friday Liturgy

807 Jesus, our true and only Saviour,
     you died like a criminal on the cross;
     but you are God, the one who forgives.
     You were broken, helpless and in pain;
     but you are God, in whom there is hope.
     You have shown us a love beyond words:
     give us your forgiveness, hope and love.

                    A New Zealand Prayer Book (adapted)

808 God our Father, the contradiction of the cross
     proclaims your infinite wisdom.
     Help us to see that the glory of your Son
     is revealed in the suffering he freely accepted.
     Give us faith to claim as our only glory
     the cross of our Lord Jesus Christ,
     who lives with you and the Holy Spirit,
     one God, for ever and ever.

                              The Liturgy of the Hours

809 O Christ, your cross speaks both to us and to our world.
     In your dying for us you accepted the pain and hurt
     Of the whole of creation.
     The arms of your cross stretch out across the
     Broken world in reconciliation.
     You have made peace with us.
     Help us to make peace with you by sharing in your
     Reconciling work.

                              Ali Newell
                         Colossians 1:15–20

810 Lord, what would we have done?
         Would we have fallen asleep and then run away terrified, like
         the disciples in Gethsemane?
     Thank you that you forgive us for our weakness, when we opt
     out and run away from conflict and cost.

Lord, what would we have done?
Would we have shouted 'Hosanna' on one day, and 'Crucify'
on another?
Forgive us when we fail you because it is easier to follow the
crowd.

Lord, what would we have done?
Would we have been harsh and judgemental like the Pharisees?
Forgive us when we are quick to condemn, or hide behind
legalism.

Lord, what would we have done?
Would we have been like the soldiers, hard and callous, just
doing their job?
Forgive us when we act blindly and unthinkingly, without con-
sidering the effect our behaviour has on others.

Lord, what would we have done?
Would we have slunk away ashamed from the horror of
Calvary?

We thank you that you forgive us when we let you down, and
that your love is stronger than all the evil we could throw at you;
Lord, accept these prayers, offered in your name.

Vincent Ashwin

811   BLESSING FOR GOOD FRIDAY
May the cross of our Lord
protect those who belong to Jesus,
and strengthen your hearts in faith to Christ,
in hardship and in ease,
in life and in death,
now and for ever.

Simon, Bishop of Iran (d. 339)

EASTER

Death is swallowed up in victory.
O death, where is your sting?

1 CORINTHIANS 15:54–5

ᥫᥭ ᥫᥭ

EASTER EVE

812   Rejoice, heavenly powers! Sing, choirs of angels!
      Exult, all creation around God's throne!
      Jesus Christ, our King, is risen!
      Sound the trumpet of salvation!

      Rejoice, O earth, in shining splendour,
      Radiant in the brightness of your King!
      Christ has conquered! Glory fills you!
      Darkness vanishes for ever!

      On this holy night all evil is dispelled,
      Guilt is washed away, and peace restored.
      So we are reconciled with God.
      Alleluia!

                From the ancient Exsultet for the Easter Vigil

EASTER DAY

813   i thank You God for most this amazing
      day: for the leaping greenly spirits of trees
      and a blue true dream of sky; and for everything
      which is natural which is infinite which is yes

      (i who have died am alive again today,
      and this is the sun's birthday; this is the birth
      day of life and of love and wings: and of the gay
      great happenings illimitably earth)

how should tasting touching hearing seeing
breathing any – lifted from the no
of all nothing – human merely being
doubt unimaginable You?
(now the ears of my ears awake and
now the eyes of my eyes are opened)

e.e. cummings

EASTERTIDE

814   Resurrection Thou –
Bright Morning Star –
Lord of the Dance –
Leap of Faith –
Stillness of Joy –
    ALL HAIL!

Jim Cotter

815   If you were not risen,
Lord Christ, to whom would we go
to discover a radiance
of the face of God?

If you were not risen,
we would not be together
seeking your communion.
We would not find in your presence
forgiveness,
wellspring of a new beginning.

If you were not risen,
where would we draw the energy
for following you
right to the end of our existence,
for choosing you again and anew?

Brother Roger of Taizé

816 God of the open garden,
     we have found you
     and long to hold you fast.
     But you refuse our clinging need,
     eluding the love
     that would bind and possess you,
     sending us out
     beyond the bounds of our feeble knowing.

     Rapt in our joy and desire,
     we cannot interpret you:
     you have gone from us again,
     moving into morning,
     moving into light.

     In your great love,
     wait for us
     where you have sent us,
     go ahead of us,
     be there to meet us,
     risen, released in your world.
                                   Nicola Slee

817 Christ, you are risen from the dead.
     We are risen with you.
     May our life never deny
     this eternal life,
     this peace and hope and joy.
     Praise and glory to the God of life
     who is stronger than all kinds of death. Alleluia.
                    A New Zealand Prayer Book

818 Blessed be the God and Father of our Lord Jesus Christ! By his
     great mercy he has given us new birth into a living hope, through
     the resurrection of Jesus from the dead, and into an inheritance
     which cannot perish or be defiled, nor can it ever fade. So let us
     rejoice!
                          Traditional

819   Ever-living God,
      help us to celebrate our joy
      in the resurrection of the Lord
      and to express in our lives
      the love we celebrate.

      Grant this through our Lord Jesus Christ, your Son,
      who lives and reigns with you and the Holy Spirit,
      one God, for ever and ever.
                          The Liturgy of the Hours

820   O risen Lord, who in your first appearance to Mary was mis-
      taken for the gardener:

      be present with us, and show yourself to us in all our mistakes
      and uncertainties.

      O risen Lord, who appeared to your dejected disciples on the
      road to Emmaus, and opened to them the scriptures, so that their
      hearts burned within them:

      be present with us, and set our hearts on fire with love for you.

      O risen Lord, who gave to your distraught followers the assur-
      ance of healing and forgiveness:

      be present with us, and bring together all Christians in peace and
      harmony.

      O risen Lord, who mindful of the needs of your disciples, pre-
      pared a meal by the Sea of Galilee:

      be present with us, and make yourself known to us in all acts of
      hospitality and sharing.

      O risen Lord, who in your final appearance on the Mount of
      Olives, lifted up hands of blessing on all people:

      be present with us, and grant that our prayers today may be
      taken up into yours on behalf of the whole world.
                          Church of South India (adapted)

821   Today we rejoice in the salvation of the world.
Christ is risen; let us arise in him!
Christ enters new life; let us live in him!
Christ has come forth from the tomb;
let us shake off the fetters of evil!
The gates of hell are open,
the powers of evil are overcome!
In Christ a new creation is coming to birth,
Alleluia!
Lord, make us new,
Alleluia!

St Gregory of Nazianzus (c.330–389)

822   The whole bright world rejoices now:
with laughing cheer! with boundless joy!
The birds do sing on every bough:
Alleluia!

Then shout beneath the racing skies:
with laughing cheer! with boundless joy!
To him who rose that we might rise:
Alleluia!

God, Father, Son and Holy Ghost:
with laughing cheer! with boundless joy!
Our God most high, our joy, our boast:
Alleluia!

Easter carol (seventeenth century)

823   Let everyone who loves God rejoice in this festival of light!
With joy we praise our Lord! Alleluia!
Let the faithful servants gladly enter into the joy of their Lord!
Our hearts are filled with thanksgiving! Alleluia!
Let those who have borne the burden of fasting come now to celebrate the feast!
We walk from darkness into light! Alleluia!
Let those who were inwardly dead now rise and dance with Christ, the Lord of life.
We are renewed in you, O Christ! Alleluia!

St John Chrystostom (c. 347–407)

THE UPPER ROOM

824   Living God,
       for whom no door is closed,
       no heart is locked,
       draw us beyond our doubts,
       till we see your Christ
       and touch his wounds
       where they bleed in others.

                        A New Zealand Prayer Book

THE ROAD TO EMMAUS

825   O God whose greeting we miss
       and whose departure we delay:
       make our hearts burn with insight
       on our ordinary road;
       that, as we grasp you in the broken bread,
       we may also let you go,
       and return to speak your word of life
       in the name of Christ.

                        Janet Morley

826   God our Father, Creator of all,
       today is the day of Easter joy.
       May the risen Lord
       breathe on our minds and open our eyes
       that we may know him in the breaking of bread,
       and follow him in his risen life.

                        The Liturgy of the Hours

INTERCESSIONS FOR EASTER

827   Jesus has risen from the dead! Alleluia!
       By his cross he has defeated the power of evil;
       and through his resurrection
       we are set free. Alleluia!

Lord, without your resurrection
our faith would be empty
and without hope.
But you are alive,
and we rejoice and dance and wonder
in the mystery of your presence among us.

We pray for your church:
free us from the shackles of guilt and legalism,
and help us to proclaim the message of healing and forgiveness
for which you died.
Lord, in your mercy,
hear our prayer.

Lord, your friends and disciples,
must have been utterly bereft at your death,
with all their hope and purpose broken.
So we pray now
for those who are in darkness and pain today:
those facing the keen disappointment of broken hopes;
lives damaged by broken relationships and broken trust;
people with broken hearts;
bodies broken by torture;
and spirits broken by injustice;
Lord, in your mercy,
hear our prayer.

We pray, Lord for broken communities, especially in . . .; and we
ask your forgiveness for our own apathy, and our desire to wash
our hands of involvement in the plight of others.
Lord, in your mercy,
hear our prayer.

Risen Lord, surround with your presence and peace those who are
ill, and the families, friends and hospital staff who care for them.
Lord, in your mercy,
hear our prayer.

Accept our prayers,
and take them up
into your creative energy of love
which you let loose into the world
on those extraordinary Passover days.

A.A.

BLESSINGS FOR EASTER

828   May the light of Christ, rising in glory, scatter the darkness of your
hearts and minds; and may the blessing of God, the Father, the Son
and the Holy Spirit, rest upon you, and be with you always.

Ancient Western Rite for Easter

829   May the God who shakes heaven and earth,
whom death could not contain,
who lives to disturb and heal us,
bless you with power to go forth
and proclaim the gospel.

Janet Morley

830   May the power of the cross,
the joy of the resurrection,
and the presence of our risen Lord
be with you, now and always.

A.A.

831   May the risen Lord Jesus watch over us and renew us
as he renews the whole of creation.
May our hearts and lives echo his love.

Celebrating Common Prayer

See also:
    No. 655: 'This is the day that the Lord has made'

THE ASCENSION

Therefore God has highly exalted him, and bestowed on him the name above all names, that at the name of Jesus every knee should bow, in heaven and on earth and under the earth.

PHILIPPIANS 2:9–10

832 When we stand gazing upwards, bring us down to earth:
      with the love of a friend,
         through the songs of the sorrowing,
         in the faces of the hungry.

   When we look to you for action, demand some work from us:
      by your touch of fire,
         your glance of reproof,
         your fearful longing.

   As ruler over all:
      love us into action,
      fire us with your zeal,
      enrich us with your grace,
         to make us willing subjects of your rule.

                                    Janet Nightingale

833 Christ our lover
      to whom we try to cling:
      as you have reached into our depths
      and drawn us to love you,
      so make us open, freely to let you go;
      that you may return in unexpected power
      to change the world through us,
      in your name.

                                    Janet Morley

834   Ascended Christ, we worship you;
Christ, present with us now, we ask for your Spirit
to make us brave in following your way.
Reign as King in our hearts,
and, in the foolishness of the divine love,
make us wiser
than the ambitions and power-games of the world.

A.A.

835   God our Father,
make us joyful in the ascension of your Son Jesus Christ.
May we follow him into the new creation,
for his ascension is our glory and our hope.
We ask this through our Lord Jesus Christ.

The Liturgy of the Hours

836   Sing to the Lord, who ascended above the heaven of heavens,
our Christ, our Sunrise, our Joy, our King, crowned in glory –
Alleluia!

Source unknown

837   Blessed are you, Sovereign God, reigning in glory.
Cloud and deep darkness proclaim your holiness;
radiant light shows forth your truth.
Jesus has entered the cloud of your presence;
he has taken his seat at the right hand of Majesty.
Perfect sacrifice, he has put away sins.
Merciful high priest, he pleads for our weakness.
Always our brother, he prepares our place in heaven.
Ruler of all, he establishes your reign.
Dawning light for the righteous, hope of sinners,
Blessed are you, Sovereign God, high over all.

Michael Vasey

PENTECOST AND THE HOLY SPIRIT

May the God of hope fill you with all joy and peace in believing, so that by the power of the Holy Spirit you may abound in hope.

ROMANS 15:13

ↄ৩ ৩ↄ

838   Holy Spirit of God,
           baptize me with your grace
           like early morning dew.
           Divine Comforter,
           heal my wounds,
           and soothe and calm my mind
           with your message of peace.

A.A.

839   Breathe in me, Holy Spirit,
      that I may think what is holy.
      Move me, Holy Spirit,
      that I may do what is holy.
      Attract me, Holy Spirit,
      that I may love what is holy.
      Strengthen me, Holy Spirit,
      that I may guard what is holy.
      Guard me, Holy Spirit,
      that I may keep what is holy.

St Augustine of Hippo (354–430)

840   O Spirit of God, mighty river, flow over me, in me, through me.
      O Spirit of God, cleanse me, purify the channels of my life.
      O Spirit of God, bear me along with thy flood of life-giving
         service.

O Spirit of God, mighty river, bear me down to the ocean,
the ocean of thy love.

O Spirit of God, mighty fire, glow in me, burn in me,
until thy radiance fills my soul.
O Spirit of God, mighty fire, may thy light illumine my mind.
O Spirit of God, mighty fire, may thy heat consume my will
until I burn for thee alone.
May the flames of thy love ever blaze upon the altar of my heart.

Chandran Devanesan

841   O thou who camest from above,
The pure celestial fire to impart,
Kindle a flame of sacred love
On the mean altar of my heart.

There let it for thy glory burn
With inextinguishable blaze,
And trembling to its source return
In humble prayer, and fervent praise.

Charles Wesley (1707–1788)

842   O Holy Spirit, when you dwell in someone's heart,
you live in what is infinitely lower.
Spirit of Holiness,
you live in the midst of impurity and corruption;
Spirit of Wisdom,
you live in the midst of folly;
Spirit of Truth,
you live in one who is deluded in many things.
Oh, continue to dwell there,
you who do not seek a desirable dwelling-place,
that one day you may finally be pleased
by the dwelling which you yourself have prepared in my heart,
foolish, deceiving and impure though it is.

Søren Kierkegaard (1813–1855)

843   Hail, O power of the Son!
      Hail, O beauty of the Father!
      Hail, O Spirit most pure,
      Bond of the Son and the Father!
      O Christ, send down on me
      This Spirit with the Father,
      That he may sprinkle my soul with his dew
      And fill it with his royal gifts.

Synesius of Cyrene (c. 370–c. 414)

844   Come down, O Love divine,
      Seek thou this soul of mine,
      And visit it with thine own ardour glowing;
      O Comforter, draw near,
      Within my heart appear,
      And kindle it, thy holy flame bestowing.

      O let it freely burn,
      Till earthly passions turn
      To dust and ashes, in its heat consuming;
      And let thy glorious light
      Shine ever on my sight,
      And clothe me round, the while my path illuming.

Bianco da Siena (d. 1434)

845   Come Holy Spirit,
          enter our silences.
      Come Holy Spirit,
          into the depths of our longing.
      Come Holy Spirit,
          our friend and our lover.
      Come Holy Spirit,
          unmask our pretending.
      Come Holy Spirit,
          expose our lives.
      Come Holy Spirit,
          sustain our weakness.
      Come Holy Spirit,
          redeem our creation.

Enter our trusting,
enter our fearing,
enter our letting go,
enter our holding back.

Flood our barren spaces,
make fertile our deserts within.
Break us and heal us,
liberator of our desires.

Come Holy Spirit,
    embrace and free us.

Neill Thew, Oxford, 1990

846   O God, life-giving Spirit,
Spirit of healing and comfort,
of integrity and truth,
we believe and trust in you.
Warm-winged Spirit, brooding over creation,
rushing wind and Pentecostal fire,
we commit ourselves to work with you
and renew our world.

Janet Morley

847   Father in heaven,
fifty days have celebrated the fullness
of the mystery of your revealed love.
See your people gathered in prayer,
open to receive the Spirit's flame.
May it come to rest in our hearts
and disperse the divisions of word and tongue.
With one voice and one song
may we praise your name in joy and thanksgiving.
Grant this through Christ our Lord.

The Liturgy of the Hours

848   Holy Spirit, hover above the chaos and make new this world.
Rest on us and change us
– give us peace that we may share it gladly.
– forgive our sins that we may forgive others gently.
– send us out that we may care for the weak graciously.

Tony Burnham

849 Fire of God,
     Wind of God,
     Spirit of God,
     purify us in the flame of your mercy,
     change us by the breath of your power,
     and take possession of us in the warmth of your love,
     so that we may rediscover
     your image in us.
                              A.A.

850   Spirit of God,
              Lord and Giver of Life,
           moving between us and around,
              like wind or water or fire;
     breathe into us your freshness that we may awake;
       cleanse our vision that we may see more clearly;
       kindle our senses that we may feel more sharply;
              and give us the courage to live
                   as you would have us live,
               through Jesus Christ our Lord.
                        John V. Taylor

851 God of power,
     may the boldness of your Spirit transform us,
     may the gentleness of your Spirit lead us,
     may the gifts of your Spirit
     be our goal and our strength
     now and always.
                      A New Zealand Prayer Book

852 Spirit of truth
     whom the world can never grasp,
     touch our hearts
     with the shock of your coming;
     fill us with desire
     for your disturbing peace;
     and fire us with longing
     to speak your uncontainable word
     through Jesus Christ.
                         Janet Morley

853   Almighty and all-loving God,
          through the fire of your Spirit
       you have drawn the hearts of men and women
          to share in the mystery of your being;
             by the power of the same Spirit
             infuse our lives with your presence,
       that, as your beloved Son was transfigured in prayer,
             we too may be transformed,
       and our lives become a flame of self-giving love.
                    Mark 9:2–3; 2 Peter 1:4
                         A.A.

854   O Holy Spirit,
          Giver of light and life,
       impart to us thoughts higher than our own thoughts,
             prayers better than our own prayers,
             and powers beyond our own powers,
       that we may spend and be spent
       in the ways of love and goodness,
             after the perfect image
             of our Lord and Saviour Jesus Christ.
   Eric Milner-White (1884–1963) and G. W. Briggs (1875–1959)

855   Spirit of God, with your holy breath
       you cleanse the hearts and minds of your people;
       you comfort them when they are in sorrow,
       you lead them when they wander from the way,
       you kindle them when they are cold,
       you knit them together when they are at variance,
       and you enrich them with many and various gifts.
       We beseech you daily to increase
       those gifts which you have entrusted to us;
       that with your light before us and within us
       we may pass through this world
       without stumbling and without straying.
                    Erasmus (1466–1536)

856   Exuberant Spirit of God,
       bursting with the brightness of flame
       into the coldness of our lives
       to warm us with a passion for justice and beauty,
       we praise you.

       Exuberant Spirit of God,
       sweeping us out of the dusty corners of our apathy
       to breathe vitality into our struggles for change,
       we praise you.

       Exuberant Spirit of God,
       speaking words that leap over barriers of mistrust
       to convey messages of truth and new understanding,
       we praise you.

       Exuberant Spirit of God,
       flame
          wind
             speech,
       burn, breathe, speak in us;
       fill your world with justice and with joy.
                          Jan Berry

857   Lord, may we bear the fruits of your Spirit:
       give us love,
       that boundless, healing energy which transforms the world; *(pause)*
       give us joy,
       because no darkness or evil can overcome you; *(pause)*
       give us peace,
       to quiet our hearts, and to free us from bitterness; *(pause)*
       give us patience,
       to go on following you even when it is hard; *(pause)*
       give us kindness,
       to reach out to our neighbour and to the person who needs to be
          loved; *(pause)*
       give us goodness,
       to give with a generous heart and without ulterior motive; *(pause)*
       give us faithfulness,

to stay at your side, come what may; *(pause)*
give us gentleness,
to respect the freedom and integrity of others; *(pause)*
give us self-control,
to see our weaknesses and overcome them in your strength. *(pause)*
Lord, may we bear the fruits of your Spirit.

A. A.
Galatians 5:22–23

BLESSINGS FOR PENTECOST

858   May his tongues of flame
burn out all evil from your hearts,
fill you with his love and peace,
and give you the gifts of his Spirit,
and a voice to praise him for ever.

The Roman Missal *(adapted)*

859   May the Spirit, who hovered over the waters when the world
was created, breathe into us the life he gives.

May the Spirit, who overshadowed the Virgin
    when the eternal Son came among us, make us joyful in the
service of the Lord.

May the Spirit, who set the Church on fire upon the day of
Pentecost, bring the world alive with the love of the risen Christ.

And the blessing of God Almighty, the Father, the Son, and the
Holy Spirit be upon us and remain with us always.

Michael Perham

THE TRINITY

Holy, holy, holy is the Lord God Almighty, who was and is and is to come.

REVELATION 4:8

860   O God, Father, moment by moment you hold me in being,
      on you I depend.
      O God, eternal Son, friend and brother beside me,
      in you I trust.
      O God, Holy Spirit, life and love within me,
      from you I live.

Richard Harries

861   The Trinity
      Protecting me
      The Father be
      Over me
      The Saviour be
      Under me
      The Spirit be
      About me
      The Holy Three
      Defending me
      As evening comes
      Bless my home
      Holy Three
      Watching me
      As shadows fall
      Hear my call
      Sacred Three
      Encircle me
      So it may be
      Amen to Thee
      Holy Three
      About me

David Adam

862   O God, you are the one to whom I reach out,
       mystery beyond human thinking, love beyond our
         comprehending.
       Yet because you are love, you have reached out to me, joined
         me to Christ,
       taken me into the very heart of your divine life,
       come close to me as father and brother.
       And even more. You yourself have come to dwell in me,
       so it is your love within me reaching out to your love beyond me.
       O God beyond me, God beside me, God within me!

Richard Harries

863   Mysterious, threefold God,
       visit my heart
       and there find a welcome
       as Maker,
       Mender
       and Builder.
       Come, my Source,
          my Saviour,
          my Comforter;
       take me up into the movement of love
       which flows in your timeless unity,
       threefold God,
       Father,
       Son
       and Spirit.

A.A.

864   I bind unto myself the name,
       The strong name of the Trinity,
       By invocation of the same,
       The Three in One, and One in Three,
       Of whom all nature hath creation,
       Eternal Father, Spirit, Word.
       Praise to the Lord of my salvation:
       Salvation is of Christ the Lord.

*From 'St Patrick's Breastplate', translated by
Mrs C. F. Alexander (1818–95)*

865   O God our mystery,
      you bring us to life,
      call us to freedom,
      and move between us with love.
      May we so participate
      in the dance of your trinity,
      that our lives may resonate with you,
      now and for ever.

                              Janet Morley

866   You are holy, God the Creator, giving us richly all things to enjoy.
      You are holy, Christ the Saviour of the world, made flesh to set
      us free. You are holy, Spirit of truth and love, willing to dwell
      in us. You are holy and blessed, O God, eternal Trinity, and we
      worship you.

           The Service Book of The United Reformed Church

867   Holy, holy, holy God,
      Holy and strong,
      Holy and immortal,
      have mercy on us and hear us.

          Great Vespers of Pentecost in the Byzantine Rite

868   Holy, holy, holy God,
      we pray as pilgrims in your temple,
      dancing in the mystery of your encircling love,
      and finding everywhere is holy ground.
      We pray for your Church;
      may the mystery of the Trinity be unfolded in our life together
      like a flower in the desert,
      that we may be enfolded in your one love.

                              Graham Keyes

869   God, we praise you,
      Father all-powerful, Christ, Lord and Saviour, Spirit of Love,
      drawing us to share in your life and your love.
      One God, three Persons,

be near to the people formed in your image,
close to the world your love brings to life.
We ask you this, Father, Son and Holy Spirit,
one God, true and living, for ever and ever.

The Liturgy of the Hours

870   Come, ye people, let us adore God in three persons:
the Father in the Son, with the Holy Spirit.
For the Father from everlasting begets the Word,
and the Holy Spirit is in the Father,
glorified with the Son,
a single power,
a single essence,
a single godhead.
Come, let us adore.

Great Vespers of Pentecost in the Byzantine Rite

871   Father, you enfold us with wings of love, as a bird protects her
       young.
In our sin we have spurned your love.
Lord, have mercy.
Lord, have mercy.

Jesus, you gather us around you that we may learn your ways.
In our sin we have strayed from your presence.
Christ, have mercy.
Christ, have mercy.

Holy Spirit, you feed us with the seed of your holy word:
In our sin we have chosen the chaff.
Lord, have mercy.
Lord, have mercy.

John Townend

872   Glory to the Father,
through the Son,
in the Holy Spirit,
now and for ever, and unto ages of ages.

from an ancient form of the Gloria

873   Holy God, who didst create all by thy Son with the aid of the
       Spirit;
      Holy and Strong, word of the Father, by whom the Spirit has
       come into the world;
      Holy and Immortal, Spirit of Consolation, proceeding from the
       Father and dwelling in the Son:
      Glory be to thee, O Holy Trinity!
         Great Vespers of Pentecost in the Byzantine Rite

BLESSINGS BASED ON THE TRINITY

874   The weaving of peace be thine
      Peace around thy soul entwine
      Peace of the Father flowing free
      Peace of the Son sitting over thee
      Peace of the Spirit for thee and me
      Peace of the one
      Peace of the Three
      A weaving of peace be upon thee

      Around thee twine the Three
      The One the Trinity
      The Father bind his love
      The Son tie his salvation
      The Spirit wrap his power
      Make you a new creation
      Around thee twine the Three
      The encircling of the Trinity.
         David Adam

875   May the Binding One unite you,
      May the One Belov'd invite you,
      May the Loving One delight you,
        Three-in-One, joy in life unending.
         Brian A. Wren

Harvest and Our Responsibility for Creation

The earth is the Lord's and all the good things in it; the whole world, and those who live in it.

PSALM 24:1

ᴄᴏ⊙ᴏᴗ

See also:
Prayers of thanksgiving for Creation are in Praise for Creation, 207–22

876 Lord, bless our farmers and all who work on the land; strengthen them when they are discouraged, and help us all to work together as good stewards of this earth, its crops and its creatures; for your love's sake.

A.A.

877 In a world whose web of life is intricate and beautiful,
  save us, Lord, from carelessness and blindness.
In a world whose creatures are so varied and vulnerable,
  save us, Lord, from plundering and cruelty.
In a world whose waters are fresh and whose oceans should cleanse,
  save us, Lord, from wanton polluting.
In a world whose forests protect our air and wild-life,
  save us, Lord, from the systems that drive us to destroy them.
In a world whose fruits are rich and plentiful,
  save us, Lord, from waste and greed.

A.A.

878 Lord, your works are wonderful,
  in wisdom you have made them all.
Forgive us for the madness that abuses the earth
  for short-term ends,

and give us the wisdom,
  to cherish and share
  with daring and delight
the abundant gifts of our fragile planet.

A.A.

879 O God,
you have made us creatures of this earth,
hungry and thirsty and needy,
that you might satisfy all our longings
with your abundant love.

Satisfy the hunger of our bodies
for food and shelter, health and human touch.
Satisfy the hunger of our spirits
for dignity and freedom
in giving and receiving.
Satisfy the hunger of our minds
to understand our world,
the reasons for its pain,
the ways we are connected to each other.
Satisfy the hunger of our hearts
that all who share this loving earth with us
shall share our satisfaction.
And satisfy the hunger of our hands
to help you make it so
through Jesus Christ.

Janet Morley

880 We have faith in One God, one Source of all life,
one Ground of the whole earth, with all her creatures.
(pause)
And thus we have faith in the goodness of earth's life,
in the innate worth of all her dependants,
in human partnership in the life of nature.
(pause)
And we have faith that in Christ we have been shown
the special role of the human race

to bear God's likeness
in working and caring for the earth,
in seeking to understand her mysteries and powers,
in gently working with these powers
for the well-being of all children of the earth.
(pause)
And we have faith that God's Spirit will lead us
to sensitive closeness with earth's life,
to that meek, unselfish and compassionate life-style
by which the earth is inherited in peace,
by which her life is transformed
for all creatures to share justly in her bounty.
So be it, Amen.

Worship in an Indian Context

CONFESSIONS FOR HARVEST

881   Lord, we acknowledge our past indifference
and exploitation of your world
including people and animals,
plants and habitats.
We commit ourselves to live sustainably
sharing earth's gifts in the future.
We ask your assistance that we may recognize
that we are not above your creation
but members of a diverse created community
with special responsibility to love and let be.

Edward P. Echlin

882   O God of justice and plenty,
whose generous earth was created
for its own particular beauty,
for the nourishment of its people,
and to sing of your glory:
we confess that through our sinfulness
we have harvested injustice and pollution,

and not your abundance;
the land has become strange to us,
and our songs of celebration have turned harsh.

We turn to you, O God.
We renounce evil.
We seek your forgiveness.
We choose to be made whole.

Janet Morley

883   O God, your fertile earth is slowly being stripped of its riches,
Open our eyes to see.

O God, your living waters are slowly being choked with
chemicals,·
Open our eyes to see.

O God, your clear air is slowly being filled with pollutants,
Open our eyes to see.

O God, your creatures are slowly dying and your people are
suffering,
Open our eyes to see.

God our Maker, so move us by the wonder of creation,
That we repent and care more deeply.

So move us to grieve the loss of life,
That we learn to cherish and protect your world.

Ali Newell

INTERCESSIONS FOR HARVEST

884   God of love,
we thank you for your gifts in creation:
for our world,
and the heavens which tell of your glory;
for our land, its beauty and its resources,
and for the rich heritage we enjoy.

We pray:
for those who make decisions about the resources of the earth,
that we may all use your gifts responsibly;

for those who work on the land and sea,
in city and in industry,
that we may enjoy the fruits of their labours
and marvel at your creation;
for artists, scientists and visionaries,
that through their work we may see creation afresh.

We thank you for giving us life,
and for all who enrich our experience.
We pray:
for all who, through their own or others' actions,
are deprived of fullness of life:
for prisoners, refugees, the handicapped,
and those without enough to eat.
We pray:
for the sick and disabled,
and those who look after them.

We pray:
for those in politics, medical science, social and relief work,
and for your Church,
as we seek to bring life to others.

Thank you that you have called us to celebrate your creation.
Give us reverence for life in your world.
Thank you for your redeeming love;
may your word and sacrament
strengthen us to love as you love us.

God, Creator, bring us new life.
Jesus, Redeemer, renew us.
Holy Spirit, strengthen and guide us.
            A New Zealand Prayer Book *(adapted)*

885   Let us pray for all who speak up for tomorrow's world:
      who speak out for the earth's forests and their people;
      who plant trees again to renew the soil;
      who seek to share the land with those
      who need it.

Blest are those who believe
God's word will be fulfilled.

Let us pray for those
who plant and harvest in hope,
in spite of daily danger;
who speak out against military harassment;
who put tools into the hands of the poor.

Blest are those who believe
God's word will be fulfilled.

Let us pray for those
who protest against intolerable working conditions;
who acknowledge our debt to the poor;
who refuse to eat the fruits of oppression.

Blest are those who believe
God's word will be fulfilled.

Let us pray for those
who are willing to question
the sources of our wealth;
who want compassion in the market as well as in the home;
who do not choose to compete with the
poor for a share in tomorrow's world,
but long for reconciliation.

Blest are those who believe
God's word will be fulfilled.

Janet Morley

886 O God our creator,
whose good earth is entrusted
to our care and delight and tenderness,
we pray:

For all who are in captivity to debt,
whose lives are cramped by fear
from which there is no turning
except through abundant harvest.

May those who sow in tears
reap with shouts of joy.

For all who depend on the earth
for their daily food and fuel,
whose forests are destroyed
for the profits of a few.

May those who sow in tears
reap with shouts of joy.

For all who labour in poverty,
who are oppressed by unjust laws,
who are banned for speaking the truth,
who long for a harvest of justice.

May those who sow in tears
reap with shouts of joy.

For all who are in captivity
to greed and waste and boredom,
whose harvest joy is choked
with things they do not need.

May those who sow in tears
reap with shouts of joy.

Turn us again from our captivity
and restore our vision,
that our mouth may be filled with laughter
and our tongue with singing.

Janet Morley

BLESSINGS FOR HARVEST

887   May God who clothes the lilies and feeds the birds of the sky,
who leads the lambs to pasture and the deer to water,
who multiplied loaves and fishes and changed water into wine,
lead us, feed us, multiply us,
and change us to reflect the glory of our Creator
through all eternity.

Trevor Lloyd

REMEMBRANCE DAY / VETERANS DAY

The Lord makes wars to cease in all the world; he breaks the bow and shatters the spear in sunder.

PSALM 46:9

❧ ❧

888   Lord, as we remember with sadness the horror of war,
      help us to work for a better understanding
      between races and nations.
      Open our eyes to see our own part
      in discord and aggression between people now;
      forgive us our pride and divisions,
      and renew in us the search for peace,
      so that trust may replace suspicion,
      friendship replace fear,
      and your spirit of reconciliation be known among us.

A.A.

889   We remember today, O Lord,
      all those who have died in any kind of war:
      soldiers who perished in the horror of battle,
      householders buried beneath the rubble,
      men, women and children hacked to death in their villages.

      Today we remember especially the victims of the two world wars,
      including those who were close to us,
      or to our parents or grandparents.

      We also remember those who came home with terrible injuries,
      those who became mentally ill through the trauma of war,
      and those who lost someone they loved.

Have mercy on us, Lord,
for all the damage done to people by people in war,
and strengthen those who are striving to bring peace in our
    world now.

A.A.

890   Lord, you will keep in perfect peace
       those whose minds are set upon you;
   guide us in the way of your judgements
       as we wait upon you,
       for you will give us peace;
   even if earthly rulers try to lord it over us,
   we will acknowledge your name alone.

based on Isaiah 26:3, 8, 12–13

891   Lord, we remember those who died when madness ruled the
world and evil dwelt on earth, those we knew and those whose
very name is lost. Because of their sacrifice, may we renew our
fight against cruelty and injustice, against prejudice, tyranny, and
oppression. Still we cry to God out of the darkness of our divided
world. Let not the hope of men and women perish. Let not new
clouds rain death upon the earth. Turn to yourself the hearts and
wills of rulers and peoples, that a new world may arise where
men and women live as friends in the bond of your peace.

Jim Cotter

892   Grant, O Lord, for the sake of those whose lives were lost in
war, and for the sake of the generation to come, that the nations
of the world may learn your way of peace; and that all may have
a chance to enjoy the life you have given them, free from war,
tyranny and oppression.

Roger Tomes

SAINTS AND ANGELS

And the twenty-four elders fell down before the lamb, and
with golden bowls of incense, which are the prayers of the
saints, they sang, Worthy are you, our Lord and God, to
receive glory, honour and blessing.
REVELATION 4:10–11; 5:8

৵৹ ৹৵

893   We remember and praise you
       For the saints and martyrs of this and every age,
       Whose lives, like seeds, dropped to the ground,
       Yet whose witness has inspired us and borne fruit.
              John L. Bell (extract from a longer prayer)

894   Lord, we thank you for your saints,
       and ask for grace to follow them:
       make us open like Mary your mother,
       and bold like Paul;
       joyful like Francis,
       and faithful like Clare.
       Help us to reflect
       Mary Magdalene's great love for you,
       John the Evangelist's understanding of you,
       and Peter's steadfast devotion to you;
            and, when we feel we have failed you,
            remind us that all your saints
            knew they were sinners in need of your mercy;
            for your love's sake.
                              A.A.

895   Eternal God,
       you have always taken men and women
       of every nation, age and colour

and made them saints;
like them, transformed,
like them, baptized in Jesus' name,
take us to share your glory.
A New Zealand Prayer Book

896 Father, today we rejoice in the holy men and women of every time
and place. May we who aspire to have a part in their lives be filled
with the Spirit that blessed them, so that, having shared their faith
on earth, we may also know their peace in your kingdom.
The Roman Missal *(adapted)*

897 We thank you, O God, for the saints of all ages; for those who,
in times of darkness, kept the lamp of faith burning; for the great
souls who saw visions of larger truth and dared to declare it; for
the multitude of quiet and gracious souls whose presence has
purified and sanctified the world; and for those we knew and
loved, who have passed from this earthly fellowship into the
fuller light of life with you.
Anon.

898 Let us pray
that like St . . .
we may be loyal to our faith in Christ.
May our lives bear witness
to the faith we profess,
and our love bring others
to the peace and joy of your gospel.
The Roman Missal

899 For all the saints
who went before us
who have spoken to our hearts
and touched us with your fire,
we praise you, O God.

For all the saints
   who live beside us
   whose weaknesses and strengths
   are woven with our own,
   we praise you, O God.

For all the saints
   who live beyond us
   who challenge us
   to change the world with them,
   we praise you, O God.

Janet Morley

900   O Christ,
   your call draws us but never ensnares us;
   show us what it means
   to leave self behind
   and follow you all our days.
   Teach us to trust you enough
   to give you everything
   as raw material for your work
   of healing and reconciliation in the world;
   for your love's sake.

A.A.

MARTYRS

901   Lord, give us grace to follow the example of your martyrs,
   in a spirit of joy and not of self-righteousness;
   may our lives be ruled,
   not by fear of what anyone can do to us,
   but by delight in your will,
   trust in your presence
   and freedom in your service.

A.A.

902 Almighty God,
     by whose grace and power your holy martyrs
     triumphed over suffering and were faithful unto death:
     strengthen us with your grace,
     that we may endure reproach and persecution,
     and faithfully bear witness to the name
     of Jesus Christ our Lord.
                    Celebrating Common Prayer *(adapted)*

903 ST PETER
     God of grace,
     your Church is built on Peter's faith;
     grant that we, like him, forgiven and restored,
     may overcome our weaknesses
     and serve you without wavering,
     now and for ever.
                    A New Zealand Prayer Book

904 God of mercy, we are as Peter;
     we lose our nerve
     and deny you in the time of trial.
     Calm our anxiety, heal our cowardice,
     take away our shame, and make us free.
                    A New Zealand Prayer Book

905 ST PAUL
     Convert us,
     Jesus the persecuted,
     as you converted Paul
     and sent him as apostle to the world.
     May our love, our prayers, our suffering
     carry your Gospel at whatever cost
     to all who wait to hear it.
                    A New Zealand Prayer Book

906 ST PAUL
All-perceiving Lover,
    sensing each disguise,
kindly you uncover
    bruised and aching eyes.
Wake us into wonder
    at your dawning day.
Halt us with your thunder
    on our stubborn way.

Brian A. Wren

And as they journeyed to Damascus, a dazzling light flashed from
heaven, and a voice said, 'Saul, Saul, why do you persecute me?' And
Saul arose, and could see nothing, until Ananias laid hands on him, and
he regained his sight, and was baptized. (from Acts 9:1–19)

907 ST MARK
We give thanks, O God, for your servant John Mark: for the
grace by which he triumphed over early failure, and for the inspiration by which he penned the story of the strong Son of God.

Teach us through his life and writings the secret of victorious
living, and deepen our faith in your redeeming love and power,
made known to us in Jesus Christ our Lord.

Frank Colquhoun

908 JULIAN OF NORWICH
Gentle God, ground of our beseeching,
you enfold us in goodness
and wrap us tenderly as in a garment;
we praise you for Julian
and her knowledge of your love.
God our Father, our Mother, our Spouse,
let love be our meaning
as it is yours,
and make us your bliss, your honour and crown,
in the love with which you loved us
before we were born.

A.A.

909 MARY THE MOTHER OF JESUS—HER VISITATION WITH ELIZABETH
Lord Jesus, grant us the double joy of Mary and Elizabeth: the
joy of carrying you in our hearts, and the joy of recognizing you
in the hearts of others, that out of joy may come praise, telling
out the greatness of God our Saviour.

Susan Williams

See also:
Prayers about Mary in the section on the Annunciation, 704–7

910 ST BARNABAS
Free us, Lord, from a spirit of cynicism
or the desire to condemn,
and make us, like Barnabas,
generous in our judgements,
bold in trusting others,
and loyal to our friends.
Fill us with your Spirit of peace,
that we may be a source of support and comfort
to all in need; for your love's sake.

A.A.

911 ST ALBAN, FIRST MARTYR OF BRITAIN
Father, by your grace St Alban gave himself up for his friend, and
was the first in Britain to shed his blood for Christ. May we,
after his example, endure all suffering for the love of you, and
seek you with all our hearts, for you alone are the source of life;
through Jesus Christ our Lord.

Roman Missal

912 ST JOHN THE BAPTIST
Who was this man,
wild and unkempt,
ascetic and outspoken?
Jesus, you knew him and loved him
and grieved at his death.
Unblock our ears

to the voice of your cousin:
refine our wills in your winnowing wind,
and help us, like John,
to bear witness to you,
for the coming of your kingdom
and the fire of your love.

A.A.

913 ST THOMAS
Christ our light,
like Thomas we want to see,
need to touch,
need to be sure before we believe.
When we don't know, help us to trust;
when we can't see, help us to keep on walking.

A New Zealand Prayer Book *(adapted)*

See also:
'Forgive us, Lord, when we want proofs'

914 ST BENEDICT
This prayer could be adapted to apply to any saint.
Almighty God,
by whose grace St Benedict,
kindled with the fire of your love,
became a burning and a shining light in the Church;
inflame us with the same spirit
of discipline and love,
that we may walk before you
as children of light;
through Jesus Christ our Lord, Amen.

The Alternative Service Book 1980

915 ST MARY MAGDALENE
Sweet is your friendship, Saviour Christ;
Mary you accepted,
Mary you drew to the foot of the cross,
Mary you met in the garden;

grant us a like redemption
that we may be healed
and serve you in the power of your risen life.
                    A New Zealand Prayer Book *(adapted)*

916   ST JAMES
       O God, we remember today your apostle James, first among the
       Twelve to suffer martyrdom for the name of Jesus; and we pray
       that you will give to the leaders of your Church that spirit of self-
       denying service which is the hallmark of true authority among
       your people; through Jesus Christ our Lord.
                    The Book of Common Prayer
              of the Episcopal Church, USA *(adapted)*

917   ST MATTHEW
       Lord, thank you
       for loving Matthew enough
       to believe in him
       and call him
       out of the chaos and corruption of tax-collecting
       into life with you.
       Open our eyes to see
       that you believe in us too,
       and give us grace to receive
       the freedom you offer
       when you say, 'Follow me.'
                    A.A.

918   ST FRANCIS
       Lord Jesus Christ,
       who when the world was growing cold,
       to the inflaming of our hearts by the fire of your love
       raised up blessèd Francis
       bearing in his body the marks of your passion:
       mercifully grant to us, your people, true penitence,
       and grace to bear the Cross for love of you;
       who live and reign with the Father and the Holy Spirit,
       one God, now and for ever.
                    Celebrating Common Prayer

919   ST LUKE
Healing God,
we thank you for Luke,
the 'beloved physician',
and for his faithful recording
of the life of your Son
and the birth of the Church.
Continue in us your work of healing:
may we never pass by on the other side,
but rather reach out to the poor and sick
and those on the margins,
in the love of Jesus our Lord.

A.A.

Colossians 4:14

920   ST ANDREW
Lord God,
whose servant Andrew told his brother
the good news of your Son,
and followed you without delay;
give us grace
to serve you with generous hearts,
and to proclaim you through our words and deeds;
through Jesus Christ, our Lord and Saviour.

A.A.

921   ST STEPHEN
For the courage of Stephen
    we thank you;
for the strength to stand up for what we believe
    we ask you.
For the courage of all who died for you,
    we thank you;
for the strength to stand firm when the crowd disagrees
    we ask you.
For the joy of your saints,
    we thank you;

for delight in the gift of each moment of life
we ask you.
Father of mercy,
bless our efforts to love you,
and help us, in spite of our uncertainties,
    to hear your call,
      follow your way,
    and surrender our lives into your hands.

A.A.

922   ST JOHN THE EVANGELIST
Shed upon your Church, O Lord, the brightness of your light,
that we, being illumined by the teaching of your apostle and
evangelist John, may walk in the light of your truth, and abide
in you for ever; through Jesus Christ our Lord.

The Book of Common Prayer
of the Episcopal Church, USA *(adapted)*

ANGELS

923   Everlasting God,
you have ordained in a wonderful order
the ministries of angels and mortals.
Grant that, as your holy angels always serve and worship you in
    heaven,
so they may help and defend us here on earth;
through Jesus Christ our Lord.

The Book of Common Prayer
of the Episcopal Church, USA *(abridged)*

924   Father in heaven, in all times of our testing and trial send your
angels to strengthen and support us, that the prince of darkness
may have no power over us; through Christ our Lord.

David Silk

925   Lord of all creation, an angel foretold your birth and the birth
      of many of your chosen servants: let us rejoice in the wonderful
      orders of angels.

      Angels announced your birth to the shepherds with great joy and
      praise: may our lips be always praising you.

      Angels ministered to you in your temptation and trial: be pres-
      ent, we pray, to all who are in trouble or oppression.

      Angels announced your resurrection to Mary Magdalen: fill us
      with the assurance of your risen power.

      Angels were present at your ascension into heaven: make us
      ready for your coming again in great glory.

                     John Michael Mountney

926   Blessèd Lord of angels and archangels,
      we praise you for the brightness of your love.
      Give your angels charge over us,
      to guard us against the powers of evil.
      May these beings of light
      encircle and protect us,
      so that we may serve you better
      and never lose our vision of your heavenly glory.

                          A.A.
                      Psalm 91:11

927   A BLESSING
      God keep you in the fellowship of his saints.
      Christ protect you by the ministry of the angels.
      The Spirit make you holy in God's service;
      and the blessing of God almighty,
      the Father, the Son and the Holy Spirit
      be upon you and remain with you always.

                     Michael Perham

part fifteen

SPECIAL OCCASIONS AND THEMES

BAPTISM

*Make disciples of all nations, baptizing them in the name of
the Father and of the Son and of the Holy Spirit.*
MATTHEW 28:19

ৎৎ ৩৩

928   Creator Spirit,
       who in the beginning hovered over the waters,
       who at Jesus' baptism descended in the form of a dove,
       and who at Pentecost was poured out under the signs of fire and
           wind:
       come to us, open our hearts and minds,
       so that we may hear the life-giving word and be renewed by your
           power,
       in the unity of the Father and the Son, now and for ever. Amen
                        Source unknown

929   God of water, Lord of life,
       we thank you for the moments in history
       which have pointed towards the mystery of baptism:
       your Spirit brooding over the waters of creation,
       bringing order out of the chaos;
       your people striding out of Egyptian slavery
       through the wind-blown passage in the Red Sea;
       and Jesus' baptism in the Jordan River,
       with the shock of the voice saying: 'You are my Son.'
       May we who are baptized already
       be renewed in our baptismal promises,
       in a spirit of love and trust;
       and may . . . your beloved child baptized today
       be blessed, and stay close to you
       now and always.
                        A.A.

930   The Lord is here
His Spirit is with us.

We need not fear
His Spirit is with us.

We are surrounded by love
His Spirit is with us.

We are immersed in peace
His Spirit is with us.

We abide in hope
His Spirit is with us.

We travel in faith
His Spirit is with us.

We live in Eternity
His Spirit is with us.

The Lord is here
His Spirit is with us.

David Adam

931   FOR GODPARENTS
Lord, we pray for all godparents; give them wisdom as they seek
to encourage those entrusted to them in the ways of generosity
and love, so that the children who are baptized may want to follow Jesus Christ, and freely choose to serve him.

A.A.

JESUS' BAPTISM

932   Beloved Son of God,
baptized by John,
we praise you
and marvel at your humility.
You are one with us in baptism:
take us with you into the kingdom.
You are one with us in humanity:

lead us into the love of the Father,
to whom be thanksgiving
now and always.

A.A.

933 O Christ, you humbled yourself and received baptism at the hands of your friend and cousin, John, showing us the way of humility;
help us to follow you, and never to be encumbered with pride.

O Christ, by your baptism, you took our humanity into the cleansing waters;
give us new birth, and lead us into life as sons and daughters of God.

O Christ, by your baptism the material world became charged with your holiness;
make us instruments of your transformation in this our world.

O Christ, by your baptism you revealed the Trinity, your Father calling you his beloved Son, and the Spirit descending upon you like a dove;
renew our worship, rededicate us in the spirit of our baptism, and mould us into our true nature, in the image of God.
For your love's sake.

after the Chaldean Rite

934 Servant-Christ, help us to follow you deep into the waters of baptism;
to link our lives with all those who grieve about the injustice in human life;
to break free from the chain of past wrongs;
to become ready to face your coming age;
and to be renewed by your Spirit,
and anointed to preach good news
to the poor, the oppressed and the prisoner.
Servant-Christ, help us all to follow you.

Worship in an Indian Context *(adapted)*

I will pay my vows to the Lord, in the presence of all his people; O Lord, I am your servant.

PSALM 116:14, 16A

935　Accept me, O Lord, just as I am, in my frailty, my inadequacy, my contradictions and my confusions.
Accept me, with all those discordant currents that pull me in so many directions.
Accept all of this, and help me so to live with what I am, that what I am may become my way to you.

> *based on the 'Suscipe me,' a prayer made by a novice on entering a Benedictine Community.*

936　Weave us, O Christ,
　　　into your people,
　　　and bless our belonging.
Hold us, O Christ,
　　　in your love,
　　　and bless our pledging.
Stay with us, O Christ,
　　　in darkness and doubt,
　　　and bless our trusting.
Fill us, O Christ,
　　　with your Holy Spirit,
　　　and bless our new beginning.

A.A.

937 Father, we dedicate ourselves to serve you faithfully and to
   follow Christ,
   to face the future with him, seeking his special purpose for our
   lives.
   Send us out now to work and to witness,
   freely, gratefully and hopefully, in the power of the Holy Spirit,
   and for the honour and glory of your Son, Jesus Christ our Lord.
                              Michael Perry

938 O Christ, bless these your servants
      who have opened their lives and hearts to you.
   By the power of your cross,
      protect them from evil.
   In the passion of your love,
      save them from half-heartedness.
   In the depth of your mercy,
      pick them up when they fall.
   Be close to them
      when they face difficulty and distress,
   and dance in their lives
      with your light and delight.
                              A.A.

939 In the Power of the Creator,
   In the Peace of the Redeemer,
   In the Presence of the Spirit,
   We welcome you.

   Three in your coming
   Three with you staying,
   Three until your going,
   We welcome you.

   In the Love of the Father,
   In the Joy of the Saviour,
   In the Strength of the Spirit,
   We welcome you.
                              David Adam

940   May the Maker's blessing be yours,
                    encircling you round,
                    above you
                    within you.

May the Angels' blessing be yours,
                    and the joy of the saints
                    to inspire you
                    to cherish you.

May the Son's blessing be yours,
                    the wine and the water,
                    the bread and the stories
                    to feed you
                    to remind you.
May the Spirit's blessing be yours,
                    the wind, the fire,
                    the still small voice
                    to comfort you
                    to disturb you.
And may our own blessing be yours,
                    a blessing rooted in our common pilgrimage,
                    the blessing of friends.
God bless you and cherish you
                    and keep you holy,
                    this day, this night,
                    this moment and for ever.
                              Ruth Burgess

THE EUCHARIST

For as often as you eat this bread and drink this cup, you proclaim the Lord's death until he comes.

1 CORINTHIANS 11:26

941   Jesus, I receive your love
      poured out for me
      in bread and wine.
      Accept this gift of my life,
      brought to the altar
      without conditions.
      Do your work in me,
      and let me be, like you,
      taken, blessed,
      and given for others;
      for, in spite of my sin,
      you know that I love you.

                                        A.A.

942   Lord, do not let the familiarity of the words in this service lull
      me into apathy about the cost of your love. Surprise me again
      with the power of your powerlessness, as I glimpse the sublime
      in the ordinary, the mystery in the meal.

                                        A.A.

943   Here, O my Lord, I see thee face to face;
      Here would I touch and handle things unseen;
      Here grasp with firmer hand the eternal grace,
      And all my weariness upon thee lean.

      Here would I feed upon the bread of God;
      Here drink with thee the royal wine of heaven;
      Here would I lay aside each earthly load,
      Here taste afresh the calm of sin forgiven.

                              Horatius Bonar (1808–1889)

944   Almighty God, let the Eucharist we share fill us with your life.
       May the love of Christ which we celebrate here
       touch our lives and lead us to you.
       The Roman Missal

945   As this bread was once scattered seed, O Lord of Life,
       sown in the earth to die and rise to new life,
       so gather all peoples together
       in the one humanity that is your purpose for us.
       Restore the broken life of your creation,
       heal the disfigured body of your world,
       and draw us all into yourself
       through your cross and in the power of your risen life.
       Worship in an Indian Context *(adapted)*

946   Most merciful Lord,
       your love compels us to come in.
       Our hands were unclean,
       our hearts were unprepared;
       we were not fit
       even to eat the crumbs from under your table.
       But you, Lord, are the God of our salvation,
       and share your bread with sinners.
       So cleanse and feed us
       with the precious body and blood of your Son,
       that he may live in us and we in him;
       and that we, with the whole company of Christ,
       may sit and eat in your kingdom.
       The Alternative Service Book 1980

947   Lord Jesus Christ, Living Bread:
           vulnerable as bread placed in the hand,
           to be accepted with joy or cast aside;
           satisfying as bread to the hungry,
           and giving life for the future;
           broken like bread that all may share,
           and as necessary as bread to sustain our living.
       You are for us our bread of life.

       Lord Jesus Christ, Living Wine:
           rich as the blood-red, sun-filled grape,

taken, pressed, and destroyed, to new-create;
welcome as the clean, fresh draught
from the host to the visitor
and refreshing the traveller on the weary journey;
poured out in love that all may share,
and gift to our thirst to meet our need.
You are for us our spiritual drink.

Donald Hilton

948   As bread is broken for the world
may we see the world's brokenness.

As we share bread with others,
may we share our time and our money.
Make us good stewards
of what we leave in our pockets,
as well as accountable for what we give.
In our common life,
may we remember the God of Creation,
the mothering, enfolding, naming God,
the God who never abandons us.

As wine is poured for the world
may we see the world's pain.

As we share the cup of suffering
with our neighbour,
may we also share our experience.
Make us good stewards of opportunity
to listen, to confront, to work
for healing, peace, and community.
In our common life,
may we remember the God of redemption,
the saving, salving, suffering God,
the God who never forgets us.

Thanks be to God,
whose broken hands
are inscribed with our names
and whose Spirit calls us to account.

Kate McIlhagga

AFTER COMMUNION

949   Lord Jesus Christ,
       though we have held and handled bread and wine,
       we can never confine or contain you;
       yet, in this sacrament, you are closer to us than our own thoughts.
       Fill us with your peace,
       and come into every corner of our complex lives,
       O Lord of love.

A.A.

950   Strengthen for service, Lord, the hands that have taken holy
          things;
       may the ears which have heard your word be deaf to clamour
          and dispute;
       may the tongues which have sung your praise be free from deceit;
       may the eyes which have seen the tokens of your love
       shine with the light of hope;
       and may the bodies which have been fed with your body
       be refreshed with the fullness of your life;
       glory to you for ever.

Malabar Liturgy

951   Generous God, you have fed us at your heavenly table.
       Kindle us with the fire of your Spirit
       that when Christ comes again we may shine like lights before his
          face;
       who with you and the Spirit lives for ever.

Westcott House (adapted)

952   O God, the Eternal Fullness and centre of light, we offer you
       thanks for your boundless kindness. You made us, who are
       weak, able to enjoy the sweetness of your words, and to share in
       the divine mysteries. Eternal praise be to you!

New Orders for the Mass for India (adapted)

ORDINATION OR COMMISSIONING TO MINISTRY IN THE CHURCH

May you be filled with the knowledge of God's will, in all spiritual wisdom and understanding, to lead a life worthy of the Lord, fully pleasing to him, bearing fruit in every good work, and increasing in the knowledge of God.

COLOSSIANS 1:9–10

953 O Lord my God, I am not worthy to have you come under my roof; yet you have called your servant to stand in your house, and to serve at your altar. To you and to your service I devote myself, body, soul, and spirit. Fill my memory with the record of your mighty works; enlighten my understanding with the light of your Holy Spirit; and may all the desires of my heart and will centre in what you would have me do.

The Book of Common Prayer of the Episcopal Church, USA

954 Dear, God, as we struggle to understand and use the power aright that you entrust to us, set before us again the way of Jesus, and work through us in your Spirit, that we may steward our power in ways that do not bind others but free them to take their share in the inheritance of life. May we grow not tall but humble.

Jim Cotter

955 Lord, may these your servants be men and women of peace, prayer, strength and gentleness. Make them transparent with your love, and always open to your grace, in which alone lies their hope and joy.

A.A.

956   Lord,
    you make your messengers winds
      and your ministers flames of fire;
    stir up and strengthen the gifts of grace
    in all stewards of your mysteries,
    that they may remove from your kingdom
      all that prevents its growth,
    and may kindle in the hearts of us all
      the fire which you came to send on earth;
    to the glory of your name.

after Henry Liddon
Psalm 104:4

957   Holy Spirit, equip . . . to be a steward (or stewards) of the mysteries of word and sacraments–the signs of your coming kingdom.
May *she* be sustained by the heartbeat of praise and Eucharist offered at *(this church)*, with . . . *(other clergy or leaders)*, serving and leading the Christian community here.
May *she* search with others for the holiness of the God who lives in the ordinary and childlike.

(a short period of silence)

May *her* ministry be nourished by solitude, silence and simplicity, as well as by creativity and action.
May *she* dare to stray to the margins of the life of the Church and the world, discovering new images and symbols in your wilderness.
May *she* continue to be enriched by the love, support and understanding of family and friends *(names could be mentioned here)*, as they work out priorities for ministry together.

(a short period of silence)

Come, Holy Spirit, breathe into *her* the comfort and stability of your presence; baptize her(him) into the vulnerability of the crucified Christ;

and immerse *her* into the giving and receiving of love, as *she* ministers the sacrifices of the wounded Christ.

(a short period of silence)

In worship, in study, in listening and caring, in laughter and tears and at prayer, may *she* live the mysteries of God, for *her* people's sake.

Graham Keyes

The short silences in this sequence are important, to create spaces around the words and enable people to enter more deeply into the prayers. This works best either if the congregation is warned just before the prayers that there will be short periods of silence or if they have the full text in front of them.
It can also be effective to have music played in the background, e.g., a simple tune on a solo instrument. On the occasion when this prayer was first used (see Note), the song 'As the Deer Pants for the Water' (by Martin Nystrom) was played on an oboe.
For a non-sacramental ministry the following version of the first two paragraphs of the above may be more appropriate:

957a Holy Spirit, equip . . . to be a steward (or stewards) of the mysteries of word, worship and service – the signs of your coming kingdom.
May *she* be sustained by the heartbeat of praise and prayer offered at *(this church)*, with . . . *(other clergy or leaders)*, serving and leading the Christian community here.

I was glad when they said to me, 'Let us go to the house of the Lord!'

PSALM 122:1

🙟 🙝

958 How lovely is your dwelling-place,
         O Lord of hosts!
     My soul desires and longs
         to enter the courts of the Lord.
     My heart and my flesh sing joyfully
         to the living God.
     Happy are those who dwell in your house;
         they will sing your praises for ever.
                    Psalm 84:1–2, 4

959 O God, make the door of this church wide enough
             to receive all who need human love and fellowship,
             but narrow enough to shut out all envy, pride and strife.
     Make its threshold smooth enough to be no stumbling-block to
             children,
             nor to straying feet, but strong enough
             to turn back the tempter's power.
     God, make the door of this church
             a gateway to your eternal kingdom.
                    Thomas Ken (1637–1711) (adapted)

960　Living God:
　　　in this building, used to the sound of singing;
　　　this building which has seen baptisms and funerals;
　　　this building where people have come to be married,
　　　or to celebrate the birth of a child;
　　　this building where people have wept, and been filled with joy;
　　　this building where people have wrestled with the deep things
　　　　　of life,
　　　have prayed urgently, been stirred and changed;
　　　in this building where you have so often been with your people,
　　　be with us now.

　　　　　　　　Patterns and Prayers for Christian Worship

OPENING AND CLOSING A MEETING

Jesus said, 'When two or three are gathered together in my name, I am there in the midst of them.'
MATTHEW 18:20

෴ ෴

961 Lord Jesus, help us to put aside all the cares which separate us from you. Calm our minds and fill us with the knowledge that you are present with us. So enrich our meeting that we may grow in fellowship with one another as members of your family.
The Mother's Union Prayer Book

962 *This prayer needs to be followed by a few moments of silence, after warning people that this will be the case.*

Go deep, Lord,
to the point beneath our thinking, discussing and planning,
so that, in the stillness beneath all words
we may open our hearts to you,
and be soaked in your love,
from which all wisdom springs.
Go deep, Lord,
as we remain quiet before you,
and offer our gathering to you.
A.A.

963 Let us ask for God's blessing on this committee, especially for vision to see the purpose of God in our work, and for wisdom, strength and courage to carry it out.
The Mother's Union Service Book

964 O Holy Spirit, be with us in this time of prayer and grant us living touch with you. Give us an insight of your kingdom, a vision
of your purpose, the guidance of your wisdom, and grace to be
fellow workers with you in doing your just and loving will;
through Jesus Christ, our Lord.

The Mother's Union Service Book

965 Creator of rainbows,
come through the closed doors
of our emotions, mind and imagination;
come alongside us as we walk,
come to us at work and worship,
come to our meetings and councils,
come and call us by name,
call us to pilgrimage.

Kate McIlhagga

966 May the grace of joy be ours;
May the grace of peace be ours;
May the grace of patience be ours;
May the grace of kindness be ours;
May the grace of goodness be ours;
May the grace of faithfulness be ours;
May the grace of love be ours;
May the grace of love be ours.

Holy Spirit of sevenfold power,
Pour out on us your light.
Each day, every day,
Keep us faithful and true.

W. Mary Calvert

BIRTH, ADOPTION AND FOSTERING

Children are a heritage from the Lord, and the fruit of the womb is his gift.

PSALM 127:3

ᛌᵒ ᵒᛌ

967   FOR A WOMAN WHO WILL SOON GIVE BIRTH
God of love,
bless our friend who will soon be giving birth;
hold her in the pain,
strengthen her in the weariness,
breathe in her,
labour in her,
and bring forth through her this child
whom we await with loving anticipation.

A.A.

968   Heavenly Father, creator and giver of life, there is such joy in our hearts at the news of a baby's birth, a most special and complete gift from God, a new being and a wonder of creation. Be with the mother and father of ... in their happiness and their praise to you, our Lord and Creator.

The Mothers' Union Prayer Book *(adapted)*

969   We praise you, Lord, for this most precious gift of a child;
may God the Father, guard her,
may God the Son, guide her;
may God the Holy Spirit fill her
with gentleness and peace
all the days of her life.

A.A.

970   O God, the presence of a child among us fills us with joy and
      awe. Help us to make our world a welcoming place for all
      children–free from fear of war, hunger, violence and all forms of
      abuse. May this child know you through those of us who love
      her/him, and may she/he grow in wisdom, age and grace all the
      days of her/his life. We ask this in the name of Jesus, who invited
      all children to come to him.
                    The Woman's Prayer Companion

971   Into your hands, O God, we place your child. . . . Support
      her(him) in her(his) successes and in her(his) failures, in her(his)
      joys and in her(his) sorrows. As (s)he grows in age, may (s)he
      grow in grace, and in the knowledge of her Saviour Jesus Christ.
      The Book of Common Prayer of the Episcopal Church, USA

972   PRAYER OF PARENTS
      Parents of the child may say together:
      God our Creator,
      thank you for the waiting and the joy,
      thank you for new life and for parenthood,
      thank you for the gift of . . .
      entrusted to our care.
      May we be patient and understanding,
      ready to guide and forgive,
      that in our love . . . may know your love.
      May (s)he learn to love your world
      and the whole family of your children;
      through Christ our life.
                    A New Zealand Prayer Book

973   THE BIRTH OF A CHILD WITH A DISABILITY
      Thank you, Heavenly Father, for the precious gift of . . . .
          We pray for all children who are handicapped in any way. We
      know that they will love us, as we are, with our many weak-
      nesses, just as you love us.
          Give to *(. . . the parents)* strength, courage, wisdom and love
      to care for . . . , so that *he* may become as independent as possible.

We thank you for entrusting *him* to loving parents. May the
love they show to *him* be a shining light in this troubled world,
to bring healing and wholeness to us all. And help us to learn
from them what it means to love.

Janet Owen (adapted)

ADOPTION AND FOSTERING

974   Lord, thank you that ... has been chosen to be part of ... and
...'s family.
Bless *her,* and *her* new parents.
May they grow together in love, laughter, learning and sharing,
so that the world may be enriched
by their openness to others,
and their delight in living.

A.A.

975   Lord bless us as we receive *this child* into our family with
thanksgiving and joy.
Through the love of God we receive *him;*
with the love of God we will care for *him;*
by the love of God we will guide *him;*
and in the love of God may we all abide for ever.

The Alternative Service Book 1980 *(adapted)*

976   Lord Jesus, you took a little child in your arms and said, 'Anyone
who welcomes a little child in my name is welcoming me, and
anyone who welcomes me is welcoming my Father who sent me.'
Help us to welcome our foster-children in your name,
and to love and care for them.
Help us to give them something of you,
and to give them back to you every day.

Winifred Wilson

BLESSING FOR PARENTS

977   May the Lord bless you all the days of your life;
       may you see your children's children,
       and in your home and country let there be peace.

based on Psalm 128:5–6

BIRTHDAYS

You have created my inward parts: you knit me together in my mother's womb; You knew my soul, and my bones were not hidden from you when I was formed in secret. How deep are your thoughts to me, O God.

PSALM 139:13, 15, 17

978   Which day is your birthday, God?
      How do you celebrate it?
      You are the maker
      You are the one who births everything that lives.
      For you the candled cake would outshine the Northern Lights
      The fireworks would wake the living and the dead.

      Thank you for my birthday, God.
      Thank you that you are part of it
      As you were from my beginning
      And will be when I meet you face to face.

      Today is the day you have made.
      Today I remember your making of me.
      Today I give thanks to my maker and rejoice.
                                          Ruth Burgess

979   O God I thank you for giving me another year of life.
      I thank you for all the people who have remembered me today,
          and who have sent me cards, and letters, good wishes, and
          presents.

      I thank you for everything I have been enabled to do and to be
          in the past year.

      I thank you for all the experiences of the past year;
          For times of success which will always be happy memories;

For times of failure which reminded me of my own weakness
    and of my need of you;
For times of joy when the sun was shining;
For times of sorrow which drove me to you.

Forgive me
    For the hours I have wasted;
    For the chances I failed to take;
    For the opportunities I missed in the past year.

Forgive me that I have not made of life all that I might have
made of it and could have made of it; and help me in the days
which lie ahead to make this the best year yet, and in it to bring
credit to myself, happiness to my loved ones, and joy to you.

This I ask for Jesus' sake.
        William Barclay (1907–1978)

980   *This prayer would be suitable at any celebration:*
Party Giving God
fill us with the joy
of happy children
who know that
your hug of welcome
always awaits us when
we knock at your door.
        Ruth Burgess

EXAMINATIONS

Lord, you have shown your servant much kindness, fulfilling
your word; Give me insight and good judgment, for I trust in
your commandments.

PSALM 119:65–6

ശൈ ை

981   Lord, guide and help me through these exams, so that I may do
      justice to all I have learned. Help me, and all of us doing exams,
      to keep their importance in perspective.

      Nick Aiken

982   Lord, we need your help.
      We need a calm mind; grant us your peace.
      We need a clear head; grant us your wisdom.
      We need a careful spirit; grant us your patience.
      We need inspiration; grant us your enthusiasm.
      Keep us from all panic
      as we put our trust in your power to help and keep us this day.

      Kathleen A. Goodacre

GROWING OLD

Forsake me not, O God, in my old age, when I am grey-headed,
that I may tell future generations of your strength and might.
PSALM 71:18

⁓ ⁓

983 Lord, you know better than I know myself that I am growing older, and will some day be old. Keep me from getting talkative, and particularly from the fatal habit of thinking that I must say something on every subject and on every occasion. Release me from craving to straighten out everybody's affairs.

Keep my mind from the recital of endless details – give me wings to come to the point. Seal my lips on my own aches and pains – they are increasing, and my love of rehearsing them is becoming sweeter as the years go by. Help me listen to other people's tales of woe with patience.

Teach me the glorious lesson that occasionally I may be mistaken. Keep me reasonably sweet. I do not want to be a saint – some of them are so hard to live with – but a sour old woman is one of the crowning works of the devil.

Make me thoughtful, but not moody; helpful, but not bossy. With my vast store of wisdom it seems a pity not to use it all, but you know, Lord, that I want a few friends at the end.

based on a prayer by a Mother Superior of the seventeenth century

984 O God, we thank you for the gift of years; for the opportunity to see the pattern of our lives and to have experienced the deaths from which we have risen over and over again. As we continue our journey, give us lightness of step and lightness of heart that we may grace our world with a spirit of joy and gratitude. We ask this in the name of Jesus who has gone before and continues to walk the way with us.

The Woman's Prayer Companion

985   O God, when we experience limitation in our physical abilities,
             – increase our inner vitality and give us a youthful spirit.
       When tiredness and fatigue overcome us,
                 – mellow our tendency to be short-tempered and enable us
                 to respond to others graciously.
       As we grow more comfortable with the familiar,
                 – give us a spirit of adventure and keep us open to the new
                 and creative.
       As each year passes,
                 – fill our hearts with gratitude for the journey that has gone
                 before
       and the journey yet to come.
                         The Woman's Prayer Companion

986   FACING RETIREMENT
       Lord, as we go forward to retirement
       we thank you for the blessings of past years.
       Help us to adjust to our different lifestyle;
       to grasp the new opportunities given,
       remembering the needs of others;
       to use our leisure creatively,
       and in the newfound joy of time together,
       may we continue in your love and service.
                         Margaret Wilson

987   In the floodtide of the day, be with us;
       In the ebbtide of the day, be with us;
       Be with us all the day.
       In the floodtide of our life, be with us;
       In the ebbtide of our life, be with us;
       Be with us alway;
       Be with us alway.
                         W. Mary Calvert

part sixteen

PRAYERS FOR USE BY CHILDREN AND YOUNG PEOPLE

CHILDREN

When the chief priests and scribes saw the wonderful things
he did, and the children crying out in the temple, Hosanna to
the Son of David, they were indignant; and Jesus said to them,
Have you never read, Out of the mouths of children and babes
at the breast you have called forth praise?

MATTHEW 21:15–16

988   Dear God, thank you for a lovely day
      and my friends and family.
      Sorry for the wrong things I have done.
      You have given us a beautiful world to live in,
      and trusted us to take care of it.
      Sometimes we don't treat it very well.
      Please show us how.
      Please guard me for ever,
      and please give me sweet dreams.

John Livesley (age 9)

989   Almighty God,
      help us never to pass by on the other side
      but always to be ready to help,
      through Jesus Christ our Lord.

Growing in Faith, *ASB Year 1*

990   Jesus, friend of sinners,
      who called Levi to follow you,
      call me too;
      and grant that I may stay near you
      forever.

Growing in Faith, *ASB Year 1*

991   Almighty Father,
       help us to know how much you love us,
       so that we may never be afraid
       to come home to you
           when we have done wrong.

                              Growing in Faith, ASB Year 1

992   ADVENT
       Lord Jesus,
       Lord of the angels,
       help us to prepare ourselves
       to greet the God of all
       at Christmas.

                              Growing in Faith, ASB Year 1

993   CHRISTMAS
       Lord Jesus,
       as the angels sing
       and the shepherds run,
       and the innkeeper is busy
       and the wise men are travelling,
       we too are excited,
       preparing for your birth.
       Thank you for all that Christmas brings,
       in church services,
       parties, presents and fun.

                                                A.A.

994   GOOD FRIDAY
       Jesus our Brother,
       thank you for loving us so much
       that you died for us,
       lonely and in pain;
       and thank you that you are close to us
       when we are hurt or miserable,
       for you are our Friend.

                                                A.A.

995 EASTER

Alleluia! He is risen!
Alleluia! He is light!
Alleluia! He is joy!
Alleluia! He is strength!
Alleluia! He is love!
Alleluia! Jesus!

A.A.

996 PENTECOST

Holy Spirit,
you are like a strong wind –
blow away our selfishness.
You are like fire –
burn up our sins,
and make us warm-hearted.
You are like a gentle dove –
help us to be peace-makers.

A.A.

997 HARVEST/CREATION

For shelves full of food,
    thank you, Lord.
For the colour of chocolate, carrots and cherries,
    thank you, Lord.
For the feel of wood, bedclothes and cats' fur,
    thank you, Lord.
For sunshine and snowflakes,
roses and oak trees,
the songs of the birds
and the waves of the sea,
    thank you, Lord.

A.A.

998   A BEDTIME PRAYER

May the peace of Jesus fill me,
the love of Jesus surround me,
and the presence of Jesus guard me,
now as I sleep, and all my life.

*The above prayer can be used as a blessing in the following way,
perhaps placing a hand on the child's head:*

May the peace of Jesus fill you,
the love of Jesus surround you,
and the presence of Jesus guard you,
now as you sleep, and all your life.

A.A.

TEENAGERS

Young men and maidens together, praise the name of the Lord!
PSALM 148:12, 13

999   Father, when I am lost and lose sight of you,
        when I forget my prayers
        and I'm swept away with life and all its difficulties,
        when I cannot answer my friends' questions about my faith
        even though I know the answer,
        when I'm too busy,
        and, like homework I cannot do,
        you get shoved to the bottom of the pile,
        remind me that all I have to do is to STOP!!
        For I know that you will find me
        and will meet me wherever I am.

                              Nick Aiken

1000   Lord, the future stretches before me
        like a long dark tunnel,
        leading into the unknown.
        After my exams,
        will I get to university?
        Or will I begin the endless search
        for a job?
        Will I make enough money?

        Lord, my future is in your hands.
        Help me to look honestly
        at my own ability
        and to know if I have the right skills
        for the jobs that attract me.
        Lord, hear my prayer.
        My future belongs to you.

                        written by young people in Kenya

1001 They say we can destroy the world
       twenty times over with nuclear bombs –
       it's probably more by now.
       I see those pictures of the mushroom cloud
       and I shiver –
       the world is too beautiful for that,
       people are too beautiful.
       Father, it's so wrong – and so frightening.

       Jesus told us to love our enemies –
       I don't think you can love your enemies with a bomb.
       It's such a mess but somehow, somewhere
       we have to turn round and really say:
       'We want to live in peace together.'

       So send your Spirit to remind our leaders
       how beautiful things are,
       how beautiful their 'enemies' are,
       to remind them to keep telling themselves:
       'We want to live in peace together.'

                                    Simon Bailey

1002 Lord, I know I've done things wrong.
       I don't want to admit to it;
       neither to my friends nor family nor you.
       Lord, it's hard to live with myself.
       I want to ask for your forgiveness
       but I feel I don't deserve it.
       But thanks to you I know it's still there for the taking,
       so I ask that I may be given a fresh start
       and be directed again on the right path.

                                    Nick Aiken

1003 It's strange, but I feel as if
I can stop talking to you
and simply be with you.

I want to be quite empty,
quite still,
and then you can come
slowly, gently,
filling me with yourself.
Come then, now –
the words end here.

Simon Bailey

INDEX OF FIRST LINES

INDEX OF AUTHORS

INDEX OF THEMES

NOTES AND ACKNOWLEDGEMENTS

13   Ateliers et Presses de Taizé, 71250 Taizé-Communauté, France.
14   *All Desires Known*, SPCK (1992).
15   *Tides and Seasons* © (1989). Used by permission of The Society for Promoting Christian Knowledge.
21   Also in *Touching the Pulse: Worship and Where we live*, Ed. Sandy Williams, Stainer & Bell, 1995.
26   Based on words in *Conferences Book X*.
34   *Prayer Is My Life* Copyright © 1966 The United Society for the Propagation of the Gospel (USPG), London. Used with permission.
36   *Power Lines* © (1992). Used by permission of The Society for Promoting Christian Knowledge.
40   *The Edge of Glory* © (1985). Used by permission of The Society for Promoting Christian Knowledge.
42   *Prayers of Life* (1963), Gill & Macmillan.
43   Care and Resources for People Affected by AIDS/HIV.
44   Exact source unknown.
46   *A Matter of Life and Death* © 1986 SCM Press Ltd.
48   as for 13.
50   Used in Yoruba parishes in Nigeria; from *Morning, Noon, and Night*, Ed. John Carden, 1976, Highway Press/CMS (Church Missionary Society).
53   This copyright material is taken from *A New Zealand Prayer Book–He Karakia Mihinare o Aotearoa* (1989) and is used with permission.
54   *Prayers for the People* (1992) Ed. Michael Perry, Marshall Pickering, HarperCollinsPublishers.
57   Ed. Eric J. Lott, © 1986 United Theological College, Bangalore.
58   *Intercessions for use with Series 1 & 2 or Series 3 Holy Communion Services* (1978) Mowbrays. Used by permission.
59   *Widening the Web* (1985).
60   *Stations–Places for Pilgrims to Pray*, Cairns Publications, 47, Firth Park Avenue, Sheffield S5 6HF.
63   *Faith in Flames* (1990), Hodder & Stoughton Ltd.
64   *Letters and Papers from Prison*. SCM Press, 1953. From a prayer written Christmas 1943, while in the prison where he was later hanged by the Nazis.
66   as for 14.
68   Reprinted from *Daily Prayer* edited by Eric Milner-White and G.W. Briggs (1941) by permission of Oxford University Press.
69   *Prayer in the Morning*, Cairns Publications, 47, Firth Park Avenue, Sheffield S5 6HF.

71   as for 14.
73   *Surprised by Light,* Ulrich Schaffer. Copyright © 1980 by Ulrich Schaffer.
     Reprinted by permission of HarperCollins*Publishers,* Inc., New York.
76   as for 73.
78   *Isaac de l'Étoile, Sermons I,* Ed. A. Hoste and G. Salet (Paris: Sources
     Chrétiennes 1967), Sermon 5.
84   as for 40.
86   *God to Enfold me.* Copyright © 1993 W. Mary Calvert. All rights
     reserved. Reproduced by permission of *The Grail,* England.
91   Source untraced.
92   *Eucharistic Liturgy of the Church of South India* © 1985.
100 *A Pilgrim's Book of Prayers* (1960) Mowbrays. Used by permission.
103 *Hebridean Altars,* Ed. Alistair MacLean, Edinburgh 1937.
107 *The Alternative Service Book* 1980, copyright © The Central Board of
     Finance of the Church of England.
108 as for 14.
109 Verse 1 of the revised version of the hymn *Great God, your love has
     called us here, in Faith Looking Forward* 1983, reprinted by permission
     of Oxford University Press. More verses from this hymn appear under
     prayers for Maundy Thursday, see No. 787.
118 as for 14.
119 *My God My Glory* (1961) SPCK. Used by permission of The Friends of
     York Minster.
121 *Approaching Light* (1994), The Canterbury Press.
122 *The Cry of the Deer* © (1987). Used by permission of The Society for
     Promoting Christian Knowledge.
126 as for 46.
131 *Each Day & Each Night* (1994) © Wild Goose Publications/The Iona
     Community.
134 Inspired by the traditional invocation of Christ (the *Anima Christi*).
146 This was his prayer before the crucifix at San Damiano, from which he
     heard the voice of Christ saying, 'Rebuild my Church'.
152 Excerpts from the English translation of *The Roman Missal,* © 1973,
     International Committee on English in the Liturgy, Inc. All rights reserved.
153 © Mrs. Ursula Niebuhr, P.O. Box 91, 7 Yale Hill, Stockbridge,
     Massachusetts 01262, USA. Originally published in *Justice and Mercy,*
     Harper & Row. This prayer was written in 1943, and has been used all
     over the world by Alcoholics Anonymous and other organizations.
154 as for 14.
157 *Ministry to the Sick: Authorized Alternative Services,* copyright © The
     Central Board of Finance of the Church of England, 1983.
159 as for 68.
161 as for 68.
163 Collect for the Fourth Sunday after Trinity. Extracts from The Book of
     Common Prayer, the rights in which are vested in the Crown, are repro-
     duced by permission of the Crown's Patentee, Cambridge University Press.

165 *A Wee Worship Book (Wild Goose Worship Group, 1988)* Copyright ©
1988 WGWG, Iona Community, Glasgow G51 3UU, Scotland.

166 as for 68.

169 as for 53.

171 This version of the prayer is in *Patterns for Worship, A Report by the
Liturgical Commission,* © The Central Board of Finance of the Church
of England 1989.

172 Reprinted from *Patterns and Prayers for Christian Worship* (1991), worship book of the Baptist Union of Great Britain, by permission of the
Oxford University Press.

174 *Contemporary Parish Prayers* (1975), Ed. Frank Colquhoun, Hodder &
Stoughton Ltd.

180 Based on lines from the poem *Gratefulnesse.*

187 From *Read, Mark and Pray,* The Prayer Handbook 1992 © 1991.
Published by the United Reformed Church in the United Kingdom.

190 Used with permission of the Dean and Chapter of York.

191 as for 172.

192 Copyright © The Mothers' Union, reproduced with permission.

196 *The Iona Community Worship Book* (1991) Wild Goose Publications.

197 Copyright © Brian A. Wren, 3, Union St, Apt.2, Topsham, ME 04086,
USA. Used by permission.

201 Prayer adapted from World Day of Prayer services. Used with permission.

207 Original version in *Prayer in the Shadows* (1990), published by
HarperCollins.

208 *Praying Round the Clock* (1983) Mowbrays.

210 Original version in *Patterns not Padlocks* (1992), published by Eagle,
Guildford.

212 *Pied Beauty*

213 *Patterns for Worship:* A report by the Liturgical Commission, © The
Central Board of Finance of the Church of England 1989.

214 as for 172.

219 Reprinted by permission of the General Synod of the Scottish Episcopal
Church.

222 From *Say One for Me,* The Prayer Handbook 1990 © Tony Burnham
1989. Published by the United Reformed Church in the United Kingdom.

223 *The Wonder of a Love,* Mowbrays. Used by permission.

225 as for 207.

226 *Christ the Light of the World Prayer Book* Highway Press/CMS (Church
Missionary Society).

233 First published in *Pushing the Boat Out* (Wild Goose Worship Group
1995).

234 as for 207.

235 The poem 'Messiah' © Ralph Wright, OSB, St Louis Abbey, 500 South
Marston Road, Saint Louis, Missouri 63141–8500.

242 as for 64.

243 as for 86.

249 *Woman Prayer/Woman Song,* New York: Crossroad, 1987, 1995, page 46. Sr Miriam Therese Winter is a Medical Mission Sister.

250 as for 63.

252 as for 15.

253 as for 53.

254 *The Face of Love, Meditations on the Way of the Cross,* Mowbray 1959, p.100. The language has been modernized. A revised edition was published by SLG Press in 1977.

255 *By Stony Paths, A Version of Psalms 51–100,* Cairns Publications, 47, Firth Park Avenue, Sheffield S5 6HF.

256 as for 53.

257 *The Woman's Prayer Companion* © 1994 by the Carmelites of Indianapolis. Used by permission.

259 as for 210.

260 as for 36.

262 as for 207.

264 Copyright Kevin Mayhew Ltd. Reproduced by permission from *Morning, Noon and Night* (1993) by Michael Forster, Licence number 594072.

266 From *Encompassing Presence,* The Prayer Handbook 1993 © Kate McIlhagga 1992. Published by the United Reformed Church in the United Kingdom.

269 First published in *Bread of Tomorrow,* Christian Aid/SPCK (1992).

273 *Lord of the Morning* (1977), © The Lutterworth Press, Cambridge.

275 as for 36.

277 From the poem *The Temper* (1). The spelling has been modernized.

279 as for 208.

280 The English translation of the concluding prayers from *The Liturgy of the Hours* © 1974, International Committee on English in the Liturgy, Inc. All rights reserved.

282 as for 207.

286 as for 73.

287 as for 207.

288 as for 14.

291 Based on, 'He meets you in Gentleness' on page 46 of *Surprised by Light,* by Ulrich Schaffer, HarperCollins*Publishers* Inc. (1980).

294 From the poem *The Wreck of the Deutschland* (1976).

295 Parts of the poem *Affliction IV.* The spelling has been modernized.

299 From *The Road to Daybreak* ©1988, by J. M. Nouwen. Used by permission of D.L.T. Ltd. UK, and of Doubleday, a division of Bantam Doubleday Dell Publishing Group Inc., U.S.A.

302 From the poem *The Prayer, in Selected Poems 1946–1968,* William Collins.

303 Verse 1 of the hymn 'When on life a darkness falls', in *Praising a Mystery* 1986, reprinted by permission of Oxford University Press.

304 Ed. Ronald Jasper. The Joint Liturgical Group of Great Britain, 52 Gisburn Road, Barnoldswick, Lancs. BB8 5HA. This version is as adapted by *A New Zealand Prayer Book,* and is also in *Patterns for Worship, A Report by the Liturgical Commission,* © The Central Board of Finance of the Church of England 1989.

315 *The Shade of His Hand* (1973), McCrimmon Publishing Co. Ltd.
317 © Ann Shepherdson, *Comfort for the Journey Home* (1991) published by Methodist Publishing House. Used by permission.
318 as for 207.
319 as for 207.
323 as for 42.
325 Copyright © 1986 Kingsway's Thankyou Music, PO Box 75, Eastbourne, East Sussex, BN23 6NT, UK. Used by kind permission of Kingsway's Thankyou Music.
327 *From Holy Sonnet XIV.* The punctuation has been altered slightly.
329 Copyright © 1990 Sovereign Lifestyle Music, PO Box 356, Leighton Buzzard, Beds., LU7 8WP, UK. Used by kind permission.
330 *Said or Sung* (1960) London: Faith Press.
332 Extract from the poem *Good Friday 1613, Riding Westward.*
333 as for 100.
335 *Daily Prayer and Praise* (1962) © The Lutterworth Press, Cambridge.
337 Reprinted from *A Diary of Private Prayer* (1936) by John Baillie, by permission of the Oxford University Press.
339 as for 14.
340 *The Iona Community Worship Book (Wild Goose Worship Group, 1991)* Copyright © 1991 WGWG, Iona Community, Glasgow G51 3UU, Scotland.
341 *Women Included,* © 1991 The St Hilda Community, SPCK.
342 as for 53.
343 as for 213.
344 as for 269.
345 In *Morning, Noon and Night,* Ed. John Carden 1976, Highway Press/CMS (Church Missionary Society).
346 *The Prayer Tree* © Copyright Michael Leunig 1991. Used with Permission. HarperCollins*Religious,* Melbourne, Australia.
348 What Does the Lord Require of Us? (1989).
349 *Prayer at Night's Approaching,* Cairns Publications, 47, Firth Park Avenue, Sheffield S5 6HF.
351 as for 107.
352 as for 213.
353 as for 53.
354 as for 57.
355 Collect for the Twenty-First Sunday after Trinity. Permission as for 163.
356 © 1989 *World Council of Churches.*
359 as for 53.
360 *New Parish Prayers* (1982), Ed. Frank Colquhoun, Hodder & Stoughton Ltd.
361 as for 57.
362 as for 208.
367 In *The Mothers' Union Anthology of Public Prayers.* Copyright The Mothers' Union, reproduced with permission.
371 as for 192.
372 as for 257.

373 *Book of Worship, United Church of Christ* © 1986. United Church of Christ, Office for Church Life and Leadership, New York. Used by permission.
374 as for 192.
376 *More Prayers for the Plain Man* (1962) Fontana, HarperCollins*Publishers.*
378 *Through Desert Places, A Version of Psalms 1–50,* Cairns Publications, 47, Firth Park Avenue, Sheffield S5 6HF.
379 as for 192.
380 *Celebrating Together,* the Corrymeela Community, Northern Ireland.
381 as for 53.
382 as for 367.
384 as for 367.
385 *Daring to Speak Love's Name, A Gay and Lesbian Prayer Book* edited by Elizabeth Stuart (Hamish Hamilton, 1992) compilation copyright © Elizabeth Stuart, 1992, copyright © Jane Robson, 1992. Reproduced by permission of Hamish Hamilton Ltd.
386 as for 385.
387 *Prayers for Use at the Alternative Services* (1986) Mowbrays.
388 *Prayers for Today's Church,* (1972), Ed. Dick Williams, Falcon Press. Also in *Lord of our World* (1973) by Susan Williams, Falcon Press. Falcon Books were published by CPAS, who are now at Athena Drive, Tachbrook Park, Warwick, CV34 6NG.
389 as for 213.
390 The tape *Laudate* is produced by The Taizé Community, 71520 Taizé, France. The prayers are based on material in *Praying for the World,* a leaflet for use at a Prayer Vigil for the Decade of Evangelism, devised by the Diocese of Southwell.
393 as for 165.
395 as for 165.
396 as for 13.
397 *Songs and Praises of the Church* (1990), compiled by John Michael Mountney. Mowbrays. Used by permission.
398 as for 207.
401 In its original form, the first and last lines of this prayer were in Latin, i.e. *Anima Christi, sanctifica me,* and *Fiat voluntas tua!*
403 *With All God's People* (1990) World Council of Churches, Geneva.
407 *Love from Below,* by John L. Bell & Graham Maule, Copyright © 1989 WGWG, Iona Community, Glasgow G51 3UU, Scotland.
408 as for 210.
409 *Contemporary Themes for Worship (The Ashram Community).*
410 as for 360.
411 as for 192.
412 as for 273.
415 *The Book of Common Prayer of the Episcopal Church, USA.* In the public domain, so no copyright permission necessary. Format: The Church Hymnal Corporation, New York, USA.
417 as for 201.
419 as for 192.

422 as for 192.
424 as for 43.
425 as for 367.
426 Used by the Bishops' AIDS Ministry Group, Durham.
427 as for 43.
430 *Pray with Us,* edited by Maureen Edwards, Lion Publishers.
431 *New Every Morning* (1973).
432 © The Mother Theresa Committee. *In Something Beautiful for God,* Malcolm Muggeridge (1972) Fontana.
433 as for 201.
435 *Sursum Corda,* Mowbrays. Used by permission. This prayer is also in *Lent, Holy Week and Easter: Services and Prayers,* © The Central Board of Finance of the Church of England 1989.
437 as for 122.
438 as for 432.
440 Used by permission. Based on a passage in *Jesus Man of Prayer,* 1987. Hodder & Stoughton, p. 185.
441 as for 430.
442 as for 57.
444 *The One who Listens* (1971), McCrimmon Publishing Co. Ltd.
447 Based on information in Christian Aid booklets: *Ways of Life* (1993) and *Invitation to Life* (1994).
448 *City Prayers* (1994), The Canterbury Press.
449 as for 360.
450 *Companions of God* (1994) © Christian Aid.
453 UK Committee for the United Nations Children's Fund.
454 April–June 1986. Copyright © The United Society for the Propagation of the Gospel. Used with permission.
455 as for 68.
456 From *Prayers for the Disappeared,* Latin American Federation of Relativesof Disappeared Prisoners, London. In *With all God's People* (1990), WCC.
458 *Towards the City, A Version of Psalms 101–150,* Cairns Publications, 47, FirthPark Avenue, Sheffield S5 6HF.
459 as for 266.
461 as for 208.
462 as for 415.
463 Published by kind permission of Lady Ryder of Warsaw.
464 Original version in *Heaven in Ordinary* (1985), McCrimmon Publishing Company Ltd.
465 as for 450.
466 Christian Renewal Centre, Rostrevor, Co. Down, N. Ireland.
467 From the inauguration of Nelson Mandela as State President of South Africa in Pretoria in 1994.
468 as for 345.
469 as for 13.
470 as for 450.

471   as for 53. The original version of this prayer was written by religious leaders for the second special session on disarmament of the United Nations in 1982.
473   Material from *Celebrating Common Prayer* (Mowbray), © The Society of St Francis 1992, is used with permission.
475   *Liturgies and Worship Guides,* 1986 (p.24). The Philippine Episcopal Church National Commission on Social Justice and Human Rights. National Council of Churches in the Philippines, Quezon City.
477   Exact source untraced.
478   as for 192.
479   as for 280.
480   as for 57.
482   as for 172.
483   *We Wait, A Litany for Good Friday,* in *Let All the World: Liturgies, litanies and prayers from around the world,* Edited by Wendy S. Robins. USPG, London, 1990.
484   as for 53.
485   as for 107.
486   as for 403.
487   as for 360.
489   as for 53.
490   as for 36.
491   as for 201.
492   as for 360.
493   This prayer originally appeared in the annual *Methodist Prayer Handbook.*
494   as for 174.
495   *The World is our Community* (1990) © Christian Aid.
498   as for 57.
499   *Prayers for Today's Church* No. 324, (1972), Ed. Dick Williams, Falcon Press. Falcon Books were published by CPAS, who are now at Athena Drive, Tachbrook Park, Warwick, CV34 6NG.
500   as for 397.
502   From the leaflet for Unemployment Sunday, February 25th 1990. 'Church Action with the Unemployed.'
504   Used with permission.
506   as for 53.
507   as for 431.
508   as for 192.
509   as for 360.
510   as for 58.
513   as for 360.
515   The original version of this prayer is found with the prayers for guidance and discernment (No. 149).
516   as for 192.
517   as for 53.
519   From the leaflet of the Week of Prayer for World Peace for 16th–23rd October 1994.

520 *Gloria Deo Worship Book,* 9th Assembly of the Conference of European Churches, © 1986.

521 as for 431.

522 as for 360.

523 as for 378.

525 as for 187.

526 as for 34.

529 Used by permission of The Council of Churches for Britain and Ireland.

534 In *Celebrating Community–Prayers and Songs of Unity* (1993) WCC (World Council of Churches).

535 as for 534.

536 as for 53.

537 as for 14.

538 as for 53.

539 *Limping Along; Confessions of a Pilgrim Theologian* (1985), William B. Eerdmans Publishing Co., Grand Rapids, Michigan.

543 as for 53.

544 Used at the 8th Assembly of the Christian Conference of Asia, Seoul, Korea. In *With All God's People* (WCC 1990) page 195.

545 as for 14.

547 *Lord, Let me Share: Meditations following a Heart Attack* (1978), Canon Subir Biswas of Calcutta Cathedral; Church Missionary Society (CMS).

548 as for 152.

549 as for 121.

550 *Lord of our World* (1973) Falcon Press. Falcon Books were published by CPAS, who are now at Athena Drive, Tachbrook Park, Warwick, CV34 6NG.

552 as for 68.

553 as for 54.

554 as for 213.

555 as for 122.

556 From *An Order of Service for the Laying-on of Hands,* Burrswood.

558 as for 556.

559 as for 556.

562 as for 415.

563 as for 53.

565 as for 73.

569 as for 317.

570 Founder of the Focolare Movement. From *Spiel mit gottlichen Rollen.*

572 as for 345.

575 as for 257.

579 as for 152.

581 as for 53.

585 as for 415.

588 'Prayer to the Alchemist', in *Selected Poems* (1979), published in aid of the charity Cruse.

589 as for 14.

590   as for 499.
592   *The Service Book* © 1989, the United Reformed Church in the United Kingdom. Published by Oxford University Press.
594   Excerpts from *The Order of Christian Funerals* © 1985, ICEL. All rights reserved.
596   as for 415.
597   as for 172.
598   as for 594.
600   as for 592
602   as for 415.
603   The liturgy arose out of the shared experience of many bereaved women. Obtained from Frances Blodwell.
604   as for 255.
608   From the poem 'Kneeling', in *Selected Poems 1946–1968,* William Collins.
610   *Journey Within* (1968), Darton, Longman & Todd.
612   as for 100.
613   as for 42.
614   as for 40.
616   as for 40.
620   as for 448.
623   as for 190.
624   as for 346.
625   as for 13.
629   as for 273.
631   as for 264.
632   as for 547.
635   as for 86.
638   as for 86.
642   as for 86.
644   as for 337.
645   as for 53.
646   as for 473.
647   *Your Will be Done,* 1985 Christian Conference of Asia Youth, Quezon City, Philippines.
649   as for 340.
650   as for 53.
651   as for 280.
654   as for 473.
657   as for 86.
660   Carmina Gadelica, translated by Alexander Carmichael, © 1971 Scottish Academic Press. Used by permission.
663   *Tides and Seasons* © (1989). Used by permission of The Society for Promoting Christian Knowledge.
665   as for 36.
666   *The Plain Man's Book of Prayers* (1959) Fontana, HarperCollinsPublishers.
667   as for 473.

669 *Supplemental Liturgical Resource 5,* p.69. Westminster John Knox Press, 100 Witherspoon Street, Louisville, Kentucky 40202–1396, USA (adapted). This version of the prayer is in *Patterns for Worship, A Report by the Liturgical Commission,* © The Central Board of Finance of the Church of England 1989.
671 as for 107.
672 as for 657.
673 as for 280.
681 *Festivals, Family and Food,* © Hawthorn Press.
689 as for 165.
691 'Friday Blessing', as for 349.
695 as for 107.
700 as for 660.
702 as for 57.
703 Inspired by ancient Celtic 'journey prayers', and by the custom of The Society of Our Lady of the Isles on Fetlar, one of the Shetland Islands, to send off all their visitors with a blessing.
704 as for 69.
705 as for 53.
707 as for 174.
708 as for 14.
710 as for 266.
711 as for 53.
712 as for 152.
713 as for 36.
714 as for 152.
716 as for 174.
720 as for 213.
728 From a Christmas letter included in the book of extracts from her writings, *The Hidden Joy,* SLG Press, 1994, p.7.
730 From a *Litany of Intercession* © World Council of Churches, Geneva. Used by permission.
732 © 1972, Saint Andrew Press.
734 as for 269.
735 as for 213.
736 The copyright owner has not been traced. The prayer appears in *The Promise of His Glory,* © The Central Board of Finance of the Church of England 1989.
738 as for 415.
739 as for 269.
741 as for 657.
747 *The Promise of His Glory: For the Season from All Saints to Candlemas,* copyright © The Central Board of Finance of the Church of England, 1990, 1991.
750 © The Society of St Francis.
751 as for 387.
752 as for 192.

753   as for 264.
754   as for 219.
755   *Prayers for the Church Community,* The National Christian Education Council.
756   as for 187.
757   as for 53.
760   as for 187.
763   Copyright © 1981 Integrity's Hosanna! Music/Sovereign Music UK, PO Box 356, Leighton Buzzard, LU7 3WP, UK. Reproduced by permission.
764   as for 14.
765   as for 378.
767   as for 187.
770   as for 53.
771   as for 57.
772   Verse 1 of the hymn 'Dust and ashes touch our face', in *Bring Many Names* 1989, reprinted by permission of Oxford University Press.
776   as for 387.
777   Copyright © 1979 by GIA Publications, Inc., Chicago, Illinois. All rights reserved.
780   as for 388.
782   as for 53.
783   as for 174.
784   as for 187.
785   as for 172.
786   as for 53.
787   Verses 3 & 4 of the revised version of the hymn 'Great God, your love has called us here', in *Faith Looking Forward* 1983, reprinted by permission of Oxford University Press. The first verse of this hymn appears under prayers of self-dedication, No. 109.
789   as for 57.
790   *Disguises of Love* (1983), © The Leprosy Mission International.
794   Based on words by Johann Heermann (1585–1647).
795   as for 100.
796   From 'The Thanksgiving'. The spelling has been modernized.
797   Translated by John Henry Newman (1801–1890).
799   Translated from a German original by P. Gerhardt, based on *Salve caput cruentatum* (ascribed to St Bernard).
801   as for 14.
803   as for 430.
804   as for 473.
807   as for 53.
808   as for 280.
809   as for 196.
813   'i thank You God', in *Selected Poems 1923–1958,* page 76, Faber & Faber Ltd. The verses here could refer to any moment of new life and joy following an experience of inner pain and 'dying', but they are particularly apt for Easter. The poems of e.e. cumming are always unorthodox in the use of small and capital letters. Here the 'i' at the beginning

reminds us of our smallness when face to face with the divine 'unimaginable You'.

814 *Prayer in the Day–A Book of Mysteries,* Cairns Publications, 47, Firth Park Avenue, Sheffield S5 6HF.
815 as for 13.
816 *Easter Garden* (1990) Fount, HarperCollins*Publishers.*
817 as for 53.
819 as for 280.
820 From a Resurrection Litany in the Service of the Lord's Supper. OUP Madras.
824 as for 53.
825 as for 14.
826 as for 280.
829 as for 14.
831 as for 473.
832 as for 269.
833 as for 14.
835 as for 280.
837 *Enriching the Christian Year* (1993) Ed. Michael Perham. Used with permission.
840 as for 345.
844 Translated R.F. Littledale (1833–90).
845 as for 269.
846 as for 14.
847 as for 280.
848 From *Say One for Me,* The Prayer Handbook 1990 © Tony Burnham 1989. Published by the United Reformed Church in the United Kingdom.
850 as for 46.
851 as for 53.
852 as for 14.
854 as for 68.
856 as for 269.
858 as for 152.
859 as for 837.
860 as for 208.
861 as for 40.
862 as for 208.
865 as for 14.
866 as for 592.
868 First used on the Festival of the Holy Trinity at St. Peter's Church, Harrogate, at the Thanksgiving Eucharist for Wendy Wilby's ordination to the priesthood, May 29th 1994.
869 as for 280.
871 as for 837.
874 as for 40.
875 Verse 3 of the hymn 'May the Sending One sing in you,' in Bring Many Names 1989, reprinted by permission of Oxford University Press.

879 *They Shall be Satisfied* (1993) © Christian Aid.
880 as for 57.
882 *Till All Creation Sings* (1989) © Christian Aid.
883 as for 196.
884 as for 53.
885 *Tell Out My Soul* (1990) © Christian Aid.
886 as for 882.
887 as for 837.
891 as for 69.
892 Address not traced. Prayer originally published in *Contemporary Parish Prayers* (1975), Ed. Frank Colquhoun, Hodder & Stoughton.
893 as for 165.
895 as for 53.
896 as for 152.
898 as for 152.
899 as for 269.
902 as for 473.
903 as for 53.
904 as for 53.
905 as for 53.
906 Verse 1 of the hymn 'All-perceiving Lover', in *Bring Many Names* 1989, reprinted by permission of Oxford University Press.
907 as for 174.
909 as for 550.
911 as for 152.
913 as for 53.
914 as for 107.
915 as for 53.
916 as for 415.
918 as for 473.
922 as for 415.
923 as for 415.
924 as for 387.
925 as for 397.
927 as for 837.
930 as for 122.
934 as for 57.
937 as for 54.
939 as for 15.
940 Ruth Burgess originally wrote this for a friend taking final vows in a religious community.
944 as for 152.
945 as for 57.
946 as for 107.
947 Reproduced from *Liturgy of Life* (1991), compiled by Donald Hilton, with the permission of the National Christian Education Council.
948 as for 266.

951 This version of the prayer is in *Patterns for Worship, A Report by the Liturgical Commission,* © The Central Board of Finance of the Church of England 1989.
952 The National Biblical, Catechetical and Liturgical Centre, Bangalore 560005.
953 as for 415.
954 as for 255.
956 Exact source unknown.
957 as for 868.
960 as for 172.
961 as for 192.
963 as for 192.
964 as for 192.
965 as for 266.
966 as for 86.
968 as for 192.
970 as for 257.
971 as for 415.
972 as for 53.
973 as for 367.
975 as for 107.
976 as for 367.
979 as for 376.
981 *Prayers for Teenagers* (1989) Marshall Pickering, HarperCollins*Publishers.*
983 *A Diary of Prayer* by Elizabeth Goudge. Used by permission of David Higham Associates Ltd., 5–8 Lower John Street, Golden Square, London W1R 4HA.
984 as for 257.
985 as for 257.
986 as for 367.
988 Written for the Hammick's/Lion Publishing children's prayers competition. In *The Lion Prayer Collection* (1992) compiled by Mary Batchelor, Lion Publishing Plc.
989 Leaders' Resource Book 2, The Canterbury Press.
990 Leaders' Resource Book 1, The Canterbury Press.
991 as for 989.
992 as for 990.
999 as for 981.
1000 as for 430.
1001 © Simon Bailey, from *Still with God,* (1986), National Society for Promoting Religious Education/Church House Publishing.
1002 as for 981.
1003 as for 1001.

Every effort has been made to obtain permission for the copyright material in this anthology, and I hope that no copyright has been infringed. I apologize in advance if correction is needed, and, should this arise, the necessary amendments will be made in any reprint of this book.

A LITTLE BOOK OF HEALING PRAYER
Angela Ashwin

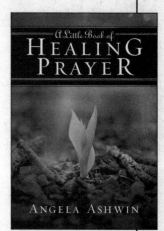

Whenever we pray, we open
ourselves to receive God's
transforming love. When we
pray for others, we are offering
ourselves as channels for that same healing love.
The prayers in this exquisite collection recognize
that each person is bruised, weary, or hurt in some
way. Whether strong or weak, we each stand
alongside each other in our common need of
God's forgiveness and love.

Softcover: 0-310-24949-X

Pick up a copy at your favorite bookstore!

ZONDERVAN™

GRAND RAPIDS, MICHIGAN 49530 USA

WWW.ZONDERVAN.COM

We want to hear from you. Please send your comments about
this book to us in care of the address below. Thank you.

ZONDERVAN™

GRAND RAPIDS, MICHIGAN 49530 USA

WWW.ZONDERVAN.COM